REVOLUTIONARY DOCTOR

BENJAMIN RUSH, 1746-1813

Also by Carl Binger

THE DOCTOR'S JOB

MORE ABOUT PSYCHIATRY

PERSONALITY IN ARTERIAL
HYPERTENSION *(with others)*

POST MERIDIAN

BENJAMIN RUSH

Painted and Engraved by E. Savage

REVOLUTIONARY DOCTOR

Benjamin Rush, 1746-1813

BY CARL BINGER, M.D.

W · W · NORTON & COMPANY · INC · NEW YORK

For Chloë

TABLE OF CONTENTS

ACKNOWLEDGMENTS

❀ I AM HAPPY TO ACKNOWLEDGE AN IMMENSE DEBT OF gratitude to Dr. George W. Corner of Philadelphia and to my friend and neighbor, Dr. Lyman H. Butterfield, for their scholarly pursuit of trenchant facts, and for their extraordinary generosity. They have made available many of Rush's manuscripts and letters, carefully edited and annotated. These have naturally drawn my attention to other valuable material cited in their bibliographies. I am grateful, too, to Dr. Richard H. Shryock, Librarian of the American Philosophical Society, for his perceptive historical writings about Rush, and to Dr. Eric T. Carlson of the New York Hospital for his recent appraisal of Rush's contribution to psychiatry. Dr. Charles Coleman Sellers, of Dickinson College, was kind enough to provide me with a volume of the *Spahr Lectures,* some of them dealing with Benjamin Rush.

I have availed myself freely of libraries at Boston, Cambridge, Edinburgh, New York and Philadelphia; and I am indebted to the various librarians there for their generous assistance. Mr. Frederick B. Adams of the Morgan Library permitted me to inspect the manuscript of Rush's *French Journal.*

The Library Company of Philadelphia, as well as the Library of the American Philosophical Society, put manuscript material in my hands, and the College of Physicians in Philadelphia gave me permission to use the engraving of Rush by Savage as a frontispiece. For these kindnesses I am greatly indebted, as I am to the Princeton University Press for permission to quote both from the Rush *Autobiography* and the published *Letters,* and to the University of Pennsylvania Press for the quotations from Goodman's biography.

It is impossible to thank all the living and dead whose works have furnished me with material for this biography. A partial list of

9

them will be found in the bibliography at the back of this book. Where material has been quoted, the page and line of my text in which the quote occurs is provided, in the Notes.

I have not seen the *Scottish Journal*, which is at the University of Indiana, in Bloomington, but Dr. Butterfield lent me his typescript copy of it. Dr. Douglas Guthrie introduced me to the Library of the Medical School at the University of Edinburgh and directed my steps toward Monymail in Fifeshire, where I visited the former country seat of the Melvilles and Leslies.

Others have helped me in less official ways. My friend the late Van Wyck Brooks read the first draft of the first few chapters and encouraged me greatly to go on. Catherine Drinker Bowen gave me a whole day of her precious time and with a few telling comments from her glowing mind taught me something about the biographer's art.

My old friends Stanley and Betty Cobb stood by as always and listened to parts of the manuscript. Other willing, if captive, ears were my children's. To all of them I express my special appreciation. In particular, my thanks go to my son, David Garrison Binger, for his careful reading of the page proofs.

In the preparation of the manuscript Mrs. Cora Holbrook lent invaluable aid by her painstaking editing of the first draft. Miss Constance Grosvenor—fortunately familiar with my scrawl—put much of the first draft in typewritten form. I am most grateful to both of them. Miss Marjorie E. Sprague is responsible for the final editing and typing and for helping in arranging the notes, bibliography and index. It was a great pleasure to me to have worked with her.

My colleague Dr. John C. Nemiah read the last three chapters and gave me the benefit of his precise and scholarly criticism. The editing of the final draft was accomplished with the assistance of Mr. Dudley C. Lunt. His seasoned judgment and great experience as an editor encouraged me to discard much irrelevant material and to mass the rest in a more coherent way.

Finally, my thanks go to my wife, who suffered a stranger to move in with us for a number of years and, in spite of the nuisance, preserved her usual good nature.

INTRODUCTION

✿ IN THIS BOOK I HAVE TRIED TO DRAW A PICTURE OF A man who lived two centuries ago. This is no easy undertaking. Time blurs outlines. Images are constantly shifting both with the author's position and with the particular aspect of the subject he is trying to bring into focus. Everyone who has looked at a marble bust from different angles has found that the contour of the head, the set of the jaw, the tilt or slope of the nose keep changing until at last he asks, "What did this man really look like?" He should know that he cannot find out by analyzing and scrutinizing the features. To have a picture of the whole man calls for an act of re-creation and this can come only from a tolerant attentiveness, a readiness, even a capacity to identify oneself with him.

There are several particular reasons for my interest in Benjamin Rush and for my having chosen him as the subject of this biography. Our professional interests had many similarities. I too had much to do with epidemic diseases, both in France and in Eastern Macedonia. Like Rush, I turned from medicine to psychiatry, passing just as he did through a concern with body-mind relationships —with what we today would call psychosomatic medicine. At an early age I was drawn as if by a magnet toward my profession and the possibility of relieving suffering, and of lessening the total burden of misery in the world. This was significantly true of Benjamin Rush.

I do not mean to push these analogies too far. It is enough that they awakened my interest. In writing of him, I have learned something of myself and this has been all to the good. No one can describe another man, nor paint a portrait, without, unwittingly, revealing himself. It is well to be on guard against this if one wants to achieve a fair presentation. An author who has been trained in psychiatry and psychoanalysis is constantly tempted to apply his knowledge in portraying a character, especially as it has become fashionable to do so. But this has its risks. It has ruined many a biography. Far better just to tell the story and let the reader interpret. There is enough knowledge abroad these days to make parlor psychoanalysts of us all.

In the case of this subject I have occasionally yielded to the temptation, partly because Rush was so devoid of insight and so given to noble rationalizations of his behavior, and partly because he provides us with much dream material and the associations so necessary for interpretation. I have stuck pretty much to Rush's own words and those of his contemporaries and I have striven to reduce speculations and fantasies about him to a minimum. At no point have I said, "Rush must have thought." When I recount what he thought, it is based on his own record. He was an indefatigable keeper of records—letters, articles, treatises, lectures, textbooks and diaries. As did many of his contemporaries, he had his *Commonplace Book*. He said of himself that when he wasn't reading he was writing. After a crowded day's work with his patients, he would spend long hours at his desk, making notes and keeping up his gigantic correspondence.

The bibliographical material and other sources will be found at the back of the book. In the case of the autobiography and the edited letters, modern spelling has been used. For Rush's *Scottish* and *French Journals* and at a few other places the original spelling has been preserved.

Much of this written material, though by no means all, has been edited, annotated and published. Were it not for its availability, I could never have come to grips with this task. Such a wealth of biographical material can be a source of embarrassment. The late Albert Deutsch, a most knowledgeable layman in the field of mental health and mental illness, once told me that it would take a poet to do justice to this subject. I wish I could lay claim to the distinction.

*   *   *

In telling this story, I started out to do so chronologically, but after a while this became impossible, because of the overlapping of Rush's interests and activities. I then had to proceed topically. The result is a description of a life growing like a tree, beginning with a straight trunk but branching out into full-leafed maturity. Perhaps this is the pattern of any vigorous life. The book was not intended to be a definitive biography.

Instead, I have tried to reveal the significant facets of Benjamin Rush's personality and character as they are highlighted by the important events of his life. These are brought into focus against the background of the medical teaching and learning of his day and of the political climate that so greatly affected him. It is impossible to separate the two, the man from his social environment. We can understand him only in the setting of the revolutionary movement which swept around him and through him.

If one sets out to describe a globule of quicksilver in purely physical terms, one can hardly convey the magic of its glint and dance. In many respects, Benjamin Rush was like quicksilver, constantly changing and reflecting the myriad images around him. And what images they were: the Philadelphia and Edinburgh, the London and Paris of the mid-18th century and such men as Samuel Johnson, Benjamin West, Benjamin Franklin, Thomas Paine, George Washington, Thomas Jefferson, John Adams. These are a few of the stars in his firmament. Because they outshone him, he has been somewhat lost to popular history. Few people recognize his name. But his was by no means a reflected light. It burned in him fiercely and made him the champion of justice and the enemy of cruelty, ignorance and bigotry.

Many of the things that preoccupied him and plagued him are still in the forefront of our concern: civil rights and the fair treatment of minority groups, alcoholism, crime and punishment, public education and especially the education of women, inflation and depreciation of the currency, loyalty oaths, and democratic government without abnegation of the rights of individuals. Added to these were the myriad and perplexing medical problems that confronted him at a time when factual scientific knowledge was sorely lacking, especially about communicable diseases. It is of great interest to see how he maneuvered by careful observation, quick intuition and lucky guesses. By dint of these he often managed well when not seduced and misled by insufficiently tested theories. These prompted him to resort to heroic measures which no doubt sometimes resulted in the death of his patients. But he applied them with such faith and enthusiasm that it gave him courage to expose himself to stupendous dangers. And his faith alone helped some of the sick recover.

It is a natural thing for an author to make a sentimental journey to the familiar haunts of the man he has tried so hard to know and understand. Even to sit in the pew in Christ Church where Rush worshipped seemed to bring him closer. To the left of his accustomed seat is a stained glass window, executed in London. It shows the bespectacled Dr. Rush and many of his contemporaries at worship: General and Mrs. Washington, Alexander Hamilton, Robert Morris, Benjamin Franklin with his daughter Sarah, Joseph Hopkinson and Francis, John Penn with his family, and Betsy Ross. Rush's elegant, almost globular, gold watch and his shoe buckle set with rhinestones are preserved at the College of Physicians, and these bring him to life. But precious above all else are the pages upon pages of closely written cursive script with many corrections and emendations, to be found, for the most part, in the Library Company of Philadelphia.

In studying Benjamin Rush I have been constantly aware of the gaps in our own knowledge, of our gropings in the face of a wide and varied ignorance. Benjamin Rush's most lasting contribution was to an understanding of the diseases of the mind. Here he was confronted by the dilemma which still confounds us as between a mechanistic and a psychological interpretation of facts.

If one wants to know where one is going, it is not a bad idea to get one's bearings from time to time by looking backward. This makes the present more comprehensible and the future more meaningful.

CARL BINGER, M.D.

Cambridge, Massachusetts

REVOLUTIONARY DOCTOR

BENJAMIN RUSH, 1746-1813

"I think that, as life is action and passion, it is required of a man that he should share the passion and action of his time at peril of being charged not to have lived."

Mr. Justice Holmes

1

THE FORMING TIME

✧ OFF CAPE HENLOPEN ON THE SOUTHERN SHORE OF Delaware Bay the *Friendship* dropped her pilot on the 2nd of September 1766. She had cleared the port of Philadelphia two days before and had sailed downriver past the little hamlets of Chester, Wilmington, and New Castle, into Delaware Bay, which was heaving and swelling with great billows. The pilot made for Lewes, his home port, carrying with him "Cape letters," those parting words of greeting from anxious passengers who know they are embarking on a perilous voyage. The *Friendship* headed out to sea, bound for Liverpool.

One of the letters in the pilot's pouch was written by Benjamin Rush, a young man of twenty, who had never been to sea before, nor indeed farther away from his home in Philadelphia than Princeton, New Jersey. In this letter he admitted that he dreaded the morrow. On the evening of the second day out the poor young man was "seized wth: a vomiting & sea sickness which continued On me wthout any Intermission for ten or 12 days." He lay on his bunk, suffering as much pain and anxiety as he had ever done in his life and trying without success to get relief from laudanum, an opium derivative then in common use.

Rush was not alone in his misery. He shared his cabin with two others—his friend Jonathan Potts from Philadelphia, who like Rush was bound for Edinburgh to study medicine, and a Mr. Cummins, a young merchant on his way home to visit his parents in Northern Scotland. On September 19, at about two in the morning, they were awakened by a violent gale. "Nothing could equal ye terror," young Rush reports in his journal. "Was now impressed upon my mind . . . how Often did I wish myself at home, and how much did I condemn that Thirst for knowledge which induced me to leave my native country." He felt that his end was at hand and that all the pleasing prospects for usefulness and happiness in the world were doomed.

In this peril he was sustained, as he would be throughout the rest of his stormy life, by his piety and his unquestioning faith in the goodness and wisdom of the Creator, whom he now implored for a happy transition to Eternity. Fortunately, the captain of the *Friendship*, Thomas Pearse, shared these beliefs and ascribed their final safe deliverance "to that Being whose tender mercies are over all his works." Rush was reassured by the fact that the Captain's conduct was always beyond reproach, that he never swore ("What, never!") and that he had been educated by a pious mother. "Then it pleased God to put an end to the storm and to our fears."

But their joy in hearing the hail of "Land ho!" from the crow's nest was short-lived. In mid-October off the coast of Ireland the *Friendship* came close to being dashed to pieces against the Shillochs. And Rush wrote:

"Many hundred ships have been lost upon them within this last Century . . . the Country around them is inhabited entirely by Roman-Catholics who are as savage as their remote situation and Religion can make them. They live chiefly upon potatoes—fish—& the Eggs of wild Birds wch they procure at the Hazard of their Lives from the Clefts of the Rocks."

The next day the *Friendship* again narrowly escaped being wrecked at Holyhead on the coast of Wales. That night Mr. Cummins suddenly awakened with a cry of great distress. He had had a terrifying dream which he told to the Captain and to Potts and which Rush learned of only later. It prophesied his own death and Rush's as well. Two days later, on October 21, 1766, after a passage of seven weeks and two days, the *Friendship* docked in Liverpool. Three days after that Cummins died suddenly in a convulsion.

This unhappy occurrence was described by Rush as "a most afflicting event, for he became very dear to us by our fellowship in dangers. We shewed our respect for him by burying him at our

expense in a graveyard belonging to an Episcopal church in town."
And he adds, "This expense was afterwards honorably reimbursed
by his father."

So ended the first leg of Benjamin Rush's voyage through life.
Soon he would be embarked upon a new venture as a student in the
Medical School at the University of Edinburgh, whose faculty was
then pre-eminent in the world. At this time he was within three
months of attaining his majority.

*   *   *

Young Rush came from a long line of dissenters, who clearly
and significantly helped shape the style of his life. First to come to
America were John and Susanna Rush, who arrived in Pennsylvania in 1683 in the second year of William Penn's "Holy Experiment." They were accompanied by eight children and several
grandchildren. Benjamin was especially proud of this ancestor, the
"Old Trooper," as he affectionately called him, because he had distinguished himself as the Commander of a troop of horse in Cromwell's army. As the eldest surviving son in his own family, Benjamin was the proud inheritor of this forebear's watch and sword. Of
him he wrote in his *Autobiography:*

"It is sufficient gratification to me to know that he fought for
liberty, and migrated into a remote wilderness in the evening of his
life in order to enjoy the priviledge of worshipping God according
to the dictates of his own conscience."

When they arrived in the Colonies, the Rushes were Quakers,
but John Rush soon joined a separatist group of Friends known as
the "Christian Quakers." His wife Susanna was baptized when she
was close to eighty, her eldest daughter when she was sixty-five. A
search for salvation by the sampling of sects began early and seems
to have become a tradition in the Rush family. They settled in
Byberry, an agricultural community, predominantly Quaker, situ-
ated on the bank of the Delaware River twelve miles upstream
from Philadelphia. Here five generations of Rushes lived, including
Benjamin's grandfather James, a gunsmith, and his father John,
who was named for the progenitor and who inherited the 500-acre
family farm and his father's trade as well.

On this farm Benjamin Rush was born on the 4th of January
1746. When he was five years old his father died. It is unlikely that

at such an early age Benjamin could have retained vivid memories of him, though he recalls his agreeable personality and engaging manners. But his mother, Susanna, kept alive in her young son the picture of a man whose opinions and sayings and observations were far above his education and rank in life—a man honest and just and exemplary, who lived and died in communion with the Episcopal Church.

Whether these fine characteristics correspond to the facts is less important than that they were imprinted early on Rush's mind and became a permanent image there. It has been said that the day a man's father dies is the most important day in his life. Many men cannot come into their own until this event, cannot take hold of life and become men in their own right. To lose a father at five, however, is too early. A small child is not ready to do battle either with him or with the world. Instead, he is thrown back on his mother in a defenseless and dependent way and she becomes the arbiter and authority. For a man this has its hazards. Many a father-less boy continues a poignant search for his missing father and creates for himself with varying success father substitutes. This seems to have been true for Benjamin Rush and to have been responsible for some of his most fruitful and creative relationships, but also for some painful and disappointing ones.

Not only this, but the antagonism latent in all young children just begins to erupt in a small boy of five, and his father naturally becomes the loved-hated-feared object. It takes time to come to terms with these tumultuous and conflicting feelings, which are often not resolved until late adolescence. When they are not, they may be readily displaced on other but inappropriate objects. Indeed, this ambivalence may become characteristic of a personality in all situations in which intense emotions are invested.

When John Rush died at the age of thirty-nine, he left an estate consisting of three houses in Philadelphia. He had previously moved to a house on Front Street, which had belonged to his mother, and there for a few years had followed his trade with industry and success. Three months after his death the *Pennsylvania Gazette* published this notice:

"All persons indebted to the estate of John Rush, late of this city, Gun-smith, deceased, are hereby desired to discharge the same: and all those that have any demands against said estate, are desired to bring their accounts in order to be adjusted, by William Rush, black-smith, and Susannah Rush, Execut. There is likewise to be sold, A likely negroe woman, has had the smallpox and measles. Likewise a parcel of black-smiths and gun-smiths tools, such as are fit for rifelling, to be disposed of; and a smith's shop to be lett."

Finding the income from this estate insufficient to support and educate her six children, the widow moved away and opened a grocery shop. This she called the "Blazing Star," and here, among other things, she sold liquors, both wholesale and retail, a venture successful enough to enable her to educate her children. Benjamin later described his mother as a woman of very extraordinary mind, full of energy, who had graduated from a boarding school in Phila-delphia and was well acquainted with the common branches of fe-male education. He felt that, as a mother, she had no superior in kindness, generosity, or in attention to the morals and religious principles of her children.

Some years after her husband's death, Susanna Rush married again, a distiller named Morris who was, according to Benjamin, a rough, unkind man often abusive in his treatment of her. This was naturally a source of great anguish to her eldest son, so much attached to her.

* * *

One of his mother's many brothers and sisters, his Aunt Sarah, was the wife of the Reverend Dr. Samuel Finley, a gentleman who was to play an important part in shaping Benjamin Rush's mind and character. When Benjamin was nine years old, he and his younger brother Jacob were sent to the West Nottingham Acad-emy, of which this uncle was the headmaster. The Academy was located in the Province of Maryland just across the line of the Three Lower Counties, now Delaware, in a village with the engag-ing name of Rising Sun. Rush later described the school as the out-standing one in the middle provinces of America, and Dr. Finley as a most gifted schoolteacher, both just and wise as a disciplinarian, who took uncommon pains to insure good manners among his scholars.

"I once saw him," wrote Rush, "spend half an hour in exposing the folly and wickedness of an offence with his rod in hand. The culprit stood all this while trembling and weeping before him. After he had ended his admonitions, he lifted his rod as high as he could and then permitted it to fall gently upon his hand. The boy was surprised at this conduct. 'There, go about your business (said the Doctor). I mean shame, and not pain [to] be your punishment in the present instance.' "

Finley's instruction included Latin and Greek and the reading, writing, and speaking of careful English. To his religious teachings Rush ascribed the fact that at no time did he ever entertain a doubt as to the divine origin of the Bible. Throughout his life, he preserved the greatest reverence for this old schoolmaster, who had exhibited in the governance and instruction not only of his school but also of his family "an example of apostolical prudence, piety and zeal." But Dr. Finley was a practical man as well as a devout and scholarly one. All the boarders shared in the labors of harvest and of haying; and Rush attributes to these activities the excellent health of the students, with due appreciation for the plentiful table of country food provided by his Aunt Sarah, who added that "the appetite is the ruling principle in young people."

Rush writes of his school days with nostalgia: "There is not a fruit tree, nor a rivulet of water on it that was not dear to me." He describes his melancholy pleasure as, some years later, he rambled slowly through the fields and meadows and orchard in which he had shared rural labors and festivity with his master and schoolmates. One thing only did he regret—that he might have profited so much more from the opportunities of literary and moral instruction, instead of indulging in the amusements of hunting and gunning and the like, which were so great as to overpower the relish for study. He persuaded himself that in a rural school these pleasures should be forbidden and replaced by agricultural pursuits, which would early inculcate the idea of a connection between industry and property.

In the spring of 1759, Benjamin left the West Nottingham Academy and entered the College of New Jersey, where, after an examination by two of the tutors, he was admitted to the junior class. This college was in Princeton but it retained its original name for 150 years until 1896, when it became Princeton University.

Shortly after Rush matriculated, the Reverend Dr. Samuel

Davies, a renowned orator in the pulpit, succeeded to the presidency. A self-made man, handsome, elegant of manner, dignified, and accomplished in classical literature and philosophy, Rush admired him greatly. Under him, he discovered in himself talents for poetry, prose composition and public speaking. Those of his verses that have come down to us are, at best, halting sentimental couplets conventionally written, but there is little doubt of his ability to express his thoughts in clear, forceful prose.

Even so, Rush again laments that he did not make the most of his opportunities, saying that those who knew him at that time remembered him only as an idle, playful, and sometimes mischievous boy—a description hard to reconcile with what we know of him. But he admits that he was inspired with a love of knowledge and that he was taught by Davies how to acquire it in the subsequent periods of his life. Above all, he is grateful for the habit he formed of recording facts and opinions and of constantly associating the use of pen and ink with every book he read.

His gift for public speaking and what today would be called his verbal aptitude were such that many of his friends urged him to take up the study of the law. This advice was approved and reinforced by Dr. Davies, who may, indeed, have shown good judgment. Who knows whether Benjamin Rush's many talents and the partisan side of his nature, which would later come to the fore, might not have been better adapted to the relatively stable authority of the law than to the rapidly changing uncertainties in the field of medicine, which ultimately claimed him? The opinion of Dr. Davies that he "should make a better figure at the bar, than in the walks of a hospital" fixed him in his determination, and his mother in consequence applied to a lawyer in Philadelphia to take him into his office.

After his graduation with a B.A. degree from the College of New Jersey at the age of not quite fifteen, and before he began reading law, he went to visit a schoolmate in Maryland. On his way there and back he stopped for a few days to see his aunt and his old schoolmaster, Dr. Finley.

Just before Rush took leave of him, his uncle called him to the end of the piazza and asked him whether he had chosen a profession. Benjamin told him that he had and that he expected to begin the study of the law as soon as he returned to Philadelphia. The reverend gentleman then warned young Rush that the practice of law was full of temptations and cautioned him not to think of it but, instead, to study physic. Then he added: "But before you determine on any thing . . . set apart a day for fasting and prayer, and ask God to direct you in your choice of a profession." Rush confesses that he accepted the advice but neglected the fasting and prayer; and from Dr. Davies, whom he saw later in Philadelphia, he got a recommendation to Dr. John Redman. Thus did Benjamin Rush embark upon the profession of medicine.

*   *   *

He was not without misgivings about his decision. He acknowledged "an uncommon aversion from seeing such sights as are connected with its practice." To be able to "stand the sight of blood" was once regarded as a prerequisite to becoming a doctor of medicine. One seldom hears about this today. But in Rush's time, there were no general anaesthetics, there was no asepsis or even antisepsis and, of course, there were no antibiotic drugs. How brutal surgical operations must have appeared under such circumstances and what a strong stomach was needed to withstand exposure not only to the intolerable agony of suffering patients, but to the stench of foul, suppurating wounds.

Rush was, moreover, still tempted both by the ministry and by the law. "There were periods in my life," he writes, "in which I regretted the choice I had made of the profession of medicine, and once, after I was thirty years of age, I made preparations for beginning the study of the law. But providence overruled my intentions. . . ." But about the law he also had negative sentiments. Later in life, in his *Commonplace Book*, he quotes Senator Maclay of Pennsylvania as observing, over a cup of tea, that half the Senate were lawyers, and that he had never known one of them to retract or alter an opinion, even after the fullest discussion of it, which he ascribed to their habits of contending at the bar for victory instead of truth.

Thus did Benjamin Rush vacillate. And no wonder. He was compounded of so many elements that one mold could hardly hold them all. His genius lay in finally accommodating himself to the frame of his chosen profession and at the same time allowing himself to become, before his passionate life was over, as rationally legalistic as any lawyer and as Calvinistically indignant and rhetorical as any preacher of the Gospel. This was his singlar talent—to fashion of his life what his inner needs demanded. As with some other famous men, his greatest act of creation was what he made of himself.

During his forming time he was much influenced by Finley and Davies. Not only were they his revered teachers but they also served as rôle models with whom he could identify. Thus they helped him discover himself. Today many adolescents are deprived of such figures in their lives. This may well be why so many of them flounder for so long in a state of confusion. Either they have no heroes, or their heroes have been so debunked that they are half ashamed to admit the need of them. They are, moreover, deprived of the annealing effect of responsibility and so they remain in a prolonged, rebellious and discontented dependence.

Benjamin Rush, on the other hand, at this juncture when he was nearly fifteen, had already taken his first steps—even if premature ones—into manhood. If Davies had presided over his "forming time" and had taught him good habits of study and of recording facts that served him so well, and if Finley had converted him by his authority and a few solemn words to the pursuit of physic, how fortunate Rush now was in his master, Dr. John Redman, to whom he was apprenticed for a little more than five years. By all accounts Redman was not only a personage but a great doctor and Rush venerated him as he had his other mentors. Of his apprenticeship he wrote:

"In the month of February 1761 I began the study of medicine and continued constantly in my master's family and shop 'till July 1766. During this period I was absent from his business but eleven days, and never spent more than three evenings out of his house. My master at this time was in the most extensive business of any physician in the city, and as he had at no time more than two apprentices, he kept them constantly employed. In addition to preparing and compounding medicines, visiting the sick and performing many little offices of a nurse to them, I took the exclusive charge of his books and accompts."

When Rush assumed these arduous duties he was a youth of only fifteen years. Nonetheless, there can be seen in him, as in most of us, the plan of personality already well laid down. He was a fatherless boy and a needful one—needful of a guiding hand and of a model. Both of his schoolmasters, first Finley and then Davies, and now his preceptor, John Redman, became such models to him and helped him to find his identity and to define his goals in life.

Until the end of his apprenticeship and his departure for Edinburgh, no well-established medical school existed in the Colonies. The first one was formed in Philadelphia in 1765, with Rush's slightly older contemporaries, Dr. John Morgan and Dr. William Shippen Jr., both of them graduates of Dr. Finley's West Nottingham Academy, as, respectively, professor of the theory and practice of medicine and professor of anatomy, surgery, and midwifery. Rush's only formal professional training in the Colonies was his attendance at the lectures of these two men in the year prior to his departure for Edinburgh.

Although in Europe, England, and Scotland medical schools had existed in antiquity and throughout the Middle Ages, the circumstances in the Colonies were not such as to favor their development. Even after medical schools came into being, the personal apprentice system continued to prevail and no generally accepted standards of excellence for medical schools were adopted until much later—about 1910. This preceptorial system continued for many years, remaining the principal method by which students obtained clinical experience to supplement the lectures they attended in the medical schools. In fact, teaching outside the medical colleges continued up until recent times and evolved into the so-called quiz classes, which were especially popular in New York, where even after the beginning of the 20th century they were conducted by some of the leading physicians and surgeons. The English and Scottish hospital-schools became our first models, and these were later supplanted by the Germanic university clinics and by emphasis on the fundamental medical sciences in which Rush had relatively little sophistication.

The apprentice system, suffering from parochialism and from an emphasis on the practice of medicine rather than its pursuit as a science, offered, nevertheless, the advantage of close association with men of superior character and accomplishments. In view of the tender years of the apprentices, this must have been an important consideration.

John Redman was distinguished both for his character and for his accomplishments. A closer look at him will sharpen some of the influences brought to bear on Rush at a critical time in his life. Like Rush, Redman had in his youth been to boarding school with a reverend gentleman who had taught him Greek and Latin and had given him his religious instruction. He had served his own medical apprenticeship in Philadelphia with Dr. John Kearsley Sr., a hard taskmaster with a morose and churlish temper. Kearsley's apprentices served as coachmen, messenger boys, prescription clerks, nurses, and assistant surgeons. It was with such a man that Redman had had his own rigorous preceptorship, but his good nature was such that in his turn he visited little severity on his pupils. However, he worked them hard and kept them endlessly busy. Rush, still a boy of only sixteen, writes to his friend Ebenezer Hazard, in September 1762, of the constant hurry of his employment and of the sickness that afflicted the citizens of Philadelphia, of which numbers died daily.

This was his first reference to yellow fever. According to Redman's account of it, prepared at the request of his "professional children," the epidemic began in late August, reached its peak in the fourth week of September and ceased in the fourth week of October. At its height, more than twenty people were dying daily of the disease.

Redman was convinced that it had been imported from Savannah by a sailor who came down with the fever on shipboard, whence friends had brought him in secrecy to the house of one Leadbetter, who lived near the "new" market. What happened to the sailor is not known, but Leadbetter and several members of his family contracted yellow fever and died of it.

Redman's comments in a treatise on the prevention and treatment of this disease have a quaint sound to our ears. He urged temperance in all things; also that the physician should pay no visit to a sick patient on an empty stomach. He believed that a quid of tobacco in the mouth possessed a peculiar virtue, since it prevented the swallowing of saliva; also that the danger of contagion was much reduced by the fumes that arose on plunging a hot iron into a bowl of vinegar. It is quite possible that these fumes kept away the mosquito, which later generations were to prove to be the transmitter of this infection. Redman opposed many of the prophylactic methods then in use, believing that they affected the mind with fears likely to render one "more susceptible of infection than the omission of them." Though an enthusiastic bloodletter, he reserved this practice in his yellow fever patients for those with a full pulse or for pregnant women. His therapeutic efforts, however, were heroic, consisting of purging with saline laxatives as opposed to the use of emetics. This was intended "to discharge the morbid matter as fast as possible" and then "to restore strength to the debilitated powers after the disease was terminated."

* * *

It was natural for young Rush to pattern himself after his teacher and to be guided in his career by Dr. Redman's experiences. After practicing in Bermuda for several years and then serving in the French and Indian War, Redman had gone abroad to study, first to Edinburgh—in its heyday in 1746, the year of Rush's birth—and thereafter to Leyden, the other center of medical learning. In Leyden he came under the posthumous influence of the great Boerhaave, who had died in 1738—a man of enormous authority, whose talents as a bedside teacher must have been incomparable and who had attracted to his wards half the leading doctors of Europe, including many of the members of the Edinburgh faculty later to become famous. Boerhaave taught his students not only the art of careful observation but of carefully recording their observations. His hospital was the cradle of modern clinical methods, the place where sound procedures for examining the sick were first worked out.

Rush was fortunate, indeed, to have had as his first teacher in medicine a man who had himself been schooled in Edinburgh and in Leyden and later at Guy's Hospital in London, and in Paris. In Edinburgh he had had a rigorous drilling in anatomy under the first of the three famous Monros. Dissection of the human body—then such a vital part of the study of medicine—often met with the angry opposition of the public. In the middle of the 16th century, when Andreas Vesalius had dissected a human corpse in Paris, he had encountered such opposition. And two centuries later, Redman's younger colleague and Rush's teacher, Dr. William Shippen Jr., would be similarly dealt with. The windows of his dissection room were smashed and he had to hide from a mob of outraged citizens. The cadavers, which Shippen was dissecting, had been taken from the graves of slaves and paupers. Indeed, body snatching was once the ghoulish accompaniment of the study of medicine.

When Dr. Redman returned to Philadelphia, he established himself in the practice of surgery and obstetrics and was appointed consultant to the Pennsylvania Hospital. With this background he was far better equipped than most of his colleagues and, in addition, he was happily endowed with great kindness and concern for his patients. One of them said that "death had nothing terrible in it when Dr. Redman spoke to her about it." He soon gave up the practice of surgery and obstetrics, confining himself to medicine, not for purposes of specializing but because of his enfeebled health. In his fortieth year he suffered from a subdiaphragmatic abscess, probably the result of amoebic dysentery, and he is supposed to have had yellow fever twice. This caused him to retire from practice at a relatively early age. Nevertheless, he became the dean of the physicians of Philadelphia, and its leading medical teacher, and was soon to be elected first president of the College of Physicians.

Among his pupils, he counted not only Benjamin Rush, perhaps the most brilliant of them, but also John Morgan, the founder of the first medical school in North America, Caspar Wistar, the first American contributor to the science of anatomy, and John Redman Coxe, the founder of medical journalism in Pennsylvania. With Morgan and Shippen he was on the staff of the Pennsylvania Hospital and this enabled his youthful apprentice Rush to attend their lectures and to visit the sick. Both Morgan and Shippen, as well as their teacher Redman, had studied in Edinburgh before Rush. Such coveted foreign training was reserved for the favored sons of the relatively well-to-do.

Redman's contributions to medical literature were, to be sure, sparse. His treatise on yellow fever has already been mentioned. As early as 1759 he published a pamphlet on the defense of inoculation for smallpox, which convinced many of the soundness of this practice. The use of variolation or direct arm-to-arm inoculation had been introduced by the celebrated Lady Mary Wortley Montagu and was then supported in England by Dr. Richard Mead, one of the leading physicians in London, whose word had great weight. In France it was defended by Voltaire and in America by the Mathers, Increase and Cotton, who turned from their preoccupation with witchcraft to urge its employment. But Redman had

much to do with its acceptance and so prepared the way for vaccination, which was not discovered until 1796.

His very appearance bespoke restless energy. It is no wonder
that he kept his young apprentices endlessly busy. He lived to the
age of eighty-four, and long after his death he was remembered as
the prototype of the good physician and wise medical teacher, who
had brought to his practice sound judgment and high ideals.

In his old age he was described by a younger contemporary as
below average height, with a dark complexion, lively black eyes,
and an eagle-pointed nose, quick of speech and gesture and nimble
of step. He dressed in a broadskirted dark coat with a pair of Baron
Steuben's military boots reaching above his knees, and a hat cocked
up behind over a full-bottomed powdered wig. With hardness of
hearing he developed a habit of lifting the corner of his wig from
one ear when spoken to. He rode a fat pony mare, which he
hitched to the shutter of the house he was visiting so that she stood
on the foot pavement. Such was the young apprentice's preceptor
—the man who with a few others temporarily filled the gap in the
training of American physicians when medical schools and scientific discipline were unknown.

*   *   *

On his part Rush was an industrious and ambitious pupil. He
took much pleasure in reading physic in Latin and Hippocrates in
the original Greek, and he translated the Hippocratic aphorisms
into English—this, despite a lament that his knowledge of Greek
was deficient.

Toward the end of his apprenticeship he wrote to his friend
Ebenezer Hazard, saying that with Dr. Redman out of town he
was so busy from morning to evening in visiting his patients that he
had little time to devote to friendship, although here as always he
protested his devotion and affection. In another letter to Ebenezer,
he wrote: "I have experienced kindness from Dr. Redman I had
little reason to expect. I have ever found in him not only the in-
dulgent master but the sincere friend and tender father." It was
good that he found this at this time of his life for it was just what
he needed. Then he added: "This, my dear Ebenezer, is our forming time. . . . Let us then be more diligent in preparing ourselves
to serve our generation."

In the last month of his apprenticeship, July 1766, Rush took care of Dr. Finley in his final illness. He had been president of the College of New Jersey since 1761, having succeeded Davies. For several weeks the young doctor sat up with his old schoolmaster every other night and finally he performed the sad task of closing his eyes, doing his best to conceal the tears in his own. This deeply moving event marked the end of a chapter for Benjamin Rush.

In a month he would be leaving his master and quitting his familiar and taxing round of duties. Yet, even before he left home for study abroad, the hidden man in him began to emerge and presaged a concern for public affairs and a bent for controversy which would characterize much of his later life.

The Stamp Act was a particular affront to a lettered man such as Rush. For it levied a tax upon newspapers, almanacs, pamphlets and documents of all types, including insurance policies and ships' papers. It covered fifty-five articles; the excise on a college degee was £2. He was outraged that the Quakers should have openly spoken in favor of it.

Rush again wrote to Hazard, this time saying, "We begin to fear the news of the Stamp Act's being repealed is premature." Albeit this letter was dated March 29, 1776, the Act had, in fact, been repealed eleven days earlier, primarily because of the ringing oratory of the elder Pitt. There was general rejoicing after the repeal and, while this may well have been shared by Rush, it did not diminish his smouldering antagonism to the British Crown, a sentiment of which he had not yet become fully aware. But the ferment of republicanism and politics was already at work in him despite his youth.

2

THE GRAND TOUR—
EDINBURGH

⌘ THE MORNING AFTER THE FUNERAL OF THEIR FRIEND
Cummins, Rush and Potts set out early from Liverpool by stagecoach bound for Edinburgh. Passing through Lancashire, West-
morland, and Cumberland, they arrived at their destination after a
journey of four arduous days. In the 18th century the traveler
was at the mercy of the condition of the roads. After heavy
rains these were often a slough of mud in which horses floun-
dered and coaches sank to their axles. Only the newest coaches
had springs. Although at the close of the war with Frederick
the Great in 1763 new highways had been constructed, their
upkeep was not looked upon as a part of public responsibility. The
demand for toll money was often refused and, indeed, led at times
to rioting.

The ancient city of Edinburgh was to be Benjamin Rush's home
for the next two years. He came to regard his sojourn there as the
most important influence on his character and the future course of
his life. Indeed, he considered the University of Edinburgh as his
birthplace in the profession of medicine.

At this time Edinburgh was a city of some 80,000 inhabitants.
The area that it covered was about a third less than Philadelphia,
although the population was more than twice as large. This fact
Rush ascribed to the height of the houses, in each of which seven
or eight families were crowded. A common pair of steps which

communicated with all the rooms of a house were open and exposed and used almost like public thoroughfares. Although the people lived together so closely in these human hives, they were in the main strangers to each other.

Rush boarded in one such dwelling belonging to two maiden ladies named Galloway, but he knew nothing about the people immediately above or below him, not even their names. There were many inconveniences in such living arrangements, especially as there were no yards or cellars or even outhouses. Filth of every kind was thrown out of the windows generally at night, to be carried away in carts the next morning. After ten o'clock at night one walked out at one's peril. It was no uncommon thing to receive a pailful from an upper story window. This was called being *naturalized*, a ceremony which Rush happily escaped, but not his unfortunate friend Potts.

In spite of these crude practices, the city presented, as it still does, the picture of somber nobility, dominated by the fastness of the Castle, atop its perpendicular rock, 300 feet above elegant Princes Street.

* * *

The University of Edinburgh was ancient, going back to 1583, but a century passed before a medical college was founded in 1681 with a charter from King Charles II. Forty years before Rush arrived there, the Faculty of Medicine had become part of the University. But even before then it had been famous for its line of distinguished anatomists, all named Alexander Monro—distinguished by *Primus, Secundus,* and *Tertius.* The birthdates of these men of three successive generations spanned the century from 1697 to 1773. It was the second of these professors with whom Rush studied—the one for whom the foramen of Monro, or the opening which connects the ventricles of the brain, is named. His son shared the Chair of Anatomy, but during his tenure the quality of teaching declined owing to the scarcity of cadavers for dissection. A contemporary surgeon and anatomist, John Bell, wrote this of *Tertius:*

"In Dr. Monro's class, unless there be a fortunate succession of bloody murders, not three subjects are dissected in the year. On the remains of a subject fished up from the bottom of a tub of spirits, are demonstrated those delicate nerves which are to be avoided or divided in our operations; and these are demonstrated once at the distance of 100 feet!"

This shortage of material for dissection led to grave robbing by determined students, who were given the macabre name of "Resurrectionists." Among them were John Bell's younger brother Charles, who contributed greatly to our knowledge of the anatomy of the brain and central nervous system and who was the first to distinguish between sensory and motor nerves, and also the famous anatomist and surgeon, John Hunter, with whom Rush would later study in London.

A brisk trade in corpses developed between Dublin and Edinburgh, and the high price offered for cadavers drew professional criminals into the business. Two of them came to trial after having murdered at least sixteen victims. One turned King's evidence, but the other was hanged and, in true Scottish fashion so that the punishment might fit the crime, his brain was publicly dissected and his skeleton is still on view in the anatomy museum of the University.

Edinburgh was famous not only for its surgeons and anatomists but for its physicians as well. At this time its medical faculty was the most celebrated in the world. On his arrival, Rush promptly obtained tickets of admission to the different lectures; besides Monro he mentions especially Cullen, Black, Gregory, and Hope. Of these professors, Hope taught botony and *materia medica*; Gregory, a physician and a philosopher, taught the practice of medicine; and Joseph Black had just succeeded Cullen in the Chair of Chemistry. Black is renowned still for having laid the foundations of quantitative analysis, for having evolved the theory of latent heat, and for founding the doctrine of specific heats. It is to Rush's credit that even as a young student he recognized the value of Black's work.

But the most important in his influence on Benjamin Rush was Cullen. From him Rush got his notion that all life is an expression of nervous force and that disease is due to a failure of its regulatory powers, leading either to exaggeration of nervous functions or to weakness of them. The idea was that in most acute febrile diseases the energy of the brain is diminished and this brings on general debility, setting up the "cold fit" or chill stage. But then the self-regulatory mechanisms come into play, inducing a spasm of the small arteries, especially on the surface of the body. This spasm then acts as an irritant to the heart, setting up the "hot fit" or fever stage.

Although one can detect in this theory a precursor of the *homeostasis* or the self-regulatory mechanism of Claude Bernard and Cannon, it was deductively derived and not based on sound empirical observation. But it was the more stoutly defended, especially by Rush, who later all but broke his lance, if not his lancet, on it. It led, moreover, to an extravagant kind of therapy, designed rather toward a logical consistency with theory than toward any statistically tested appraisal of results. Treatment, it declared, must aim to build up nervous energy by restorative drugs and diet or to reduce it by bleeding, purging, and semi-starvation. Rush swallowed all this teaching uncritically, and later he would push it to its limits.

Even so, Cullen was a great teacher. An amiable and generous man of strong philosophical bent, he was a popular clinical lecturer, who spoke in English rather than Latin, which had previously been the custom of the faculty. A contemporary portrait shows him dressed in academic robes, wearing a full-bottomed wig, his face distinguished for its high forehead and long-pointed intelligent nose, one of his sensitive hands clasping a scroll and the other with uplifted forefinger in the perfect posture of the persuasive pedagogue. It is no wonder that he made such a strong impression on Rush—the more so because he had been the teacher of his teachers—and he quickly joined the gallery of Rush's heroes. In his *Scottish Journal* Rush writes of him, "It is scarcely possible to do Justice to this great man's Character either as a scholar—a physician—or a Man."

Benjamin Rush was still a youth of only twenty, and it is not surprising that he should have idolized his teacher and seen in Cullen the mirrored image of his own coming eminence. He and his friend Potts had been commended to Dr. Cullen by one of their former teachers, and with this introduction they were made welcome to Cullen's house and introduced to his family. In almost every letter written from Edinburgh, Rush sings the praises of his new hero and emphasizes his genius, his wisdom, and his learning. In his *Scottish Journal* he again writes:

"D^r: *Cullen* in particular will always be dear to me. I have experienced not a little of his private friendship. I never asked a Favour from him but wt: I obtained it. in a word I loved him like a Father, & if at present I entertain any Hopes of being eminent in my Profession I owe them entirely to this great man."

It was Dr. Cullen who some years later provided the occasion for an extremely interesting communication to Rush from Benjamin Franklin. This letter reveals the professional point of view of both Cullen and of his young protegé, Rush. Franklin wrote in July 1773:

"I have not seen Dr. Cullen's book, but am glad to hear that he speaks of catarrhs or colds by contagion. I have been long satisfied from observation, that besides the general colds now termed *influenzas*, (which may possibly spread by contagion, as well as by a particular quality of the air), people often catch cold from one another when shut up together in close rooms, coaches, etc., and when sitting near and conversing so as to breathe in each other's transpiration; the disorder being in a certain state. I think, too, that it is the frouzy, corrupt air from animal substances, and the perspired matter from our bodies, which being long confined in beds not lately used, and clothes not lately worn, and books long shut up in close rooms, obtains that kind of putridity, which occasions the colds observed upon sleeping in, wearing, and turning over such bedclothes or books, and not their coldness or dampness. From these causes, but more from too full living, with too little exercise, proceed in my opinion most of the disorders which for about one hundred and fifty years past the English have called *colds*.

"As to Dr. Cullen's cold or catarrh *a frigore*, I question whether such an one ever existed. Travelling in our severe winters, I have suffered cold sometimes to an extremity only short of freezing, but this did not make me *catch cold*. And, for moisture, I have been in the river every evening two or three hours for a fortnight together, when one would suppose I might imbibe enough of it to *take cold* if humidity could give it; but no such effect ever followed. Boys never get cold by swimming. Nor are people at sea, or who live at Bermudas, or St. Helena, small islands, where the air must be ever moist from the dashing and breaking waves against their rocks on all sides, more subject to colds than those who inhabit part of a continent where the air is driest. Dampness may indeed assist in producing putridity and those miasmata which infect us with the disorder we call a cold; but of itself can never by a little addition of moisture hurt a body filled with watery fluids from head to foot."

In this letter, Franklin, with his usual prescience, anticipated by about a century the germ theory of disease and perhaps also allergic reactions. His mind was freed from the need to build and defend a *system*, which possessed Cullen and his young American disciple, not to mention others. He was able, therefore, to look at complicated facts with the eye of the radical empiricist. In spite of being a moral philosopher and a man of universal and inventive genius, Franklin was not primarily concerned with the theoretical interpretation of natural phenomena. On the other hand, thoughtful physicians of his epoch, all but overwhelmed by the flood of facts emanating from the successful observations and experiments of the 17th and the early part of the 18th centuries, felt the need of establishing theoretical systems to explain them.

Among the scientists who uncovered these facts were such men as Newton and Harvey in England; Malpighi and Morgagni and, slightly later, Galvani in Italy; van Helmont in Brussels; von Haller of Tübingen, who later joined the famous pair of Dutch physicians, Boerhaave and van Swieten in Leyden. These men are great in the annals of medical history for having contributed to our understanding of the workings of the body or for their phenomenological descriptions of disease. Many of them were also practitioners of medicine, intellectually far superior, of course, to the average doctor, who was still a somewhat poor and confused creature now cut adrift, by the new knowledge, from the firm anchorage of classical and medieval medicine which up to this time had held him.

Thomas Sydenham, who was another one of Rush's heroes, was the exception. A 17th-century London practitioner, without academic position or pretensions, he became the first modern clinician. Although not a distinguished man of science, nor the father of any system or theory, he introduced in one volume of moderate size the ontological conception of medicine, which investigates the essential properties and relations of the organism. Sydenham was concerned with the description of symptoms and their changes rather than with speculations in natural philosophy. His accounts of gout, from which he suffered himself, of smallpox, measles, dysentery, and syphilis have become medical classics. He recognized symp-

toms as the expression of the struggle between the nature of the
sick person and the noxious influences that produced the illness. In
other words, he saw them as part of nature's healing activity, and
from this he concluded that the doctor's goal must be to assist nature in its struggle and to guide and intensify the healing power of
nature. Furthermore, he realized that illness was never a local process but a reaction involving the whole organism.

Sydenham has been well named the English Hippocrates. But
Hippocrates, with all his great clinical acumen, recognized only
sick individuals, not diseases as entities, whereas Sydenham raises
himself above the platform of antiquity and by introducing the notion of special pathology emphasizes the importance of diagnosis.
His principles are still our own and are the basis of modern medicine.

Rush, while an apprentice under Dr. Redman, had read Sydenham, as he had Boerhaave's lectures on physiology and van Swieten's practical aphorisms. Rush came to revere Sydenham above all
others. Years later he would bring out an American edition of his
works on *Acute and Chronic Diseases* and likewise pay homage to
his hero by naming his country villa "Sydenham."

Although Sydenham's important work held great promise for
the future of medicine, his classification of diseases was based
chiefly on an enumeration and description of their symptoms. This
had its drawbacks. There was no end to the number and variety of
symptom-diseases; as many as 1,800 or more different illnesses were
listed. Cullen, himself, described hundreds. The result, of course,
was the confusion which characterized 18th-century medicine. As
Professor Shryock has pointed out, the very success of observation and experiment prior to 1700 led inevitably to the subjective
and fanciful medicine so popular for more than a century thereafter.

Sydenham's contemporary, the philosopher John Locke, who
had studied medicine, seems to have been aware of what was coming. He said: "I wonder that, after the pattern Dr. Sydenham has
set them of a better way, men should return to the romance way of
physic." But return they did.

There is no doubt that Cullen was among the archromancers.
But his motives and intentions were good ones. He felt a great need
to organize the new knowledge into a coordinated whole, to pro-

vide for medicine some kind of unified field theory such as Newton
had done for mechanics in terms of relatively simple mathematical
law. Here is what Cullen said about this:

"For, when many new facts had been acquired it becomes requi-
site that these should be incorporated into a system, whereby not
only particular subjects may be improved, but the whole may be
rendered more complete, consistent, and useful."

Laudable though this aim was, it was premature and so missed its
mark. Facts were not at hand to support the dogmatic generalization which Cullen indulged in. This need to explain led not only to
what has been called a "plague of speculation" but also to an unfortunate tendency toward partisanship and propaganda, reminis-
cent of medieval medicine and perhaps anticipatory of modern
psychiatry. The "Solidists," to which camp Cullen adhered, pitted
themselves against the "Humoralists" and each side defended its
views with pugnacious zeal. Warmed by the Scottish love for
wordy metaphysical discourse and a battle of wits, they tried to
settle matters of fact by argument and disputation.

But one should not belittle these great clinical teachers of the
18th century. To be sure, they suffered from a cultural lag which
kept them from realizing the practical benefits to be derived from
the scientific discoveries in chemistry and physics of the previous
century. But they were beset on all sides by urgent problems which
they were impatient to solve. In view of the virtual disappearance
of many of the acute epidemic diseases today, the pace of medical
practice and research is now more deliberate. Furthermore, in the
18th century, the dissemination of new knowledge was slow,
whereas now we are all but swamped by a swift surfeit.

*　　*　　*

Such was the atmosphere in which Rush was immersed during
his student days in Edinburgh. In truth he lived and breathed medicine as the best of our medical students do today. In a letter to a
former classmate he wrote of the medical college:

" 'Tis now in the zenith of its glory. The whole world I believe
does not afford a set of greater men than are at present united in
the College of Edinburgh."

His youth, his enthusiasm, his diligence, his great ambition, and
his need to identify himself with figures of authority sufficiently

explain why Edinburgh took such possession of him, and why it remained his intellectual and spiritual home.

In addition to his preoccupation with his profession, Rush found time to revive his knowledge of Latin and to study Italian and Spanish sufficiently to acquire a reading knowledge. He was also taught French by "a man of uncommon genius" who forbade him to commit any rule of grammar to memory and, with his help, he made himself "master of the French language"; at least, so he tells us. Then in addition to all of this, he studied "mathematicks" under a private tutor.

On the 19th of June 1768, Rush was admitted to the degree of Doctor of Medicine. He took the usual examinations and defended his thesis—written, of course, in Latin, under the title *De Coctione Ciborum in Ventriculo*—the digestion of food in the stomach. This was a rather crude attempt at a chemical explanation of the digestive process, based on three experiments performed on himself and one on a friend. The work was published in Edinburgh as a pamphlet of thirty pages. The first three pages, written in the florid style of the period, were his formal dedication to the seven stars of his firmament. Benjamin Franklin was the most lustrous. He came first. The others were Joseph Black and his former teachers, given in this order: John Redman, William Shippen, and John Morgan; then his friend and former classmate, Jonathan Smith; and finally his brother Jacob.

When copies finally reached Philadelphia, Dr. Morgan's umbrage at being overshadowed in rank by Redman and Shippen led to an exchange of letters between him and Rush. Benjamin tried to wriggle out of his uncomfortable position. Calling Dr. Shippen his oldest friend and master—a tune which he would later change— and casting aspersions on Redman, his erstwhile venerable and venerated preceptor, he wrote that it was to Black, the Scottish chemist, who was then in his ascendancy, that he owed most of the knowledge he possessed.

His letter to Dr. Morgan ends with: "I hope therefore, my good friend, you will overlook my omission in placing your name after Dr. Shippen's." Then he adds, rather disarmingly: "My thesis has been read, and is now I dare say forgot forever. No one will remember six weeks hence whose names were mentioned in my dedication." Could it be that Rush was already angling for the Chair of Chemistry which Morgan would later help him secure?

The dissertation appears to have been well received. One of his contemporaries described it as an accurate and ingenious performance presented with lucidity. If time was to prove that Rush's inferences were wrong, since gastric digestion is not, in fact, a process of fermentation, no one should belittle his heroic attempt, which required his taking tartar emetic—a sweetish metallic salt of antimony—which made him vomit after a heavy meal, and this three times in succession. Later, one of Rush's students, J. R. Young, demonstrated the acid nature of digestion. Six decades would elapse before another American, the Army surgeon, William Beaumont, would make his classical observations and establish the true nature of gastric digestion, which depends on the action of enzymes and not on fermentation.

Amid all these activities Rush still found time for a lively correspondence and a rewarding social life, both with his fellow students and with families of influence and position. He had hitherto resolved not to form connections with persons of great distinction, but now, after a little more than half a year in Edinburgh, he found that he could not avoid such associations. Actually he had a strong inclination toward the great, by whom, throughout his life, he seems to have been welcomed and with whom he formed so many profitable relationships. Often he says as much—that he sought this man or that one out because of his instructive conversation or because he could learn from him.

But if Rush was on the make it was not because of personal ambition alone. Early in life he was aware of the destiny that awaited him; he was firm in his purpose to devote himself to the good of mankind. Thus the picture arises of an unusually personable man with energy and charm, a little deficient in humor and a little vain, but with warmth and affection and a capacity for sincere relationships. Writing to his old friend Jonathan Bayard Smith in Philadelphia and referring to the recent death of several young friends during his absence from home, Rush said:

"I sometimes wish my temper was less disposed to friendship and that I loved my fellow creatures less. It would exempt me from all those calamities which arise from sympathy, which indeed are the only calamities I at present feel."

He was happy with his fellow students who had come to Edinburgh from many parts of Europe and the British Empire. Americans and West Indians, Portuguese and Italians, Frenchmen and Englishmen, Irishmen and Dutchmen, Germans and Swiss, Russians and Danes were united in a common fraternity. "There was then no competition of interest to divide us," writes Rush. Together they pursued their clinical studies in the Old Infirmary on Drummond Street, which had been built in 1741.

He became a member of the Royal Medical Society, which met once a week in a room at the Royal Infirmary, there to "dispute upon subjects in philosophy and the practice of physic." Professors and students alike belonged to it. His own dissertations, presented before the Society, concerned bilious fever and venereal diseases. Twenty years later he would be elected an Honorary Member on account of his distinguished work.

In addition to the Medical Society, in Rush's own words he had the "pleasure of being domesticated in several very amiable private families," distinguished for their "learning, taste, or piety." Among them he mentions the Reverend Dr. John Erskine, an evangelical divine and friend of Jonathan Edwards; Mr. Thomas Hogg, the banker; Sir Alexander Dick, a prominent and wealthy physician, in whose house he dined with the philosopher and historian, David Hume; and he was received in the home of Professor Gregory, where he met Dr. William Robertson, author of *History of Scotland*, and later of a *History of America*, and at that time principal of the University of Edinburgh. Rush says that he was frequently made happy by the company of the blind poet, Thomas Blacklock, whose store of literary information and pleasant manners impressed him greatly.

Although Rush was avid for enlightening and elevating company, he was neither a social climber nor a conventional snob, in spite of his obvious ambition to get ahead in the world. He felt much indebted to the landladies with whom he boarded, for their kindness, as he did to their brother, whom he considered a living dictionary. He met from time to time an old Highlander named Dugald Buchanan, a man of original mind, who was engaged in translating the Bible into Erse. Rush found acquaintance with him most profitable.

Another acquaintance should be mentioned because of his influence on Rush's political thinking. This was one John Bostock, a student of medicine in Edinburgh, to whom Rush had been given a letter of introduction through a chance meeting in Liverpool with Bostock's aunt. This lady had happened to be in attendance at the shop where Rush and his friend Potts went to pay for the articles they had bought for the burial of poor Cummins, their shipmate. Soon after his arrival in Edinburgh, Rush breakfasted with Bostock, whom he found to be well informed upon all subjects, particularly upon history, geography, and belles lettres—all of them of great moment to Rush. They discovered in conversation that each had had a forebear in the service of Oliver Cromwell, both ancestors having commanded a Company. This discovery immediately drew the two men together.

"He now," writes Rush, "opened his mind fully to me, and declared himself to be an advocate for the Republican principles for which our ancestors had fought. . . . Never before had I heard the authority of Kings called in question. I had been taught to consider them nearly as essential to political order as the Sun is to the order of our Solar System."

For the first time in his life, Rush admits, he exercised his reason on the subject of government. He renounced the prejudices of his previous education, became convinced of the absurdity of hereditary power, and was persuaded of the fact that no form of government could be rational unless it derived its authority from the suffrage of the people.

"This great and active truth became a ferment in my mind." But he adds discreetly: ". . . the change produced in my political principles by my friend Bostock had no effect upon my conversation or conduct. I considered the ancient order of things with respect to government as fixed and perpetual, and I enjoyed in theory only the new and elevating system of government I had adopted."

Rush seems to have forgotten for the moment how indignant and outraged he had been at the passage of the Stamp Act before he ever sailed from home, but his anger was then directed more at Parliament than at the Sovereign. Although he counted his conversations with his friend Bostock among the many benefits he derived from his stay in Edinburgh, to attribute his conversion to republican principles to them alone would be incorrect. The germ had been planted earlier in Pennsylvania; perhaps it took firmer root and sprouted on Scottish soil.

No wonder that Rush found Edinburgh so much to his liking. On all sides there were people and things that delighted him. He was struck with the moral order which prevailed among all classes, with the silence of the streets at night, with the absence of drunkenness, profanity, and gambling even among the "common people," and he was pleased that dancing took the place of silence or insipid conversation at all large evening gatherings. He loved what Benjamin Franklin had called Edinburgh's perpendicular streets, so characteristic of the city.

Thus we can imagine with what extreme satisfaction Rush was presented with the Freedom of the City at "a public and very grand entertainment" held on March 4, 1767, when he was received by the Council of Edinburgh as a burgess and gild brother of the City. But by then he was soon to leave Scotland forever—to part with this fascinating company of gifted men and women, and with the great and wise Cullen, father of all his pupils, from whom no one ever went away dissatisfied.

A curiously interesting series of Rush's letters of this period reveal the extraordinary and seemingly contradictory facets of his personality. There are five such letters addressed to the Reverend John Witherspoon.

This gentleman came into Rush's life in the following fashion. With the death of Samuel Finley just before his young nephew's departure for Edinburgh, the presidency of the College of New Jersey at Princeton had fallen vacant. This had occurred at a time when the ancient factional quarrel between the so-called Old Side and New Light Presbyterians was splitting the Church, and since the College was the principal training ground for Presbyterian ministers in the Colonies, the trustees sought to heal that schism by the election of Witherspoon, an eminent Scottish divine who had had no part in the factional struggle.

At this time Rush's future father-in-law, Richard Stockton, was in London, and he was sent to present Witherspoon with the minutes of the meeting at which he had been elected. Witherspoon refused the call, largely because of his wife's reluctance to leave Paisley and her fear of crossing the ocean. But the trustees persisted, and among many of their letters to him urging his acceptance, one written on Christmas Eve 1766, by the pastor of the Wall Street and Brick Churches in New York, made mention of Benjamin Rush as "a young gentleman of singular Merit, Parts &, I hope, true Piety" who is "extremely well qualified to give You the fullest information respecting the College & the State of the Country. . . ."

This had brought young Rush into the act. He now succeeded where his future father-in-law had failed. He was well prepared for the part, a loyal graduate of Nassau-Hall, reared in the cradle of the New Light Presbyterians, and deeply concerned about finding a worthy successor to his uncle. Then follow his letters—appealing, urging, cajoling, flattering, shaming Dr. Witherspoon into a change of mind. Witherspoon, who was twice Rush's age, took him seriously.

Rush showed both consummate diplomatic skill and his usual extravagant admiration for what he felt was a good and a great man. He speaks of Witherspoon's luminous mind, calls him a man to his very fingertips, says he has never heard his equal in the pulpit and that in point of genius he is Dr. Davies and Dr. Finley revived in one man. And then Rush pulled all the stops to the point of sounding maudlin. At the end of April 1767 he wrote Witherspoon:

"Suffer me to conjure you by everything you look upon as sacred not to refuse the call, if you have any regard to religion, to your family, and to your own private happiness. . . . Let not the enemies of the College triumph over her dejected, heartbroken friends. Every tear they shed and every pang of grief they feel will be felt by you. . . . My heart bleeds within me—O Nassau-Hall, Nassau-Hall!"

That summer Rush traveled to Paisley and waited on the Reverend Doctor. He spent some time with Mrs. Witherspoon and succeeded in persuading her, having reassured her about the dangers of crossing the Atlantic. This accomplished, there was no difficulty in prevailing on her husband to accept the post. In the following spring the couple sailed for America, where Witherspoon soon became an important influence in the growth of the College and in closing the factional breach. He was partly responsible for the flowering of the Presbyterian Church in America before the Revolution and was destined to play a vital part in the impending struggle for independence. Rush's predictions thus became true.

* * *

So emotional a young man and such a gifted one could obviously not long endure isolation from the opposite sex. Before leaving Philadelphia he had weighed the possibility of marrying a Miss Livingston of New York, or Polly Fisher of Philadelphia, to whom he had been tenderly attached. But so was his friend, Thomas Bradford. Benjamin wrote the latter from Edinburgh, relinquishing any claims to Polly's hand. He said that he had received unwelcome orders from home not to think of a wife for eight or ten years and that ". . . Heaven hath ordered it so in order to enable me to provide more honorably for my dear sisters and their sons, whose only hopes of happiness in this world are now fixed on me." Both his sisters were already widowed. Nevertheless, he protests his love for Polly, saying:

"But oh! did the blessed creature know what pangs of love she has cost me. Did she know how often I have walked up and down my room for whole nights together since I came to Scotland, thinking upon nothing but her; and above all, could she see my *heart*, my honest heart, she would judge differently of me. . . . She is the only woman whom I ever loved and, I may add, ever shall. If ever I do marry, other motives of a sordid nature must influence me. *Love* never will."

But Benjamin's "honest heart" is by now in the Highlands; and Bradford marries Polly, with his friend's blessing.

In the meanwhile Benjamin had come to know the family of the Earl of Leven, who lived in a town house in Nicholson Square, just south of the University, and had a country seat at Melville in Fifeshire, about twelve miles north of Edinburgh. Rush was a frequent visitor at both places. As a homesick young man he responded naturally to the warmth and affection that this good family offered him. The head of the household he described as "the patron and friend of everything that's good" and his lady as an "angel incarnate." Soon he and their eldest son, Lord Balgonie, became fast friends. Their temperaments seemed exactly suited to each other and they enjoyed many fine philosophic walks "thro yᵉ woods &

Avenues of Melvil." When they parted, the young lord gave him "a gold ring which contained in a small circle about the size of a dime every word and letter of the Lord's Prayer." On the inside of the ring were engraved the day of the month and year on which he left the family seat at Melville. On July 5 he wrote from Melville:

"I cannot tell when I shall return to Edinburgh. My attachment to Melvill grows stronger day by day.—how insipid are all Lectures and Studies when set in Competition with the *pleasures* of *Friendship* & a rural Life!" He declares: "It was here I first saw true domestic happiness in its highest perfection."

If this only increased his nostalgia, it also opened his heart to love, for it was here that he fell in love with Lady Jane, the eldest daughter. In the private journal of his sojourn in Scotland, Rush exposes his smitten and palpitating heart. He describes Lady Jane Leslie as between fifteen and sixteen: "an Age in w^ch: the Charms of youth—Beauty—& Virtue appear to y^e: greatest Advantage. . . . But when these amiable Endowments meet in a Person of high Rank & Fortune they strike us w^th: something divine & inexpressible!"

Poor Benjamin! If he had been sleepless and walked up and down his room for whole nights together for love of Polly Fisher in the spring, what could he have done now that summer was here and the heather in bloom and his Highland lassie so adorable and virtuous, so rich and well placed! Although one half page of the manuscript of his *Scottish Journal* has been cut away, enough is extant to reveal his feelings.

"She inherits every virtue of her Mother, & has added to them a complete Knowledge of Music, ye French Language, & all ye polite Accomplishments of ye Age. what politeness! What an Address—what an insinuating Manner does she possess! *The Law of Kindness is written in her Heart.* Words like Honey drop from her Tongue. in a word *Heaven is in her Eye—Grace is in her Look—* in every step there's Dignity & Love."

Benjamin Rush had been struck with the fine lunacy, but he was by no means ready for marriage, even if he had been given the keys to the City of Edinburgh. Lady Jane sang Scottish airs to him; he never forgot one of them, "The Birks of Endermay." They called each other Edwin and Angelina after the lovers long parted and later reunited in a pathetic ballad by Goldsmith.

The idyllic days at the Melville country seat in Fifeshire came to an end. Soon young Rush would be setting forth by coach on the next stage of his grand tour which would take him to the great metropolis that was 18th-century London. Then there would become enshrined in his memory the picture of Lady Jane waving her last good-bye to him from the top of the sweeping curved double stairs that fronted the austere façade of the mansion. From there she could see the park and the gently rolling meadows, and in the near distance Bishop Hamilton's tower, as she watched the coach roll away between the twin brick gatehouses with their delicately domed roofs. Benjamin's last letter written in Edinburgh is addressed not to Lady Jane but to her younger brother, David.

"While you are reading this," he writes, "I expect to be upwards of a 100 miles on my journey. Think what sensations I must feel on my way when I reflect upon what I have left behind me in Scotland.—I can say from experience that there is no operation in surgery so painful as the separating two friendly hearts asunder. . . . May the choicest blessings that Heaven can bestow be the portion of your dear sisters, Lady Jane and Lady Mary. Pray kiss sweet little George a thousand times for me. . . . My heart is full—I can add no more."

In Edinburgh he had spent the happiest period of his life. These, as he said, were his halcyon days.

3

THE GRAND TOUR—
LONDON AND PARIS

✿ TRAVELING WITH TWO COMPANIONS BY STAGECOACH
through highly cultivated and beautiful country, Rush arrived
in London at the end of September 1768, after a journey of some
ten or eleven days. His friend Potts was no longer with him;
he had had to leave Edinburgh soon after their arrival to return
home. So now Rush was alone and for the first time in his life confronted by a vast metropolis twice the size of Edinburgh. What a
rude change after the compact panorama of the Scottish city and
the friendliness of his fellow students there.

This was the London of Hogarth and Dr. Johnson, the London
of alehouses and taverns and gin swigging, of filth and grime and
glitter, the London of the Adam brothers and of Christopher
Wren, of elegant lords and their ladies and liveried footmen, of dim
street lights and vice and cruelty and crime and public hangings,
and the London of stately colorful processions. Just behind the
British Museum, which Rush especially enjoyed, the land was occupied by a farm, and from Bloomsbury Square he could get a full
view of Hampstead and Highgate.

Rush took lodgings in the Strand, and during the first days of
autumn he visited the Abbey, the Tower of London, and the
Houses of Parliament. He watched George III being driven in
great pomp through the streets to the House of Lords to open a
session of Parliament. His wide-ranging curiosity was much in

evidence. It drove him to inspect most of the large manufactures in London, and to search out and observe things that were curious and rare. People interested him most. He loved to talk and to listen and to exchange ideas with all kinds. Indeed, the social contacts of Benjamin Rush sound like a *Who's Who* of 18th-century London: There were Sir John Pringle, Surgeon-General to the British Army, the founder of modern military medicine and later president of the Royal Society, whom Rush described as "a high toned Royalist;" the Reverend Mr. Whitefield, a celebrated evangelist, whom Benjamin had met as a boy at home and whom he classed with John Wesley as constituting "the two largest and brightest orbs that appeared in the hemisphere of the Church in the 18th Century." In addition, there were a series of other famous divines whom he heard preach or called upon.

He spent many agreeable evenings with the American painter, Benjamin West, who introduced him to several of the most celebrated members of the Royal Academy, including Sir Joshua Reynolds. Reynolds thereupon promptly invited him to dine with Dr. Johnson and with Oliver Goldsmith. Rush's account of this dinner, written nearly a quarter of a century later, can be found in a letter addressed to James Abercrombie, a Philadelphia cleric with strong Tory leanings, who idolized Dr. Johnson and furnished Boswell with material for his *Life*. Rush's letter was sent to Boswell, who died before he could use it. Here are a few excerpts from this interesting communication:

"At dinner I sat between Dr. Johnson and Dr. Goldsmith. The former took the lead in conversation. He instructed upon all subjects. . . . A book which had been recently published led to some remarks upon its author [Boswell]. Dr. Goldsmith, addressing himself to Dr. Johnson, said, 'He appears, Doctor, from some passages in his book, to be one of your acquaintances.' 'Yes,' said Johnson, 'I know him.' 'And pray, what do you think of him?' said Goldsmith. 'He is well enough—well enough,' said Johnson. 'I have heard,' said Goldsmith, 'he is much given to asking questions in company.' 'Yes, he is,' said Johnson, 'and his questions are not of the most interesting nature. They are such as this—"Pray, Doctor, why is an apple round, and why is a pear not so?"'

"During the time of dinner, Dr. Goldsmith asked me several questions relative to the manners and customs of the North American Indians. Dr. Johnson, who heard one of them, suddenly interrupted him and said, 'There is not an Indian in North America who would have asked such a foolish question.' 'I am sure,' said Goldsmith, 'there is not a savage in America that would have made so rude a speech to a gentleman.' "

Rush's visit to the Houses of Parliament also calls for his own words:

"I went a few days ago in company with a Danish physician to visit the House of Lords and the House of Commons. When I went into the first, I felt as if I walked on sacred ground. I gazed for some time at the Throne with emotions that I cannot describe. I asked our guide if it was common for strangers to set down upon it. He told me no, but upon my importuning him a good deal I prevailed upon him to allow me the liberty. I accordingly advanced towards it and sat in it for a considerable time. When I first got into it, I was seized with a kind of horror which for some time interrupted my ordinary train of thinking. . . .

"From this I went into the House of Commons. I cannot say I felt as if I walked on 'sacred ground' here. This, I thought, is the place where the infernal scheme for enslaving America was first broached. Here the usurping Commons first endeavored to rob the King of his supremacy over the colonies and to divide it among themselves. O! cursed haunt of venality, bribery, and corruption! In the midst of these reflections I asked where Mr. Pitt (alas! now Lord Chatham) stood when he spoke in favor of repealing the Stamp Act. 'Here,' said our guide, 'on this very spot.' I then went up to it, sat down upon it for some time, and fancying myself surrounded with a crowded House, rose up from my seat and began to repeat part of his speech: 'When the scheme for taxing America,' said I, 'was first proposed, I was unhappily confined to my bed. But had some kind hand brought me and laid me down upon *this* floor, I would have bore a public testimony against it. Americans are the sons, not the bastards of Englishmen. I rejoice that America has resisted.' "

These words Benjamin sent to his friend Ebenezer Hazard, to whom it was his custom to expose his deeper feelings. But his convictions were relatively newly won, perhaps still not too securely held, and, with the exception of his friend Bostock in Edinburgh, there were few in Britain with whom he could share them.

Thus, here again there comes into focus the political side of the future man. But at this time his mind and heart were first of all in medicine and in making the most of his new opportunities.

Finding that his lodgings in the Strand were too far from the hospitals and lectures he was to attend, he moved after a few days to the house of a widow named Jeffries in the Hay Market and here he remained for the rest of his stay in London. This was near the three hospitals—Middlesex, St. Thomas' and Guy's—and just across Shaftesbury Avenue from the end of the Hay Market was the famous Hunter's School of Anatomy in Great Windmill Street. It was still September and the London weather was too warm to permit bringing dead bodies into the theater.

*   *   *

Rush came to regard his attendance at the lectures and dissections of Dr. William Hunter, the elder of the two famous brothers who conducted the school, as the greatest of his new opportunities. Here many of the best British surgeons were trained, and Americans, too. In fact, Benjamin Rush's former lecturers in Philadelphia and his future professional colleagues, Doctors Morgan and Shippen, had both studied with the Hunters.

A word should be said about these remarkable brothers. The lectures which Rush attended were given by Dr. William Hunter, the celebrated Scottish anatomist, surgeon and obstetrician. His ability as a lecturer attracted many outside the medical profession— among them Edmund Burke, Adam Smith, Edward Gibbon, and the Scottish historian William Robertson, whom Rush had met in Edinburgh. William Hunter was also distinguished for his illustrated folio called *The Anatomy of the Gravid Uterus*.

He had come to London from Edinburgh about 1740. There he, too, had been a student of Monro (*Primus*) and of Rush's mentor Cullen. He devoted himself to dissection and midwifery, and six years later he set up his own school of anatomy. Within two years he was joined by his brother John, an unschooled boy from Lanarkshire, who became his pupil. This brother John, who was ten years his junior, became known as "Mr. H" after he had established himself as a practicing surgeon. But, above all, he was a pioneer in comparative anatomy who, in the end, far outdistanced his older brother William as a man of scientific genius.

At this time when Rush was his pupil, Dr. Hunter, though directing the affairs of the school of anatomy, was devoting more and more time to his private practice. In the month before Rush's arrival in London he had attended the Queen in childbirth —in his own words he had had "the sole direction of Her Majesty's health as a child-bearing lady." This led to his appointment as Physician Extraordinary to the Queen, a post which must have kept him pretty well occupied, since Her Majesty gave birth to fifteen children. Dr. Hunter did not, to be sure, deliver all these babies himself. Apparently he directed the operations of a midwife from the side lines in an anteroom, out of consideration to royal modesty.

Even more important than these royal accouchements was the fact that Dr. Hunter's reputation for skill and learning became such that people of wealth and rank employed him, and so he paved the way for the modern obstetrician who gradually replaced the midwife. Long before the classical work on puerperal sepsis or childbed fever, done in Boston in 1843 by Oliver Wendell Holmes, William Hunter had had the wit to protect his women patients from the risk of infection by separating the place where he conducted his practice from the house where dissections were made.

At the time that Benjamin Rush was attending his lectures and those of his associate Mr. Hewson, Dr. Hunter had introduced the Parisian method of providing each of his pupils with one entire body and from time to time inspecting the dissections himself. While Rush was engaged in a dissection, Mr. Hewson succeeded in an experiment that proved the existence of lymphatic vessels in fishes. The function of the lymphatics in absorbing fluids and foodstuffs from the intestines was a matter of dispute—the great Swiss physiologist Albrecht von Haller claiming that animals other than mammals had no lymphatic vessels. Hewson's experiment proved him in error.

The Hunters—and John in particular—did not confine their studies to man, but embraced all of nature with the hope of establishing a true comparative anatomical physiology. In fact, what Dr. Hunter did for obstetrics, Mr. Hunter did for surgery—freeing it from the crude practice of the barber-surgeons and the tooth extractors and helping to establish it as a biological medical science. We owe especially to John Hunter the perfection of the art of preparing and mounting anatomical and pathological specimens and of demonstrating the blood vessels and lymph spaces of the animal body by the injection of colored materials. It would take us too far afield to enumerate all the important discoveries of this unusual and indefatigable man, who had resisted all attempts to subject him to a formal education. Of his short sojourn at Oxford he said, "They wanted to make an old woman of me, or that I should stuff Latin at the University; but these schemes I cracked like so many vermin. . . ." His contribution to our knowledge of inflammation and of the collateral circulation ranks high among his researches and in their influence on medical thought.

How different was this approach from the one which had enthralled Rush at Edinburgh, where metaphysical Scottish physicians had argued about the blood vessels and their state of tension or relaxation—but never looked at them. It is good that Rush was exposed for a short time at least to the careful experimentation and the tough-minded thinking that prevailed in the house on Great Windmill Street. He also walked the wards of the Middlesex Hospital and of St. Thomas'. There he had occasion to see an immense variety of diseases and of practice.

St. Thomas' was more than two centuries old, having been granted its charter by Edward VI. In the 18th century it had been rebuilt and enlarged to meet the needs of the expanding population in the neighborhood of London Bridge. The building was arranged in a series of quadrangles, with women patients in the wards in front, then the administrative quarters, then the male wards, and finally the "Foul Wards," where patients of both sexes with venereal diseases were housed.

Every Thursday was "taking in day," when new patients were admitted to the Hospital after examination, a routine at which Rush as a pupil assisted. It gave him the opportunity not only to observe new patients but to watch his masters at work and to try to emulate their skill. Before precise laboratory techniques were available, diagnosis depended on looking, hearing, touching, smelling, and tasting and on inferences arrived at by intuition and experience and by happy guesses. Even such simple procedures as counting the pulse and taking the temperature were not practiced, although Galileo had measured both. Indeed by the time of our Civil War there were probably not half a dozen clinical thermometers employed in the largest Union army. And this was some 250 years after their first introduction. The same can be said of measuring blood pressure, which was first done by Stephen Hales in 1733. This did not come into common clinical usage until a century and a half later, with the invention of the modern sphygmomanometer.

If diagnostic procedures were primitive, therapeutic ones were even more so. The kind and number of prescriptions written for the men, women and children who crowded the out-patient department of St. Thomas' Hospital on Wednesday, Thursday and Friday mornings were legion. It has been true in medicine, and it still is, that the less we know about a disease, the more remedies are used for it. The *London Pharmacopoeia* of the previous century (1618) listed such remedies as bile, blood, hair, perspiration, saliva, and wood lice, and even as late as 1724 Cotton Mather wrote to the Royal Society that physicians in Boston advised the swallowing of leaden bullets for "that miserable *Distemper* which they called the *Twisting of the Guts*," to which the old Puritan added, "I think, I should endure abundant, before I tried such a remedy."

But by mid-18th century, when Rush was in London, such practices had probably been abandoned even if bleeding, purging and blistering continued to be used with unabated and uncritical fervor.

Some notion of contemporary therapeutics can be gleaned from the writings of Dr. John Fothergill, a celebrated London physician and friend of Franklin's, to whom Rush had letters of introduction. He was kind and welcoming to the young American, who breakfasted with him at eight o'clock once a week and enjoyed his animated if methodical conversation. His wide knowledge of botany and his skill as a gardener drew him closely to John Bartram, the famous American botanist. The study of botany and the compounding of medicaments from herbs and other plants were then an important part of the medical curriculum, an activity now largely taken over by the drug companies.

In 18th-century England, herb or physic gardens were common. Some of them were already quite old—the one of the College of Physicians dating back to 1587, and the Society of Apothecaries, which can still be seen in Chelsea, to 1673. Dr. Fothergill had such a garden on his estate in Essex, equal in the number and variety of its exotic specimens to the Royal Botanic Gardens at Kew. Nursery catalogues today list a shrub, not unlike witch hazel, called *Fothergilla major,* which was named for him by the great Linnaeus. It was one of nearly a hundred varieties of plants that he had imported into England.

In Fothergill's time a revolution had begun in the use of medicines, although tradition dragged heavily and impeded its progress. Formulae handed down from antiquity were still among the sovereign remedies of the 17th and 18th centuries, some of them containing as many as sixty-nine ingredients and possessing magical names such as *Athnasia Magna, Aurea Alexandria,* and *Theriaca Andromachi* or Venice treacle, and claiming to possess magical properties. Wolf liver, goat and stag horn, dried vipers, crabs' claws, and the bellies of lizards went into their make-up. Fothergill and his even more renowned colleague William Heberden, who first described angina pectoris, were pre-eminent in breaking the fetters of these superstitions, although actually the introduction of more rational methods of therapy was the natural result of the more rational medicine of Sydenham and Boerhaave and the Edinburgh School.

It was out of an herb brew with twenty ingredients, long kept secret by an old woman in Shropshire, that yet another 18th-century physician, trained in Edinburgh, William Withering, extracted digitalis from the leaf of the common foxglove. This was first thought to be a cure for dropsy, but later observation was to prove that it was effective only in the dropsy resulting from heart failure, because of its action in slowing the heart rate and increasing the force of contraction. The drug had been used as an emetic and a purge, because of its toxic effects, long before Withering's discovery, but in spite of the clear rules which he enunciated for its use, it took another century before its value was properly appreciated.

The pharmacology of the time when Rush was in London, and therefore the medical practice to which he was exposed, are further illustrated in the writings of Dr. Fothergill. He used Winter's bark, first obtained by one of Drake's captains, named Winter, from a magnolia-like tree growing on the shores of the Straits of Magellan, and employed it as a remedy for scurvy. Fothergill not only obtained some of the bark in 1768 but introduced the tree, which is said to flourish still in parts of Ireland. He obtained sassafras from

North America, and used it as a diaphoretic to induce sweating; rhubarb from Turkey, and elaterium, a violent purgative no longer used, from the cucumber. He also, of course, used Peruvian bark or Cinchona, from which quinine is extracted, but he gave this to scrofulous children with enlarged glands, adding calomel and antimony to the decoction. One cannot imagine that this helped them much. He was fond of using aromatic balsams, resins and gums, and such things as soap-lees to dissolve stones in the bladder, which they probably did not do. For gout he condemned the use of opiates and instead prescribed a diuretic punch containing spa water, old hock, rum, potash, and sugar and bitters. Opium was in common use, and so also were such heavy metals as iron, mercury, and antimony, the latter now being seldom prescribed except as tartar emetic or for certain tropical parasitic diseases.

Even if Fothergill contributed much to the eventual revision of the *Pharmacopoeia*, he could not quite free himself from the conventional polypharmacy of the past and from the temptation to use a little of this and a little of that. The test of a remedy was still purely pragmatic and empirical. Careful physiological investigations and the statistical methods and controls of modern medicine had not yet come into being. Rush himself grew up with these conventional 18th-century methods, and he was never able to rise above them.

If while Benjamin Rush was in London a reform had begun in the use of medicines, there were other reforms under way which must have impressed so alert, intelligent, and receptive a young doctor. The dispensary movement had begun in 1750 with the establishment of a center which the poor might attend for advice and free medicines. In the 18th century medical practice had been chiefly among the richer classes. The poor lived depressed and degraded lives in cellars and tenements, vermin-infested and insanitary. Gin swigging, with the resultant destitution, filth, prostitution, venereal disease, and violence, was the rule. This was greatly abetted by the custom of paying laborers and artisans on Saturday nights in the alehouses, where they were kept waiting for their pay by the master or foreman sometimes from six in the evening until ten or eleven o'clock. Corrupt paymasters were in league with corrupt keepers of the alehouses, and the effect on the workers and their wives and children can easily be imagined. Crowding and dirt and poverty, of course, breed disease. The "fever" (typhus) was perennial in London, with occasional severe epidemics; the most terrible one occurred in 1740 and 1741. It was John Hunter who wrote:

"There are but few of the sick . . . that find their way into the great hospitals of London, which probably is to be imputed to there being but one day a week allotted for the admission of patients. Before a recommendation can be procured and the stated day comes round, the sick person is either better or so much worse that he cannot be moved, or is perhaps dead. They are carried, however, in great numbers to parish workhouses, in which it frequently happens that during the cold months the fever becomes as violent, and proves as fatal, as in the most crowded jails, hospitals or transports."

But the worst period was between 1720 and 1750, which corresponded with an orgy of drinking very cheap and intoxicating liquors and a resulting drop in births and an increase in death rates. By the time Rush reached London, conditions had improved. The change had come in about 1750, with the establishment of the first public dispensary, though certainly it was not attributable to this fact alone. The dispensary was itself an expression of a growing awareness of the plight of the poor, who till then had been treated as pariahs.

Another potent source of the improvement in general health can be ascribed to the cheapness of cotton goods, both for clothing and bedcovers. When these became available to the public, they could for the first time be washed. Personal cleanliness, therefore, took a boost. Theretofore the wives of journeymen, tradesmen and shopkeepers had worn leather stays that were never washed although worn day after day for years, and quilted petticoats, stuffed with wool and horsehair, which were worn until they were rotten. A similar beneficial change was the introduction of iron bedsteads in place of the old vermin-infested wooden ones. These facts did not escape a mind as restless and inquisitive as Rush's, and he stored them away for use later.

* * *

Being bent on further education, Rush naturally decided to visit the Continent, in accord with 18th-century tradition. On the night of February 16, 1769 he crossed the Channel from Dover to Calais and then traveled in company with two young gentlemen overland to Paris. The beauties of Picardy, which was green in spite of the early season, impressed him and he remarked in his *French Journal* that it wanted only water to make it one of the richest prospects in nature. In fact, he extols water in motion in rivers and brooks, or in fountains such as he saw at Chantilly, for the charm it lends to landscape. But his interest was not only aesthetic. While at Dr. Finley's school, he had become concerned with farming, and now, ten years later, he observed that the agriculture of France was beginning to flourish and this was bound to have a favorable influence on its liberties. Few countries in the world, he thought, could equal France for varieties of soil, climate and situation; and yet, because of the neglect of cultivation, an acre of ground in the most fruitful part of the country produced no more than did an eighth of an acre in most parts of England. Rush explained this meager state of fertility by the contempt in which agriculture and farmers had always been held in France, by the vast number of parks reserved for hunting, the short leases granted to farmers, the want of enclosures for fields and the lack of encouragement from the Crown. At the time of his visit, however, Rush noticed a change in attitude. He reflects wisely that the civilization of mankind and agriculture belong together and he writes in his *French Journal:*

"It is owing to this that the American Colonies, have in so short a Space of time arisen to such a Pitch of Grandeur & Riches. . . . where Agriculture is encouraged, there will be Riches, where there are Riches, there will be Power, and where there is Power, there will be Freedom and Independence." So Rush believed!

Rush's *Journal* proceeds in the typical style of the self-conscious young tourist—written perhaps with one eye on a guidebook— describing the architecture, churches, statuary and paintings of Paris. He tells us that he visited all the public hospitals in Paris without entering himself as a pupil in any of them. Elsewhere in his *Journal* he speaks of his disappointment in the opportunities that France offered to improve oneself in the study of medicine.

"Physic is not cultivated here by Men of Rank and Fortune, nor is the Profession look'd upon so liberal in this Country, as it is in England or America." Also he ". . . Conversed with Several of the principal Physicians in Paris, and was sorry to find them at least

50 years behind the Physicians in England & Scotland in Medical Knowledge."

Rush singled out the Hôtel de la Charité as being remarkably neat and clean, where the patients were well accommodated and nursed by nuns of noble families. But the Hôtel Dieu, which was open to the sick of all religions and countries, he found crowded and offensive, containing at some seasons 8,000 souls. As early as the Middle Ages this hospital had a special department for treating the mentally ill, but Rush makes no mention of this fact. His later interest in mental illness had not yet become evident. The Foundling Hospital, where one-eighth of the children born in Paris were said to be brought, he described as admirable. He wrote:

"One Reason why it is so much crowded is, that if a Woman brings forth a dead Child, without first declaring her Pregnancy, She is burnt alive; this puts an entire stop to Child Murther, and every poor Child of course that is born in Paris, is naturally sent to this Hospital. . . ."

Rush was touched by the motto over the door of this institution, where 8,000 children were left annually, and where the abandoned child of Jean Jacques Rousseau slept in a crêche side by side with the child of a cobbler, a robber, an imbecile, or a prince: "Mon pere, et ma mere m'ont abandonè, mais Le Seigneur a pris soin de moi." France had no laws regulating adoption. The children from the Foundling Hospital were sent, two at a time, to the country in the care of paid nurses, and within the first two years about half of them died.

Although Rush's strictures about the state of medicine in Paris during the time of his visit were well-founded, he was still too insular and too unsophisticated in medicine to appreciate what it did have to offer. The Académie Royale des Sciences, where his own teacher, William Hunter, had pursued his anatomical studies some twenty-six years earlier, had been the first school of anatomy to provide enough cadavers so that each student could make his own extensive dissections. Hunter had brought this system back with him and established it in his school on Great Windmill Street.

This same Académie, finding the treatment of the mentally ill unsatisfactory, assigned to one of its members, Dr. Jacques-René Tenon, the task of writing in 1788 a report on the reform of the hospitals of Paris. Tenon visited hospitals in the French provinces and also crossed to England to inspect the best institutions there. His report describes the Hôtel Dieu as one of the most backward hospitals in all Europe and speaks of the deplorable condition of the violently insane, which had long since aroused the attention of the Government. But the time for action had not yet arrived, although efforts at reform had started as far back as the 17th century when St. Vincent de Paul became the first person in France to show a humane interest in the mentally ill.

The great day of French medicine was yet to come when such men as Bichat, Desault, and Corvisart would flourish; and when Philippe Pinel would lead an heroic fight against the brutalities committed on the insane. All this would occur twenty years after Rush had left Paris.

Equipped with letters of introduction, as he had been in Edinburgh and London, and also with a letter of credit for 300 guineas from Dr. Franklin, Rush again soon found himself in the homes of the distinguished and the socially elevated. First among these was the physician and botanist, Barbeu Dubourg. It was Dubourg who later translated Franklin's *Experiments and Observations*, calling Poor Richard "le pauvre Henri" so as to avoid the pun *pauvre* and *richard*.

These two men, Franklin and Dubourg, were in frequent correspondence, and in July of 1768, just a few months before Rush presented his letter of introduction, the vigorous elder statesman, then in his sixty-second year, wrote his French colleague a letter on one of his favorite themes, namely, bathing and catching cold.

". . . the shock of the cold water has always appeared to me, generally speaking, as too violent, and I have found it much more agreeable to my constitution to bathe in another element, I mean cold air. With this view I rise almost every morning, and sit in my chamber without any clothes whatever, half an hour or an hour, according to the season, either reading or writing. This practice is not in the least painful, but, on the contrary, agreeable; and, if I return to bed afterwards, before I dress myself, as sometimes happens, I make a supplement to my night's rest of one or two hours of the most pleasing sleep that can be imagined."

In view of the almost worshipful attitude of young Rush toward Franklin, it is not astonishing that he took so immediately to Dubourg, his new French friend.

"In a little time," Rush wrote later in his *Journal*, "I forgot that He was a Stranger. I forgot that He was a Frenchman; I forgot that He was once the Enemy of my Country—I took him into my Arms, nay more. I took him into my very Heart. From that Moment, He became my Friend, and shou'd I gain no other Advantage by going to France, than the Benefit of his Friendship, & Correspondance, I shall esteem my Visit well bestow'd."

At this time the Marquis de Mirabeau, the father of the famous revolutionary orator, kept a coterie once a week at his house, and to this Rush was invited. When he entered the large drawing room "filled with ladies and gentlemen of the first literary characters," Dr. Dubourg announced him with these words:

"Voilà! Un ami de Mons. Franklin."

Thereupon, according to Rush, the Marquis ran toward the door and taking him by the hand, said,

"C'est assez."

One can imagine the young man's pleasure at being thus singled out. Rush was pleased as well by the behavior of the ladies, whom he called the umpires of all disputes. It was to them that, in the prevailing mode of the Parisian salon, all conversation was addressed, and a gentleman was listened to with more or less attention according to how much he entertained them. Rush was much impressed by their delightful manners and their brilliant and witty talk, and he confides to his *Journal*:

"Too much cannot be said of the Accomplishment of their Minds: A well bred Woman here is one of the most entertaining Companions in the World. . . ." And, far from agreeing that learning makes a woman vain, he protests that it would add greatly to the happiness of marriage.

He was impressed with the graceful ease and informality that prevailed between the sexes.

"There is nothing stiff or reserv'd in these Companies," he observed. "In *England* the Sexes meet only at Assemblies, plays and other Places of public Entertainment . . . every thing is conducted with a ceremony which forbids Conversation."

The young American tourist was struck, as many have been since, by the beauty of these Parisian ladies. He was pleased by their sprightliness, their good humor and their great personal charm. And he wrote:

"Much however of their Beauty is borrow'd from Art, I mean from Painting. . . . It is very common to see them take out, a little Box of Paint, which they always carry in their Pockets, together with a small looking Glass and a fine Pencil, and daub their Cheeks over, in their Coaches, when they are going out to an Assembly or any Public Entertainment."

He will allow no charge of indelicacy against them, nor does he take umbrage at the freedom of their behavior or conversation or, above all, at the fact of their admitting gentlemen to pay them morning visits in their bedchambers.

"I am far from thinking," he writes, "a Ladies Virtue should be called in Question, who receives a Gentleman in her Bed Chamber, nor can I see wherein the difference consists, between seeing a Lady in her ordinary Dress, and under a Pile of Bed Cloaths— Much more of the Body is expos'd in the former Case (even by our most delicate English ladies) than in the latter."

In Scotland he had heard ladies, otherwise remarkable for their delicacy, use expressions which he would blush to repeat, and he adds that no woman in Turkey is ever looked upon as virtuous who has been seen dancing with a man. He is convinced that there is as much real virtue among the ladies of France as among the women of any other country in the world. For a young man of his conventional and Calvinistic background, this shows an independence of thought and a remarkable degree of freedom from bias.

Of the others whom Rush met in Paris, two were of special interest. One was the academician Bernard de Jussieu, who had been trained both as a physician and as a botanist, as were Dubourg and John Fothergill of London. The other was the encyclopedist Diderot, who entertained him in his library and gave him a letter of introduction to the philosopher Hume.

De Jussieu had been appointed Botanist to the King and was in charge of the Royal Gardens of the Trianon at Versailles. He was one of a distinguished family, of whom five were famous botanists, and his nephew Antoine Laurent de Jussieu, whom he had trained, would fifteen years later play an important part with Benjamin Franklin on a Royal Commission created by Louis XVI to investigate, on behalf of the Academy of Sciences, what was then called animal magnetism.

The times that encompassed Benjamin Rush's short sojourn in

Paris were those of revolutionary ferment. The winds of coming events were already stirring, and Rush's development in later life indicates that this intellectual atmosphere had its influence on him. This was true not only of political events but scientific ones as well—certainly those related to chemistry and to the care of the mentally ill, with both of which young Rush would before very long become greatly concerned. The atmosphere of 18th-century rationalism was already becoming a part of his substance. It was an age which has been described as deficient in wisdom and depth, and as one which ignored whatever did not fit its scheme of things. One of its greatest exponents was Diderot, the philosopher and friend of Voltaire.

This then was the intellectual atmosphere of Paris when, nine years after Rush's short sojourn there, a German-born physician arrived from Vienna and took the place by storm. His name—Franz Anton Mesmer—survives to this day in the synonym for hypnotism: mesmerism. He could produce convulsions and hysterical seizures in his subjects by hitching them up to his magnets, believing that a "universal fluid" passed between them. He soon had a following among the fashionable and won the favor of the Queen. Some of the aristocracy, including Lafayette, became his ardent admirers, and ladies of high rank grew foolish about him. However, there was another side to the story. He had been expelled from Vienna and denied a license to practice medicine in France, many members of the profession believing him to be an unscrupulous charlatan.

At that time it was customary to submit new discoveries to learned bodies. But these were not always as wise and foresighted as might have been expected. The French Academy, for example, rejected in turn vaccination, lightning conductors, and the fall of meteors, and a little later a French Commission would study the plans for Fulton's steamboat and declare them to be visionary and impractical.

Now it was called upon to report on these demonstrations of hypnotism which Mesmer styled "animal magnetism." The Commission which was to investigate these sensational and disturbing demonstrations was an impressive one. It included some of the most famous men in pre-revolutionary France: Lavoisier, the founder of modern chemistry, Jean Sylvain, astronomer and statesman, and Dr. Guillotin himself—all three of whom were soon to lose their heads under the latter's celebrated knife. Benjamin Franklin, too, then Ambassador, aging and in bad health, was to preside at the meetings, but weakness kept him from attending them when they were not held at Passy, where he was staying. For the most part he was absorbed in his diplomatic duties and had little time and energy to give to these doctrines of Mesmer. With his interest in electricity, it is understandable why he should fail to perceive other possible forces at work, and thus why he missed the opportunity of becoming a pioneer in psychology, as he was in so many other fields.

The Commission's approach was entirely materialistic. Its members limited themselves to physical proofs and, of course, they could find no evidence of the existence of any such fluid, as claimed by Mesmer. The report ended with a severe condemnation of him, written with thinly veiled prejudice and hostility. Jefferson had called his beliefs a "compound of fraud and folly," and in large part because of the weight of Franklin's great authority, Mesmer and his "animal magnetism" went out of fashion and he left Paris.

There was one dissenter and that was the botanist de Jussieu. Recognizing that there was something in Mesmer's theories that could not be so easily explained away, as the other members of the Commission had believed, and that imagination was an important factor in the cures, he wrote a minority report. Mesmer himself did not understand the forces he had liberated or the implications of de Jussieu's interpretation of them. But de Jussieu's close associate, Dr. Charles d'Eslon, in reply to the Academy's verdict, said:

"I think I can lay it down as a fact that the imagination has the greatest share in the effects of animal magnetism. The new agent might indeed be no other than the imagination itself, whose power is as extensive as it is little known. . . . If Mesmer had no other secret than that he had been able to make the imagination exert an influence upon health, would he not still be a wonder doctor? If treatment by the use of the imagination is the best treatment, why do we not make use of it?"

These are the words that caused Mesmer's biographer to claim that "Dr. Charles d'Eslon laid the corner-stone of modern psychotherapy. Not for decades would his theory be recognized as a new science, but he had sown the first seeds of conscious mental therapy."

*   *   *

In spite of his opportunity to meet and converse with all the liberal intellectuals he had met in Paris, young Rush did not grasp what was in the air. He believed that Louis XV, known at one time as "le Bien-aimé," was still the idol of the nation. His slowness to discern the deeper meaning of historic events may be attributed partly to his youth and to insufficient familiarity with the French language, but chiefly, in this instance, to an ambivalence with respect to monarchy—not too remarkable in a young revolutionary. He both revered the institution and reviled it.

Curiosity drove him to visit Versailles, where he spent a whole day. He saw Louis XV pass through a large hall to a gallery in his chapel, on his way to mass. Rush followed him there, and remarking on his good eye and intelligent countenance described him as "the most sensible looking fool in Europe."

He also saw the Dauphin—then between fourteen and fifteen—and his two younger brothers, the Count de Provence and the Count D'Artois, grandsons of the King. The Dauphin he described as coarse-featured, brown of skin, and stoop-shouldered, "dull in his intellects and vulgar in his manners." He was horrified to see him take a piece of meat from his mouth and, after looking at it for some time in the presence of nearly a hundred spectators, throw it under the table. Having thus devalued the eldest, he quickly came to the defense of the youngest and extolled him in extravagant terms, saying of him, "I think he is the handsomest form, I ever saw in my Life," and speaking of "the Pregnancy of his Genius, of his great love for every thing that is Noble or Princely;" and finally declaring that it would not surprise him "to hear hereafter, that this little Prince directed the Counsels, or led the Armies of France all over the World."

Benjamin Rush's *Journal* contains many other divagations on the culture, manners and mores of France. But they are no different from the diary of many another young man making the Grand Tour, or of a student today writing home to his parents from his first trip abroad. Occasionally he will give a glimpse into himself and of his own inner development. At Amiens, on his journey back to

London, he tells us that he was struck by the figure of a venerable *abbé* whom he saw walking up and down in the church.

"His Complexion was dark, his Countenance grave, inclining a little to the melancholy. His Eyes were fix'd so intently upon the floor, that all the Noise that was made by those who passd and repassd . . . did not cause him once to lift them up or look around him."

He relates that he approached as near as possible but could not disturb him, and then goes on to say:

"Had I given Way to the Prejudices of my Education, with Regard to the Opinions which are entertaind in most protestant Countries Concerning the Popish Religion, I shou'd have Concluded that this venerable Man, this Son of the Rom^n. Catholic Church was plotting some Schemes to subvert the States or to eradicate the Tenets of the Heretics. But I was far from cherishing a Thought of this kind. This holy Man (said I to myself) has betook himself this Morning, to this Sanctuary, in Order to offer up his Morning Oblations to Heaven. The flame of Devotion can burn notwithstanding it is kindled upon the Alter of Superstition.

"The Deity pays no Regard to those little Ceremonies, in worship which divide most of the Christian Churches. He will always worship acceptably, who worships him in Spi[rit] & in Truth. The Perfume of flowers is the same on whatso[ever soil] they grow. . . ."

With these noble sentiments, Rush left Calais for Dover and reached Dartford near London the next day. En route he had been delayed by the suspicious conduct of a man who rode several times around the post chaise threatening to rob its passengers. But the delay had had its good uses. The next morning at about eight, the postilion, hearing a cry for help from a nearby wood, stopped the carriage. Rush, true to the tradition of his profession, ran quickly to the spot. There he found a poor woman in labor lying upon an old blanket on the ground. Needless to say, he delivered her of a fine boy. Then with the assistance of her husband and two old women, Dr. Rush lifted her into the post chaise and drove her to a nearby village. There, in a comfortable little house, he provided her with enough money to support her for several days, and left her. Two years later he learned that the child had been named Benjamin Rush. What a fitting introduction to the adventurous career of a young doctor.

A day or two after his arrival in London, Rush called upon Dr. Franklin and told him that he had found it necessary in Paris to draw upon his banker to the amount of 30 guineas. Franklin seemed pleased at this. He suggested that Rush should pay back the money to Mrs. Franklin at his convenience after his return to Philadelphia, and this the young doctor did out of his first earnings. At first Mrs. Franklin refused to accept the money, since her husband had never mentioned the loan in any of his letters to her. But this was no trivial matter to the young man. It was, in fact, an earnest of trust and respect and it attached him to Franklin during the remainder of the great man's life.

While in London Rush also delivered a letter from Diderot to David Hume and spent part of a forenoon in the latter's company. He had met this celebrated philosopher once before when in Edinburgh. Hume, he records, had a picture of Rousseau in his chamber and he remarks upon the resemblance—especially in having his "peevish countenance." This was Rush's last encounter with the great on foreign soil.

The end of Rush's Grand Tour was now at hand, and, taking passage on the ship *Edward*, he embarked on her at Gravesend on the 26th of May in the year 1769. From the deck of the *Edward* as she pulled slowly away from land, the young doctor looked lingeringly back at the White Cliffs of Britain, as so many have done both before him and since. He thus describes this last view from her stern:

"All the ancient and modern glory of that celebrated and highly favoured island rushed upon my mind. I enjoyed in silence this pensive retrospect of the first country in the world, 'till distance snatched it for ever from my sight."

And with it went his youth as well.

Of his companions on board, there was Daniel Coxe, whose son, John Redman Coxe, would later become one of Dr. Rush's many distinguished pupils. Another passenger was a Lieutenant Dysert, who had served in Germany in the Seven Years' War. Rush passed many agreeable hours with him on deck listening to him discourse on military history and taking lessons in German from him. During their six-weeks' passage Rush not only studied German grammar, but from a steerage passenger he obtained a Bible in German, which he read constantly, so that he was able to understand what he read without the aid of a translation or a dictionary. He also read an Italian novel, *La Contessa del Nord*, which Captain Salmon, the master of the vessel, had picked up in Leghorn and loaned him. But this was not all. From Mr. Coxe, he borrowed the first three volumes of Blackstone's *Commentaries*, and these he read with uncommon attention and pleasure; also Sir Michael Foster's *Crown Law*. To these books Rush later ascribed in part the relish for political science which he experienced at the beginning of the American Revolution.

His avid reading was not only the expression of his natural curiosity and scholarly bent. It was also a deliberate device for dealing with the discomfort both of body and mind that he experienced at sea. Although he was seasick on one day only, he never felt perfectly well. His appetite was weak; food lost its savor. Yet he was never easy except when he was eating. But it was his restless and unsettled mind that troubled him most and, for this, reading was the best remedy. The variegated and polygot intellectual diet that he enjoyed was not wholly of his own choosing, but all he could lay his hands on aboard ship, since he had sent his own books home before him.

In the midst of this intellectual preoccupation, the cry of land-ho went up. Sandy Hook was in sight and that same afternoon, July 14, the *Edward* anchored off the Battery in New York harbor after a voyage of forty-nine days.

From his first view of the American shore to his first dish of tea with bread and butter ashore, this homecoming was one of rapture and relish. He had been away on his Grand Tour for nearly three years, and from all points of view they had been pregnant and profitable ones.

4

A PHILADELPHIA DOCTOR

❀ WHEN THE *Edward* ANCHORED IN THE PORT OF New York, Rush was overjoyed to be greeted on the dock by his old friend and classmate, Ebenezer Hazard—the one to whom he had so often unburdened his heart. Directly Ebenezer took him in tow and saw to it that he was properly cared for and entertained.

On his arrival, like many another who has been abroad for so long a time, Benjamin Rush was struck by contrasts and comparisons. The people on the streets of New York had less color than those in London; they walked with a slower step; they stood less erect. But these observations were more a matter of mood than of fact because he acknowledged in himself an "uncommon depression of spirits, the usual effect of a high tide of joy upon the system." In any case, after a few weeks ashore such differences ceased to attract his attention.

In two days he set off by stagecoach for Philadelphia, meeting in the course of his journey, at Bristol, his brother Jacob and Jonathan Bayard Smith, another classmate. This reunion caused him great happiness. From Edinburgh two years earlier he had written Smith, "Your name is well known to most of my friends here. 'Mr. Jonathan Smith of Philadelphia' is my favorite toast when an old friend is called for." And this pleasure was compounded when on the evening of July 18 he was received by his mother and sister, whose tears of joy, he says in his stilted way, "soon became recip-rocal."

Within a week Rush was installed in a house on Arch Street, be-tween Front and 2nd Streets. Here he set himself up with his brother Jacob, who had just begun the practice of the law. Their sister Rebecca, who had been unfortunate in her marriage, kept house for them. Young Rush, now at the age of twenty-three, seri-ous, diligent, cultivated and humorless, set out to establish himself in business, as he called it in unadorned terms. Among his principal assets, besides a quick intelligence and a lively curiosity, were his natural dignity, an unusual charge of physical vigor, and an inde-finable quality which attracted people to him and inspired them with confidence. He was of medium height, slender but manly build, always meticulously but simply dressed, and his face was dis-tinguished by a high domed forehead and piercing, arresting eyes.

At this time Philadelphia was a fast-growing Colonial metropolis. In the twenty-three years between Rush's birth in 1746 and his re-turn from abroad, its population had more than doubled from ap-proximately 13,000 to 28,000; after London and Edinburgh it was the third largest city in the British Empire. Its growth had been greatly augmented by a steady flow of new arrivals from England, by the Scotch-Irish in the 1720's, and in the next decade by a tide of German Lutherans.

After a few months in the house on Arch Street, Rush moved to one on Front Street near Walnut. From the back of this house he had a good view of the wharves along the Delaware River and the constant coming and going of ferries and of cargo vessels bringing cotton, tobacco, spices and slaves from the South and from the West Indies. The cobbled stones outside the house were a-clatter with the iron-rimmed wheels of phaetons and chairs, of carts and drays and newly invented Conestoga wagons, bringing produce from the country, and everywhere resounded the tattoo of horses' hooves. Since there were few foot paths or sidewalks, the pedes-trian had to watch his step.

Dr. Rush at first traveled mostly on foot, but later he rode in a chair, taking his black servant, a freed slave, with him. Slaves were sold in public places, among them the old London Coffee House, where it was a common practice to sell blacks of both sexes and to display them on the head of a cask. The firm of Allen and Turner

advertised the sale of some likely Negroes from the Barbadoes, in-
cluding a likely breeding Negro woman. Messrs. Willing and
Morris advertised for sale 170 Negroes just arrived from the Gold
Coast.

The old London Coffee House was on the corner of Front and
High Streets—a stone's throw from Dr. Rush's residence. It served
as a social club and as a place to transact business. The Governor
and other persons of rank ordinarily went there at set hours to sip
their coffee. Many of them had reserved stalls. The proprietor had
to give his assurances "as a Christian to preserve decency and
order . . . and to discourage the profanation, of the sacred name
of God Almighty by cursing, swearing, &c." Moreover, he
"covenants, that under a penalty of £100 he will not allow or suffer
any person to use, play at, or divert themselves with cards, dice,
back-gammon, or any other unlawful game." But his Christian
sensibilities seem not to have recoiled at the traffic in Negroes.

The same contrasts between stately public buildings and well-
appointed comfortable patrician dwellings of the rich and the primitive ramshackle houses of the poor that Rush had seen abroad
again met his eye in his native city. He cast his lot with the poor,
and they became his first patients. Life for them and even for the
affluent must have been hard. The street gutters served as open
sewers when there were any at all. There was, of course, no running water—at best a pump in the yard. Bathing was done mostly
in the summer months in small wooden tubs lined with tin. It was
not unusual for four or five members even of a well-to-do family
to bathe in rapid succession in the same water. In gentle families the
order seems to have been mothers first, then fathers, then daughters
and then the boys, who no doubt were most in need of a bath. Elizabeth Drinker, whose family were among Rush's more affluent patients, wrote in her diary: "Nancy came here this evening. She and
self went into Shower bath. I bore it better than I expected, not
having been wett all over at once, for 28 years past." The poor
seldom bathed and were frequently infested with body lice. Public
baths were occasionally resorted to, but were looked upon as im-
moral. Street cleaning was ineffective. Cesspools where they existed
were seldom emptied, perhaps once in forty years, and the pits to
prevent their filling up were often dug down to ground water,
where they flowed into nearby wells. Flies and mosquitoes

swarmed. It is no wonder that before long Dr. Rush had too much to do.

*   *   *

Benjamin Rush had a tough row to hoe. His position in Philadelphia was an uncertain one. He was without patronage. The pattern of medical practice was well established and bound by tradition. Its founder, Dr. John Kearsley Sr., who had come from England in 1711, was an ardent Anglican who held his own with the Welsh Quakers. Until his arrival, they had pre-empted much of the practice of medicine.

This extraordinary, many-sided man combined with his expert medical knowledge the gifts of artist, politician and scientist. He was not only a vestryman of Christ Church but also its principal architect, and later he had a hand in drawing the plans for St. Peter's. He served for a long time as an assemblyman and sat on the committee to superintend the building of the State House that would later be known as Independence Hall. Added to this he published in the *Philosophical Transactions* of the Royal Society his observations on comets and eclipses. As early as 1731 he and his students had submitted themselves to inoculation for smallpox in order to set a public example, and twenty years later he recorded with pride that he was "the first that us'd Inoculation in this Place."

Most of Rush's older colleagues—Thomas Cadwalader, Thomas Bond, John Kearsley Jr., a nephew and namesake of John Kearsley Sr., John Morgan, and Redman, his former master—had been apprenticed to this remarkable physician who, in addition to being a taskmaster of exacting harshness, had enjoyed the privileges of a liberal education which led him to urge his students to go abroad for further study. And thus it was that the tradition, which Rush had so faithfully followed, had been established in Philadelphia. There were other physicians of accomplishment and reputation who, to be sure, had not studied with Kearsley, but many of the best practitioners had done so.

Thomas Cadwalader was the first native Philadelphian to attain a European medical degree, and shortly after his return there appeared, in 1745, from the press of Benjamin Franklin, his "Essay on the West-India Dry Gripes: With the Method of Preventing and

Curing that Cruel Distemper." In this essay the author demonstrated that the colic caused by drinking punch made from Jamaica rum actually resulted from distilling the rum through leaden pipes. As early as 1723 the use of lead-pipe stills in the manufacture of rum had been forbidden by law in Massachusetts. It was Cadwalader, too, who performed the first experiments on the therapeutic use of electricity in America.

Thomas Bond, another pupil of Kearsley's, had appealed to Benjamin Franklin in 1751 for help in establishing a hospital in Philadelphia; he became, in fact, its founder. He was the principal figure of the medical faculty of Philadelphia and had been selected by Franklin to represent the medical profession in the American Philosophical Society, which had been founded in 1743. Without doubt Bond was a great clinical teacher in the modern mode, who emphasized not only the need for careful observation but also the importance of autopsies. He seems to have foreseen the value of the clinical-pathological conference. In 1759 he published a paper on the uses of Peruvian bark in scrofula. His essay on "The Utility of Clinical Lectures," delivered in 1766 before an assemblage of professors, physicians, and students, laid down the guidelines for the future development of medical education in America. He was also a skillful surgeon famous for his lithotomies.

Then there were Rush's more contemporary colleagues— William Shippen Jr. and John Morgan—whom he would naturally try to emulate. And indeed, the careers of these two patrician and prominent physicians, both of whom enjoyed the advantages of birth, position and wealth, were destined to become fatefully intertwined with his own at the University and later in the Revolutionary Army.

The pattern established by Morgan was exceptional. A fascinating, gifted and brilliant man, eleven years Rush's senior, Morgan belonged to an older civilization. His early training had been similar to Rush's—Nottingham Academy, the College of New Jersey, and apprenticeship with Dr. Redman; he became probably the greatest of the Colonial physicians. In Philadelphia his name was second only to that of Benjamin Franklin. In Britain, France and Italy, where he had studied and traveled, he had blazed a luminous trail. He was a member of the most distinguished foreign scientific bodies, including the Royal Society. In Italy, Morgagni, the founder of pathological anatomy, had greeted him as a blood brother; in Edinburgh, Cullen had treated him more like a colleague than a pupil and had urged him to stay there. Morgan's doctoral thesis for the first time conceived of pus as a secretion from the blood vessels and not from solid tissues. One hundred years later, this observation would be confirmed by the German pathologist Cohnheim.

Despite the pressure brought to bear on him to remain abroad, Morgan had determined to return to his native city to try to achieve something for his profession. He wrote at the time (November 1764) to his teacher Dr. Cullen, "I am now preparing for America to see whether, after fourteen years' devotion to medicine, I can get my living without turning apothecary or practicing surgery." He was therefore, in a sense, the first medical specialist. In Edinburgh he had discussed with Shippen, who hoped to deliver lectures on anatomy, his thoughts about medical education in the Colonies. Later, in Paris, he formulated in greater detail his ideas about founding a medical school in Philadelphia, and on May 3, 1765, he presented his proposals for a medical school at a special meeting of the Trustees of the College. Morgan was soon elected Professor of the Theory and Practice of Physic. At the Commencement Exercises, he delivered his famous "Discourse upon the institution of medical schools in America," which expresses his conviction that the arduous pursuit of medicine calls for "an enlarged and benevolent mind." Of this discourse, Abraham Flexner has said that it contained the essentials of what is still sound in medical education.

Unfortunately, in this public discourse, Morgan, being ambitious, proud and somewhat arrogant, gave little credit to Shippen and thereby earned his lasting enmity. No doubt he was sometimes high-handed in his dealings with his colleagues and he often tried to put himself at the head of things. Although Shippen had proposed to establish a medical school in Philadelphia, Morgan proceeded with his plans without ever taking Shippen into his confidence, even though he had talked to many others, including Thomas Penn and Drs. Fothergill and Hunter about them. In fact, Morgan had begun to surpass Shippen in professional and social accomplishments. He had advantages of birth, breeding and wealth; and he was safely ensconced among the Anglican aristocracy, though he came of Welsh Quaker stock. In addition he was handsome and fashionably dressed, as can be seen in the portrait painted by his patient, Angelica Kaufmann. A contemporary account describes him walking . . . "down Chestnut Street, bearing one of those new fangled 'umbarilloes' and an aura of slightly foreign charm and people were proud to be able to say, 'I've seen him.' "

*   *   *

Compared with Morgan, Benjamin Rush was a man of the people and he knew it. At the outset of his career he analyzed the principal means by which success might be won and he enumerated: the patronage of a great man; the influence of extensive and powerful family connections; and the backing of a religious sect or political party. In all of these he found himself deficient. His name was unknown to any of the men who were called great in his city; his family connections were few and without influence; and the Presbyterians among whom he had been brought up were both too small in number and too divided among themselves to afford him much support. He felt himself, moreover, "too feebly attached to their principles and forms, to have any claims upon them." They were the object of the jealousy and hatred, at least so Rush believed, of both the Quakers and the Episcopalians, who between them possessed the greater part of the wealth and influence in the city. Besides, the Quakers were in the habit of confining their business to members of their own Society. Rush did not complain of this. To him it was both natural and praiseworthy, but he knew that he could not expect their patronage.

Therefore, he had recourse to the only remaining mode of succeeding in business: attending the poor. Dr. Cullen had thus established himself in Scotland. So had Dr. Fothergill in London. In fact, during his apprenticeship, Rush had already made himself acceptable to the poor, for whom he claimed a natural sympathy. His new patients were widely scattered, some living as tenants at country seats near the city. During the first year of his practice he visited them mostly on foot, and supplied them with medicine out of his own shop. His business soon grew, because of his reputation for faithful attendance and because his treatment relied more upon diet and drinks than on the use of medicines. This, too, he had learned from his master, Dr. Cullen.

Rush now enhanced his professional reputation by introducing the new Suttonian method of inoculation against smallpox. This method used as an inoculum, not the pustular material from a patient, but rather the clear serum from an early lesion in the blister stage, before it was contaminated with pus. The serum was then introduced into the arm through a small scratch or puncture, and was less liable to be followed by a secondary infection. The young Doctor was obviously alert to recent progress in medicine because Sutton, an apothecary in Norfolk, England, had published his book, *The Inoculator*, in 1769, the same year that Rush began his practice in Philadelphia. Sutton's sons had popularized their father's method in England six years earlier, and Rush had seen it used in London.

His growing practice he attributed to various persons who continued to recommend him widely. These included a sea captain, a Presbyterian minister, a Scottish merchant named David McMurtie, who had business dealings with his mother, and Mrs. Patten, a neighboring midwife. He acknowledges that he felt neglected and unknown by the leading citizens of Philadelphia, and though his practice was extensive, it was less profitable than it should have been because he was paid in paper money which had a way of depreciating by the time his bills were paid.

But in the launching of his professional career, undoubtedly what was most beneficial to Benjamin Rush was his appointment, in the month after his return from his Grand Tour, as Professor of Chemistry in the College of Philadelphia. Shortly after landing he had made formal application to the Trustees offering himself as a candidate and promising to do anything in his power to discharge the duties of a professor and to promote the reputation and interest of the College. Before he had left for Edinburgh in 1766 he had been advised by Dr. Morgan to qualify himself for it.

But he was not awarded the appointment without opposition. This had came in part from Dr. Redman, a Trustee of the College, who was not persuaded of his former pupil's readiness for such a post. Rush had reacted to this skepticism with a good deal of pique and this had been reflected in two earlier letters written to Dr. Morgan from Edinburgh in which his bitter feelings toward Redman were ill concealed. In one of them he stated that he wanted to teach chemistry as a professor because he thought that he could show its application to medicine and philosophy in a stronger light than had ever been done, and that, also, having a seat in the College would enable him more fully to cooperate with Dr. Morgan in advancing medical sciences in general. In the same letter, Rush had written: "I think I am now master of the science and could teach it with confidence and ease." He acknowledged freely that it was to Dr. Black that he owed most of the chemical learning he possessed.

Redman had written him that he could not expect formal election until he had fully qualified himself and secured satisfactory testimonials, although he assured him there was no other claimant he need fear. The young man then wasted no time in getting the necessary testimonials, the most important one being from Dr. John Fothergill. This famous physician wrote to Mr. James Pemberton, one of the leading Quakers of Philadelphia, who served on the board of the Pennsylvania Hospital, stating that Rush had pursued his studies with much diligence and success. In the end the Trustees acted favorably, and Rush's appointment was unanimously voted on the day following their receipt of his formal application. Whereupon in August of 1769, the *Pennsylvania Chronicle and Universal Advertiser* carried this notice:

College of Philadelphia, August 14, 1769

By election of Dr. Rush to be professor of chemistry in this College, the different professorships, originally intended in the medical schools, are now filled up—and a complete course of lectures in the different branches of medicine will be open on Wednesday, the first day of November, *viz.*

Anatomy, Surgery and Midwifery, by Dr. Shippen
Chemistry, by Dr. Rush
Materia Medica, by Dr. Kuhn
Theory and Practice of Medicine, by Dr. Morgan
Clinical Lectures at the Pennsylvania Hospital, by Dr. Bond.

Dr. Smith, Provost of the College, will give a course of lectures in natural and experimental philosophy for the benefit of the medical students. Dr. Kuhn also will give a course of lectures in botany, to begin as soon as the season permits. N.B. The Honorable Thomas Penn, Esq., one of the proprietors of this province, hath sent to the College, by Dr. Rush, a complete apparatus for chemical experiments.

*   *   *

This was a time of ferment in the science of chemistry. The gathering storms of revolution, about to break on the American Colonies and then on France, were already heralded by the revolution in chemistry. This discipline was gradually freeing itself from the domination, first of alchemy and the iatrochemists, and then of the phlogiston theory. Rush, then, was undertaking to teach it when the primacy of the elements was already understood and when the transmutation of baser metals into gold, with all the attendant magical rites and symbols, was no longer a proper concern for chemists. Nor was it longer regarded as a mere handmaiden to medicine, whose first task was to provide cures. These preoccupations had lasted from the beginning of the 16th century to the middle of the 18th.

One of the first of the moderns was Robert Boyle, a contemporary of Cromwell and a name still familiar, because of his Gas Law, to every student of elementary physics and chemistry. Boyle was one of the founders of the Royal Society and its first President until his death in 1691. In his chief work, the *Sceptical Chymist*, he expounded his views on the nature of chemical elements and proclaimed them simple substances incapable of further decomposition; but he saw them as composed of closely assembled clusters and thus perhaps anticipated the contemporary notion of electrons and of protons and neutrons. He became the real founder of analytical chemistry and actually introduced the word "analysis" to describe his investigations.

"The chemists," he said, "view their task as the preparation of medicines and the extraction and transmutation of metals. I have tried to deal with chemistry from quite a different viewpoint, not as a physician or an alchemist but as a philosopher [scientist]."

Boyle believed that if men had the progress of true science more at heart than their own interests, they would render the greatest possible service to the world by setting up experiments and making observations rather than by proclaiming and espousing untested theories. He conceived the chemist's task to be the experimental investigation of the properties of substances without other ulterior purposes, and so he helped establish chemistry as an independent discipline.

Boyle's work was radical, prophetic and far-reaching, but his doctrine of elements failed to gain general acceptance, perhaps because he was a private scholar who lived for years in semi-seclusion and occupied himself with problems of religion, natural science and ethics. He was not a doctor of medicine, and chemistry was still the close companion of medicine, as it was a stepping stone to academic advancement. Even though some of its best teachers—as for example Boerhaave in Leyden, Cullen in Edinburgh, and Morgan—had endeavored to free chemistry from the confines of applied magic, the fact of their medical training undoubtedly restricted its development. This was also true of Rush's influence. Medicine was still doctrinaire, untroubled by controlled observation and quantitative measurement, and given, moreover, to a kind of metaphysical dialectic.

In these circumstances it was natural that the so-called phlogiston theory with its somewhat animistic implications should have taken so firm a hold on chemistry and on the minds of these men. George Ernst Stahl, a professor of medicine in Halle, is usually regarded as its originator. Phlogiston was thought to be contained in all combustible substances and to vanish when they were heated or burned. And it was believed that the residues of these substances after phlogiston had been given off could be changed back to their previous state by the addition of phlogiston to them. Further than this, and especially important for medical teaching, it was held to play an essential rôle in decomposition, fermentation and respiration.

A modern reader will have little difficulty in recognizing the missing element as oxygen, but oxygen was not discovered until 1771. And even its discoverers, Scheele in Sweden and three years later Priestley in England, could not quite shake off this tenacious and all-pervading theory. In fact, Priestley called the gas he obtained by heating red oxide of mercury—the gas which made a candle burn more brightly and set a smouldering taper aflame— "dephlogisticated air." Neither Scheele nor Priestley was a physician. The Swede was for years apprenticed to a pharmacist and the Englishman was a non-conformist Unitarian clergyman.

A few weeks after the discovery of oxygen, Joseph Priestley traveled to Paris, where he discussed his experiments with Lavoisier. Lavoisier appears to have grasped the importance of Scheele's and Priestley's experiments and finally to have explained oxidation, not by the loss of phlogiston, but by the addition of oxygen. The proof lay in the demonstration of weight gained in the process of oxidation by the use of the chemical balance.

This started a new era in chemistry. As is so often true in the history of science, the new light came not from the discipline itself but from a neighboring one. Antoine Laurent Lavoisier was not a chemist; he was a physicist. By 1780 his views became sufficiently clear to develop his oxidation theory, based on a quantitative measurement of weight ratios, and with this he buried the phlogiston theory. By their overlapping discoveries Scheele and Priestley had contributed to its end but they continued to cling to it in spite of the weight of contrary evidence.

The value of a theory can be measured in the terms of its power to explain hitherto baffling observations, to evoke new ideas, and to enlarge the field of inquiry for further testing. As applied to a theory this is what is meant by the modern word operational. In this sense Lavoisier's theories were operational, since by careful measurements they explained not only the phenomena of combustion and oxidation but also later were extended to include the process of respiration and thus led to an understanding of metabolism. But owing to the inertia of traditional thinking and to the turbulence of the times, his theories made slow headway. In 1794, this great man went to the guillotine, the president of the tribunal stating that "We no longer need scientists."

The revolution in chemistry was finished; the revolution in politics was still going on. In this latter revolution Rush would soon take his part, as indeed he did in many other farsighted social reforms, but in chemistry he must be classed as a conservative, insisting on its utility to medicine and perhaps delaying its fruitful independence as a science. His own pupil, however, young Dr. James Woodhouse, who succeeded him to the Chair of Chemistry, did more than anyone except Lavoisier to disprove the phlogiston theory and establish the proof of the existence of oxygen. Rush's lectures both in content and organization were strikingly similar to those of his teacher, Joseph Black, and were derived as well from Cullen and from Boerhaave.

* * *

Benjamin Rush's motives in seeking this appointment had been of course not wholly disinterested. Nor was he concerned only with the scientific aspects of the discipline. Rush had a good practi-

cal sense. He knew where his bread was buttered. In fact, he admits
in his diary that his appointment as Professor of Chemistry the
month after his arrival had held his name up to public notice now
and then in the newspapers and made it familiar to the public ear
much sooner than it otherwise would have been. Then he adds the
not unimportant consideration that it was likewise an immediate
source of some revenue. After all, he was without a fortune. He
had his sisters to support and his way to make in a medically unsophisticated society in which quacks not only flourished but also
advertised their sure cures for every conceivable type of disease in
the local newspapers.

A glazier named Thomas Anderton enlarged his business by fitting up his residence next to his store on Market Street as an office
for the treatment of venereal disease, promising a sound and lasting
cure. He sold medicines:

" . . . the first ever offered in the world, that will effectually
and radically cure every symptom of the venereal disease, without
pain or sickness, or any confinement whatever. Salivation is wholly
by them rendered unnecessary. . . . They are taken by the most
delicate of both sexes, at all seasons of the year, and by fishermen in
water, without any hurt to the constitution; for they improve and
invigorate the whole nervous system."

Anderton also advertised, in the *Pennsylvania Packet* for March
16, 1772, Turlington's balsam of life; Baron Van Swieten's worm
plums for grown persons and children; and Dr. Stark's tincture
for toothache and a fine water for sore eyes.

Dr. Day from London sold a bottle and a box for a dollar each
"that infallibly cures the worst fevers and agues or the worst
rheumatisms." All families were urged to keep a ready supply of
Dr. Ryan's:

". . . worm destroying sugar plums . . . one of the best
purges in the world for gross bodied children that are apt to breed
worms, and have large bellies; their operation is mild, safe and
pleasant; they wonderfully cleanse the bowels of all stiff and
clammy humours, which stop up the parts, and prevent the juice of
food being conveyed to the liver and make blood, which is often
the case with children, and is attended with a hard belly, stinking
breath, frequent fevers, rickets, and a decay of strength in the
lower parts: Likewise settled aches and pains in the head, swellings,

old sores, scabs, tetters or breakings out, will be perfectly cured, and the blood and skin restored to its original purity and smoothness; they purge by urine, and bring away the gravel, and effectually cure all obstructions of the urine, or ulcers in the kidnies. They at once strike at the true cause of the scurvy and entirely destroy it, and all scorbutic humours and effects, root and branch, so as never to return again; and what makes them more commendable is, they are fully as agreeable to both taste and sight as loaf sugar; and in their operation as innocent as new milk."

Advertising was not resorted to by lowly quacks, charlatans and medicasters alone. Both Rush and Shippen advertised their lectures in the public press, the one in chemistry and the other in anatomy. Although this may have been done partly to satisfy personal ambition, it was entirely consistent with their philosophy and with the temper of the times. The aim was to involve and to educate the public in scientific matters.

Within a year after his appointment, the new Professor had published a syllabus of his *Course of Lectures on Chemistry*—a slim volume containing in mere outline the subjects dealt with. Two other editions are known to have been printed, one in 1774 and the other in 1783.

His lectures were widely advertised. Indeed, the *Virginia Gazette*, printed as far away as Williamsburg, carried the following advertisement:

College of Philadelphia September 4 1771

A COURSE of *lectures* and *experiments* on *chemistry* will commence on *Monday* the *28th* of *October*, at 3 o'clock in the afternoon, by BENJAMIN RUSH, M.D., professor of chemistry in the college of *Philadelphia*. In these lectures and experiments, it is proposed to deliver not only the chemical history of the various bodies in nature, such as *salts—earths—inflammables—metals—waters*, &, with their application to medicine; but also to explain and illustrate most of those curious principles in nature and art, which depend upon chemical principles. The whole will be taught in such a manner as to be intelligible to the private Gentleman and enquiring artist [i.e., artisan], as well as the student of medicine. *The price of a ticket six pounds.*

*   *   *

These lectures were well attended. People of all sorts came to hear him as one of the experiences in Philadelphia that was not be missed. They were attracted by his great personal charm and his eloquence.

Both the advertisement and the caliber of Rush's mentality clearly indicate that his lectures had a strong practical slant. They were aimed more at an application of chemistry to medicine and to the arts than to any discussion or exploration of chemical theory —this in spite of the profound changes occurring in the discipline at this very time. The culture in which Rush lived, though more sophisticated than that in many of the Colonies, was still a pioneering one. It demanded of science that it be practical and popular and that it serve patriotic aims. Or, to put it in the contemporary words of the *Transactions* of the American Philosophical Society, of which Rush was a member: "Knowledge is of little use when confined to mere speculation." Members were urged to restrict their disquisitions to such subjects as tended to the improvement of their country and to the advancement of its interests and prosperity.

How well this fitted the philosophy of Benjamin Rush, who, in spite of a fine intelligence and a hunger for information, was too restless for the steady pursuit of knowledge for its own sake. His very choice of chemistry as a field of interest had been partly based on the belief that it would unlock the hidden sources of wealth in the waters and the earth of the new continent. He wanted to share this knowledge with all who would come to hear him, and to teach such practical things as the preparation of potash from wood ash, and the use of earths in the manufacture of china and the production of fertilizers.

He even conducted a course in domestic science at a new academy for young ladies in Philadelphia, where he lectured on methods of keeping houses cool and clean, on ridding them of insect pests, on materials for making dresses, on the use of soap, starch, blue and dyes, on foods and condiments, and also on the means of preserving female beauty. According to handwritten notes in his own copy of the *Syllabus*, Rush even had thoughts on "Horse and Cow—how to be treated," on gardening and on house remedies, including "Trifling disorders in wch. Drs. are not consulted, as *warts —ring Worms*—corns—sore eyes." He introduced this course of lectures with the statement that he would teach the young ladies frugality and economy and qualify them "to shine as wives, mothers, and mistresses of families."

It is evident that in chemistry, as indeed in his other interests, Rush was more the teacher, the advocate, the patriot, and even the propagandist than he was the creative student. Such experiments as he had performed in the chemistry of digestion in Edinburgh now gave way to popularizing chemistry as an applied science which could contribute much to improving life in the Colonies. He did, to be sure, perform some experiments to find the best vermifuges and still others to discredit a fake cancer cure, but he made no substantial contribution to chemical science. This has been attributed by one commentator to "his constitutional inability to concentrate on any single one among his innumerable enthusiasms," and by Oliver Wendell Holmes to the fact that Rush was an observant man, but not a good observer. He was, in fact, an insatiable accumulator of facts with an almost evangelical gift for teaching. His fame in chemistry and also in medicine rests on these qualities rather than on those of a discoverer or an original thinker.

In his introductory lecture on chemistry which he delivered in 1771 Rush asserts that a knowledge of that science is indispensably necessary to a physician, and he ends it on the following cautionary note:

"Among many other advantages which you will derive from reading Medical Books, I shall mention only one, which to a liberal spirit will be of great consequence, & this is, it will tend to deliver you from that *servile obedience*, which young men are apt to pay to the Opinions of their Masters, & will make you dare to think for *yourselfs*. A step this which never fails paving the way for a man's becoming Eminent in his Profession."

For twenty years, until 1789, when he succeeded Morgan in the Chair of Medical Theory and Practice, Rush continued to occupy the Chair of Chemistry, with interruptions due to his military service, to his sitting in the Continental Congress, and to political dissensions in the Medical School. When he began his lectures there were no American texts for his students to consult, but there were a few foreign works—French, German and English—to which Rush referred them. He put his own teachers, Cullen and Black, at the top of the list.

Because of lack of equipment there was, of course, no laboratory instruction. He lacked the funds to import the necessary chemicals and he had no laboratory assistant. Accordingly, lecture demonstrations were rather few in number. He did, however, demonstrate the production of hydrogen by treating iron filings with sulphuric acid, and this simple exhibition caused a numerous assemblage of medical students to gather around him. He likewise showed the effervescence that follows treating marble with sulphuric acid.

Although he tried to keep his knowledge of chemistry up to date and must have been aware of the discovery of oxygen, he assumed the existence of a "principle of inflammability"—a term which his master, Joseph Black, had used—and gave no evidence of having discarded the phlogiston theory or of having accepted the theories of Lavoisier.

At a later stage Rush's work took a more practical bent and before long he was engaged in the task of supplying gunpowder for the Army. When rebellion seemed imminent, the British forbade the shipment of gunpowder to the Colonies. In 1775 the Continental Congress authorized the publication of a pamphlet on methods of making saltpeter. The subject matter of this pamphlet was taken almost entirely from two articles, one written by Rush, the other by Benjamin Franklin. Rush had previously described in the *Pennsylvania Packet*, under the pseudonym of Peregrinus, the results of experiments on producing crude saltpeter from dried tobacco stalks, and he had also reviewed the work of the German chemists, Cramer and Glauber. These short articles were combined and appeared in the *Pennsylvania Magazine* for June 1775. The result was then reprinted and widely circulated under the title, "Several Methods of Making Salt-Peter." A house on Market Street was converted into a factory and Rush was appointed to a committee to superintend the manufacture of saltpeter.

One can well imagine with what energy and enthusiasm this gifted man lent his scientific training to the exigencies of the rebellion. Although Rush is regarded by many as a great teacher of medicine, he was, in addition, the first systematic chemist and teacher of chemistry in America and the first pharmacologist, as well.

* * *

Although chemistry was Benjamin Rush's specialty, it never contained him or confined him. His livelihood was gained from the practice of medicine, and into this he put much of his restless energy. From the time of his settlement in Philadelphia in 1769 until 1775, he led a life of constant labor and self-denial. In the morning and at mealtimes his shop was crowded with the poor. Each day he visited on foot nearly every street and alley in the city. Often he would climb ladders to the upper stories of old huts where his poor patients lived and where for want of a chair he would rest his weary limbs on the bedside, at the risk not only of taking the disease but of being infested with vermin. This, indeed, happened to him more than once.

By the time he had been in practice for five or six years, the young doctor was earning up to £900 a year in Pennsylvania currency, and this in spite of the fact that several of the older and established physicians of the city had become unfriendly to him and that for the first seven years of his practice none of his professional colleagues had ever sent him a patient. Rush attributed this to his lectures, in which he expounded the system of Dr. Cullen rather than that of Boerhaave, who was then in vogue in Philadelphia. But it is probable that his uncompromising nature rather than mere differences of opinion cost him the good will of his colleagues.

At a later stage Rush would offer other explanations for the fact that his colleagues so seldom called him in consultation. The part that he was about to play in the Revolution prejudiced some wealthy citizens of Philadelphia against him, the great majority of them being Loyalists; also his "meddling with politicks," albeit he intimates that they would not have objected to this had his politics coincided with their own. Again he believed that he had offended his medical brethren by urging that the period of study of medicine should be reduced from five years to two. Added to all this he wrote out his prescriptions in English instead of in Latin as was the custom, and he likewise used English in his inaugural dissertations.

It is hard for a modern physician to comprehend the medical convictions which in Rush's time were defended with so much vehemence and passion. The intensity of the defense was a measure and a denial of the fundamental uncertainty behind such convictions and a reluctant admission of the profound ignorance of the nature of diseases. The more devastating and decimating they were, the more the need to explain them by a rational "system." This served to allay the anxiety and sense of impotence of the doctor, even if it contributed little to his real understanding or to his

ability to cope with the problems confronting him. In one of his
lectures on the Practice of Physic, Rush proclaimed:

"I have formerly said that there was but one fever in the world.
Be not startled, Gentlemen, follow me and I will say there is but
one disease in the world. The proximate cause of disease is irregular
convulsive or wrong action in the system affected. This, Gentlemen, is a concise view of my theory of disease. . . . I call upon
you, Gentlemen, at this early period either to approve or disap-
prove of it now."

Here speaks an evangelist rather than a scientist. The truth
which he proclaimed was based not on carefully documented observation or experiment but on the enormous personal authority of
the speaker. Lingering traces of medievalism clung to Rush and to
his contemporaries, both at home and abroad. The characteristics
of all these systems were their tendency to oversimplify, to develop
monistic theories and to erect elaborate theoretical structures,
flimsily based on imperfect observation, inadequate data and loose
reasoning.

Rush's system can be reduced to a simple syllogism. The Doctor observed that fever is associated with a flushed skin, which was
thought to be caused by distended capillaries. From this he concluded that fever was the result of an abnormal ("convulsive")
condition of the blood vessels. All fevers he believed resulted from
this pheonomenon, which was then attributed—without evidence
—to the veins and arteries as well as to the capillaries. By dint of a
magical gesture Rush swept other pathological conditions into the
same category with fevers. Thus he achieved in his own mind a
unitary field theory of disease. All that then remained was to convince others of this revealed truth and to derive from it logical
therapeutic procedures.

A similar kind of ratiocination had activated Cullen and his pupil
John Brown, who, disagreeing with his master, announced dog-
matically that disease was due either to excessive tension or to
equally extreme relaxation in the body, and that treatment should
be directed at correcting the existing state. This speculative
"Brunonian system" was widely accepted throughout Europe and
the United States until about the year 1800. For a while Rush
adopted it, but then he forsook it, as he had Cullen's, in favor of his
own views.

It is profitless to pursue these arguments further, since the systems were based on false premises, even though the arguments derived from them and the treatment which they appeared to support were thought to be logical. Two aspects of this trend in medical history are noteworthy. One was the pride and zeal with which the proponents of these theories defended their views and challenged to wordy battles all who differed from them. But even greater than the evil of intolerance were the extravagant, and often harmful, methods of treatment that sprang from these medical dogmas.

However, the errors of our forebears can be overstressed. Within the limits of their ignorance, these 18th-century physicians maneuvered well. And they toiled incessantly. Their dogmatism serves as a warning that while a faulty working hypothesis is perhaps better than none, it can easily imprison men and blind them to new and fruitful observations. In any case, whatever Rush and his contemporaries may have lacked in scientific discipline, they possessed in humanity and wisdom. Both these are essential ingredients for any good physician. There is no doubt of Rush's dedication to the welfare of his poor patients, nor of his compassion.

There was yet another circumstance that both marked and facilitated the progress of Benjamin Rush's professional career. The Philadelphia physicians whom Dr. John Kearsley Sr. had influenced, either directly or indirectly, formed an élite group which kept alive a tradition of inquiry and public service. As has already been noted, the older colleagues of Rush's—Bond, Cadwalader, Kearsley Jr., Morgan and Redman—had distinguished themselves by their medical writings. Benjamin Rush was a natural inheritor of this tradition and he lost little time in joining their ranks with contributions of his own to medical literature.

During the dozen years before 1776 more than thirty publications concerning medicine and the public health appeared in America. Most of these were scientific treatises and thirteen among them came from members of the faculty of the local medical school. The Philadelphia printers, Franklin and Bradford, and a shrewd Scot named Robert Bell, encouraged the publishing of these articles, and they republished important European medical works as well. Among these, two were from the pens of Rush's former teachers: a pirated edition of Dr. William Cullen's *Lectures on Materia Medica*, which, according to Bell, was in danger of being lost to the world, and a subscription edition of the London physician Dr. John Gregory's *Lectures on the Duties and Qualifications of Physicians*. Both of these American editions appeared in 1775.

Professor Shryock, whose commentaries on medical history contain so much wisdom, says of Gregory's *Observations* that they contain "a statement of principles that might well have served as a working program for the century that was to follow." To quote from Dr. Gregory himself:

"It should be seen, upon the whole, that all physicians must reason, and that the only difference among them consists in this; that some reason better than others. Some search into the cause of disease and the effects of remedies. Deeply sensible of the difficulties of enquiry, and of the various ways in which they may be deceived, they collect and arrange all the facts relating to the subject; when they have got a remote view of a leading principle, they attempt to bring a direct and conclusive proof by experiment. . . . If the proof turns out against it, they see and candidly acknowledge that there is an error somewhere. . . . These, I think, have a just claim to the title of rational physicians."

There speaks the modern pragmatist. For deep reasons of his own or perhaps, better, because of forces within himself, Rush could sustain this point of view only fitfully. In 1768 he had written from Edinburgh to his friend John Morgan, "Dr. Gregory's lectures abound with excellent practical observations, but are by no means equal to the unrivaled Dr. Cullen's, whose merit is beyond all praise." In the light of subsequent medical history, one could wish that Rush had paid more heed to Gregory's words.

Another medical book of importance to the Colonies was reprinted in Philadelphia by the patriot printer, William Bradford. This was Cadogan's "Essay upon Nursing and the Management of Children." Since the author "sought to clear away the accumulated rubbish of folklore and to replace it with a sane, empirical hygiene," this appears to have been the "Holt" and "Spock" of the day.

Like his professional contemporaries, Rush availed himself of the public press, not only for scientific contributions but to express his views on matters of social import. In 1770 he published in the newspaper some observations on *Cynanche trachialis*, called at that time the "hives," a word still used in England for croup and probably derived from "heaves." He pointed out that the cause of this condition was a spasm of the windpipe without any secretion of mucus or the formation of a membrane, thus differentiating it from diphtheria.

The next year there appeared from his pen anonymously three essays entitled "Sermons to Gentlemen upon Temperance and Exercise." These, according to their author, were well received until it was discovered who had written them—after which, he says, they were as extravagantly abused. Then followed successively "An Address to the Inhabitants of the British Settlements in America upon Slave-keeping" (1773); "Experiments and Observations on the Mineral Waters of Philadelphia, Abington, and Bristol, in the Province of Pennsylvania" (1773); and an oration delivered before the American Philosophical Society containing "An Enquiry into the Natural History of Medicine Among the Indians in North America" (1774).

This gives an idea of Rush's industry and his far-ranging concerns. Although his days were ones of constant employment, his evenings were given to study. He seldom went to bed before midnight, and often heard the watchman cry three o'clock before he snuffed his candle. When overcome with sleepiness he would increase the blaze of his fire in the winter or expose himself for a few minutes on his balcony, which projected out over Water Street.

For the five years between 1769 and 1774 Rush says he kept little company except for an occasional dinner or supper for a stranger or for a few young merchants in his neighborhood. Occasionally he would spend afternoons in the company of ladies, "upon parties of pleasure both in town and in the country." But by and large at this stage of his life he gives the impression of a rather embattled somber recluse, unlike the more social and convivial student of those earlier days in Edinburgh, London and Paris.

5

THE DOCTOR TAKES A WIFE

⌗ INTO THE LIFE OF YOUNG DR. BENJAMIN RUSH THERE
now came dancing on joyous feet the charming Sarah Eve, a free-
spirited and lovable young girl who comes alive today in the surviving fragments of her diary written with naïve vivacity and
humor.

Sarah Eve had a freely ranging mind. She was one of a group of
young ladies in Philadelphia who were unusually emancipated and
cultivated. Many of them she mentions in her chronicle, such as
Sally Wistar and Amy Horner and Elizabeth Sandwith. They
were given to reading not only current literature but also such
classics as *Don Quixote*, *Tom Jones*, *Paradise Lost*, Pope's *Homer*,
and the works of Rousseau and Rabelais; the poems of Dryden and
Thomson and plays by Congreve and Cumberland. They availed
themselves freely of libraries and were not afraid of being called
blue-stockings, despite John Adams' contemporary expostulation
to his wife Abigail: ". . . the Femmes scavans, are contemptible
Characters."

In her diary Sarah keeps a sort of almanac of the weather so that
her dear father, long absent from home and to whom she is greatly
devoted, could "form a pretty just idea of the melancholy winters
we have had since he went away." Oswell Eve, a ship's captain,
had once been in command of the ship *George* and was the owner
of shares in at least twenty-five other vessels. His prosperous
family lived in a large stone house in Philadelphia. But he had met

with financial reverses and in May 1768 he had left with his sons, Oswell Jr., who had been a classmate of Benjamin Rush's, and John, for the West Indies, where he was trying to repair his fortunes in business at Montego Bay in Jamaica. They had been gone now for five years and Sarah was waiting impatiently, almost breathlessly, for the day of his return or for news of him and her two brothers.

In spite of this anxiety Sarah Eve led an active and sociable life, with excursions into the country and much visiting back and forth with neighbors and friends and family, and always the cheering cup of tea. She greets a June morning thus:

"As soon as I got up this morning, I went out in the field to see them mow, and I could not help thinking that I walked and kicked the grass just as my dear Father used to do, the thought gave me so much pleasure I had liked to forget to eat my breakfast." Of Dr. Shippen, who calls, she says: "What a pity it is that the Doctor is so fond of kissing; he really would be much more agreable if he were less fond. One hates to be always kissed, especially as it is attended with so many inconveniences; it discomposes the economy of one's *handkershief*, it disorders one's *high Roll*, and it ruffles the serenity of one's countenance."

Her mention of Benjamin Rush is scant and formal. Referring to him as Dr. Rush or B. Rush, an occasional entry tells of a visit. Thus: "After Tea, B. Rush, Miss Harper and I took a walk, curiosity lead us to the Mineral Point and persuaded us to drink, or rather *taste* the water which is excessively disagreable, but at present is drunk for almost every disorder, and is looked upon as an universal nostrum."

A year later the *Pennsylvania Packet* reported:

"A *Mineral Water* hath lately been discovered in a lot of ground at the corner of Sixth and Chestnut Streets in this city. From the most accurate experiments, made by different gentlemen of the faculty, it appears to exceed in strength any chalybeate spring yet known in the Province. It hath already proved of great service to several persons afflicted with disorders, in which waters of this quality have generally been used."

Dr. Rush praised its virtues in his essay on the mineral waters of Pennsylvania, but unfortunately it was subsequently discovered that the spring was contaminated by sewage. This accounted for its strong sulphurous taste, if not for its medicinal value, and put a stop to its use. As a trained chemist, Rush should have known as much.

"In the evening," Sarah Eve writes in September 1773, "Mr. Rush came to see us, he did not know we were sick [she and her mother] until he came here; he seemed so distresst that he did not know how to leave us, 'You should, why did you not let us know how you were, that we might have been up before.' Are we not blest with the best of friends."

The next day he gave her mother some powders and her some elixir and they thought these had been of service to each of them. Thereafter there are more frequent visits from B. Rush.

In the end these two planned to be married. At this time Benjamin Rush was twenty-six years old. Three years earlier on his return from Europe he had declared that he could not be tempted into matrimony until he had extended his studies to the point where a family would not impede his further progress. Before that he had given as an excuse for his single state the fact that he was the sole support of his mother and sisters. Perhaps these were cogent reasons for not marrying, but they are also readily recognizable as rationalizations for a reluctance on his part to give his emotions sway and to relinquish his accustomed purposive and intellectual approach to life. He was a high-minded and rather rigid Puritan—not the stuff that lovers are made of. His two earlier amorous sallies—one with Polly Fisher, and the other with the youthful Lady Jane Leslie—were charming, tepid, literary and not wholly convincing. Now perhaps he was more ready. The year before he had written that solitude is the bane of man. There can be no doubt of his solitude and of his dark feelings of being unappreciated and dealt with severely and unfairly by his colleagues and by people of high estate. To be sure he had invited such feelings through his zeal for unpopular causes, but these feelings were no less real to him nor painful.

Then tragedy struck. Three weeks before the date set for their wedding, Sarah Eve died of tuberculosis. She was buried on the 4th of December 1774.

With her independent mind Sarah Eve was Benjamin Rush's equal and she might well have made him a suitable wife. But whether she could have infused into his Puritanical bones a little of her joy of living, it is hard to say. It has been argued that Rush could have had no deep feelings for her because he makes no mention of her in his autobiography. But it should be remembered that this was addressed to his children and it is hardly customary in such circumstances to refer to previous romances. Indeed he may have been so deeply moved by Sarah's tragic death as to prefer to seal it over with silence. To assert that he could not have loved her because he married another within two years betrays little knowledge of the human heart.

The story ends a week after Sarah Eve's death with the appearance of a short anonymous piece in the *Pennsylvania Packet* that bears the title, "A Female Character." This has been attributed to the pen of her fiancé, and from its literary style this guess may not be wide of the mark. It is a panegyric of virtues. But it is lifeless and it conveys none of the qualities of this remarkable young woman, who is breathed into life through the pages of her diary.

*　*　*

A retreat into morose inactivity because of his grief over the loss of Sarah Eve would have been inconsistent with the nature of Benjamin Rush. On the contrary he became more than ever occupied with his various interests. For some time he had been deeply involved in the slavery issue. Through his writings he tried to show the iniquity of the slave trade and he urged an increase on the duty upon Negro slaves imported into the province. But Rush was more than a pamphleteer. He helped start and he played an active rôle in many philanthropic organizations. Of these, one of the most important was the Pennsylvania Society for Promoting the Abolition of Slavery and the Relief of Free Negroes Unlawfully Held in Bondage. This society was founded in 1774.

In a letter to Granville Sharp, an Englishman, who like himself could best be described as a liberal and humanitarian, Rush admits that his "Address to the Inhabitants of the British Settlements in America upon Slave-Keeping" had been written amidst many interruptions and contained few new arguments, yet he hoped their conciseness would give them new force. Rush also speaks of a spirit of humanity and religion awakening in some of the Colonies in favor of the poor Negroes and he says that the clergy are beginning to bear public testimony "against this violation of the laws of

nature and christianity." But he believes that nothing of consequence can be done "till the ax is laid to the root of the African
Company."

This pamphlet, written under a pseudonym, he sent as well to
Barbeu Dubourg, his friend in Paris, the physician and botanist to
whom Franklin had introduced him, and, of course, to Dr. Franklin himself. He tells both that he has been publicly credited with
having written the pamphlet at the request and instigation of Anthony Benezet, whom he describes to Dubourg as "a pious
Quaker of French origin . . . whose name is held in veneration in
these parts and deserves to be spread throughout the world." In
his letter to Granville Sharp, Rush had stated that a few years
earlier Benezet had stood alone in opposing Negro slavery in Philadelphia, but that now three-fourths of the province as well as the
city cried out against it. This pamphlet was reprinted in New York
and Boston, where it gained ardent and sympathetic support, and
apparently his good work bore fruit. On January 26, 1773, an act
was passed which laid a tax of from £7 to £14 sterling per head on
Negro and mulatto slaves imported into the province of Pennsylvania, and this amounted to an almost total prohibition.

It is quite understandable why Rush should not choose to write
this address over his own name. He acknowledges that the pamphlet did some good in removing errors and prejudices on the subject of domestic slavery, but he recognizes that it probably did him
harm by exciting the resentment of many slaveholders against him.
He felt also, as many physicians have, that the public objected to
his meddling in a controversy foreign to his own business. And yet
in spite of all this, his practice continued to increase.

We next find Rush delivering the annual oration before the
American Philosophical Society, that august body which still flour-
ishes and of which Rush later became vice-president. His paper was
called "An Inquiry into the natural history of medicine among the
Indians of North America, and a comparative view of their diseases
and remedies with those of civilized nations." If the speech was
given as it appears in the first of the four volumes of Rush's *Medical Inquiries and Observations* in sixty-eight octavo pages, it must
have taken him nearly two hours to deliver. But Rush was an
accomplished orator with a fine voice and presence—and skilled in
holding the attention of his audience. Much of the address is

derived more from the observations of others than from his own. Although he extols the simple rugged life of the Indian and finds him free from those new diseases which he calls the offspring of luxury, he does not idealize him. He says that "the Indian submits to his disease, without one fearful emotion," unlike the white man who has "converted even the fear of death into a disease." And in this connection he makes the remarkable statement that he has not been able to find a single instance of mental derangement among the Indians. However, it is now recognized that one must be intimately familiar with a culture before such deviations can be detected.

Rush realized that those Indian tribes who had mingled with white people had a higher death rate than others because of the "extensive mischief of spiritous liquors." Here again was a subject that would later engage his attention for many years and to which he would make one of his most telling contributions.

Rush seems to have been free from racial prejudices and to have had at heart the welfare of those who comprised the minority groups of his time. On a later occasion he would describe the detail of a circumcision ceremony at which he was the only one who was not Jewish in a company of more than thirty. His account, detached and objective, is without comment on this, to him, alien ritual, and he ends it with these plain yet revealing statements: "After the whole was ended, the company sat down to a splendid and plentiful breakfast. The heat of the day was 84°."

He was also invited to attend a Jewish wedding. Rush writes his wife that he accepted the invitation with great pleasure because he loved to add to his stock of ideas on all subjects. The ceremony was, of course, in Hebrew, of which he did not understand a word except "Amen" and "Hallelujah." He was astounded to see that the men wore hats and conversed with each other during the whole time of worship. The bride, a most lovely and affecting object, was led by her two bridesmaids under a beautiful canopy of white and red silk. There she and the groom both sipped about a teaspoonful of wine given them by the priest. The groom then threw the glass on a pewter dish which had been placed at his feet. As the glass broke into many small pieces, there was a general shout of joy, and the ceremony was over. Needless to say, Rush inquired as to the meaning of all this. He was told that partaking of the same glass of wine denoted the mutuality of their gods, and breaking the glass was intended to teach them the brittleness and uncertainty of human life and the certainty of death, in order to temper and moderate their present joys. After the ceremony Dr. Rush had to hurry away, but not before eating some wedding cake and drinking a glass of wine. He also ministered to the bride's mother, who had fainted from excitement and the heat of a June day.

It would have been unlike Dr. Rush not to have ended this account with a homily:

"During the whole of this new and curious scene my mind was not idle. I was carried back to the ancient world and was led to contemplate the passovers, the sacrifices, the jubilees, and other ceremonies of the Jewish Church. After this, I was led forward into futurity and anticipated the time foretold by the prophets when this once-beloved race of men shall again be restored to the divine favor and when they shall unite with Christians with one heart and one voice in celebrating the praises of a common and universal Saviour."

*   *   *

Coming events were beginning to cast their shadows across Rush's path. He would not have been himself had he tried to evade or sidestep them. On the contrary, the republican principles which he had adopted in Edinburgh had prepared him to play what he called an early but obscure part in the controversy between Great Britain and the Colonies. Under a variety of signatures Rush wrote several pieces in the newspapers in favor of the claims of the Colonies. He was close to some of the leaders in Pennsylvania politics, among them Edward Biddle, George Clymer, John Dickinson and Thomas Mifflin. These men, like Rush himself, had been chosen delegates to the first Continental Congress. This body met at Philadelphia in September 1774.

Rush with several others went as far as Frankford to meet the delegates from Massachusetts, not so much to welcome them as to warn them not to utter a word about independence, which was as unpopular in Pennsylvania as the Stamp Act itself. He rode back into town in the same carriage with John Adams, and describes him as plain in dress and manners and in conversation cold and reserved. In the custom of the day Rush says that he waited upon nearly all the members of the first Congress and entertained most of them at his table. He specifically mentions John and Samuel Adams, who made themselves at home in his family and whose conversation he found animating and in favor of liberty and republicanism. John Adams enjoyed the Doctor's very best claret, Madeira and Burgundy, and found his "Melons, fine beyond description." At this time he also inoculated Patrick Henry from Virginia for the small-pox. While he never heard Henry speak in public, Rush describes him as having a deep and correct knowledge of human nature.

His conversations with these members of the first and second Congresses Rush characteristically refers to as "feasts of noble sentiments." There can be no question that, caught in the fervor of the day, he was enthralled with the republican ideal. A recent commentator accuses him of climbing on the band wagon and becoming a patriot because it was the thing to do. This is a misreading of Rush's character, especially in view of the fact that his revolutionary sentiments cost him the patronage of those wealthy citizens who remained staunch Tories.

During the session of the first Congress Rush spent a long evening at General Mifflin's in the company of General Washington, the two Adamses and General Charles Lee. On this occasion, John Adams expressed no hope of reconciliation with Great Britain, and after supper he gave a toast, "Cash and Gunpowder to the Yankees." The next evening, Washington dined in Rush's home.

Until the battle of Lexington and Concord Rush acknowledges himself a spectator of events. But this dramatic action gave a new tone to his feelings, and he resolved to assume his share of the burdens in the coming Revolution. With these first shots fired at Americans, he considered the separation of the Colonies from Great Britain as inevitable and looked upon that battle as "the signal for the commencement of our independence." From this time on, many of his publications were designed to prepare the public mind for the momentous events that were to come.

The previous autumn he had addressed a letter to his fellow countrymen on patriotism. It was printed in the *Pennsylvania Journal* for October 20, 1773. In it he warns them of the arrival of "vessels freighted to bring over a quantity of tea taxed with a duty to raise a revenue from America."

In his effusive style he wrote: "The baneful chests contain in them a slow poison in a political as well as a physical sense. They contain something worse than death—the seeds of SLAVERY. Remember, my countrymen, the present era—perhaps the present struggle—will fix the Constitution of America forever." On November 27 the first of the three tea ships, the *Dartmouth,* arrived in Boston Harbor, with consequences known to history.

Most important in Benjamin Rush's life at this juncture was his meeting with Thomas Paine. This young man—he was eight years older than Rush—had arrived in Philadelphia from Norfolk, England, in November 1774. He was armed with letters from Benjamin Franklin and his intention had been to teach school or to give private lessons in geography to young ladies and gentlemen, but Robert Aitkin, the book dealer who published the *Pennsylvania Magazine,* employed him as an editor. In this capacity Paine soon exhibited great ability.

Aitkin introduced Bejamin Rush to Thomas Paine in his bookstore. Immediately the two found much in common—not only Paine's anti-slavery convictions, but also his realization that the independence of the American Colonies from Great Britain was now a necessity. Rush invited the young Englishman to visit him, and this he did a few days later. Before their next meeting, Rush put some of his own thoughts on paper. He was about to write an address to his fellow citizens urging the final separation of the Colonies, but he hesitated to do so, for, as he wrote in his autobiography, he "shuddered at the prospect of the consequence of its not being well received." Undoubtedly one of the consequences would have been damage to his professional reputation and loss of patients, the sole source of his livelihood and of those dependent on him.

But Thomas Paine had nothing to lose. He could live anywhere. He was not tied to Philadelphia, where a great majority of citizens and some of Rush's close friends were hostile to cutting the ties between the Colonies and England. There was nothing to prevent him from coming forward as a pioneer in the heated controversy. Accordingly, Rush asked him what he thought of writing a pamphlet on the subject, and to this suggestion Thomas Paine gave his ready assent.

It was Rush who suggested the world-famous title, *Common Sense,* at least so he tells us. From time to time Paine would call upon Rush and read a chapter to him. The latter records that he was especially charmed by one sentence that never found its way into the final version: "Nothing can be conceived of more absurd than three millions of people flocking to the American shore every time a vessel arrives from England, to know what portion of liberty they shall enjoy."

A report circulated that Paine had been helped in the writing of *Common Sense* by Samuel Adams, Mr. Rittenhouse, and Dr. Franklin, but the fact is that not one of them actually saw it until it was finished, and then only at the suggestion of Benjamin Rush. Both Charles Lee and John Adams believed Rush to be the author, but he disclaimed any such attribution. Still, it is hard to conceive that he would sit by passively while Thomas Paine read his manuscript aloud. Rush also saw to its publication, sending Paine to the Scottish printer and bookseller, Thomas Bell. However, Rush's account of his share in the preparation of Paine's famous tract was written nearly twenty-five years after the event, and it is quite possible that he has claimed too much for his part.

Upon the publication of *Common Sense* on January 10, 1776, Rush declares that it "burst from the press . . . with an effect which has rarely been produced by types and paper in any age or country," and that "its effects were sudden and extensive upon the American mind." It was soon widely read and quoted by men in the public eye and repeated in schools and even from the pulpit. All of this Rush viewed as a blessing because he saw a republican form of government within his country's grasp—a fulfillment and realization of the principles which he had adopted in his student days in Edinburgh.

Rush continued to cherish Thomas Paine for his rhetorical gifts and his political and humanitarian ideals. Only his religious views struck a discordant note. For Paine was a deist. He believed that the existence of God can be proved rationally without the aid of supernatural revelation. But to his pious young friend such a persuasion as this was unchristian doctrine.

Rush, of course, had his opinions of all his revolutionary compatriots. He came to cherish and to value John Adams above all, with the possible exception of Franklin. With Adams he formed a warm and confident, an equal and unambivalent friendship—rare among his relations with men. Their friendship withstood sharp differences of opinion and endured throughout nearly four decades, terminating only with Rush's death in 1813.

Each of these American revolutionaries has left an account of the other in exchanges of letters throughout this long friendship. With a fitting and appropriate bow to the vivid and accomplished Abigail Smith Adams, Rush speaks of the many delightful evenings passed in their home; and of Adams he wrote that "He saw the whole of a subject at a single glance, and by a happy union of the powers of reasoning and persuasion often succeeded in carrying measures which were at first sight of an unpopular nature." He spoke also of Adams' pungent humor and satire, of his fearlessness of men, and of his bold assertion of his opinions. As an example of this, Rush cites Adams' comments on General Washington. The superstitious veneration paid to the latter distressed Adams and in Congress he said boldly, "I honour him for his good qualities, but in this House I feel myself his superior. In private life I shall always acknowledge him to be mine." Again Rush extols Adams' moral qualities: "a stranger to dissimulation," he calls him, "more jealous of his reputation for integrity, than for talents or knowledge." He sums it all up by calling Adams "a real American in principle and conduct."

Now what has Adams to say about Rush? Nothing too flattering: "Dr. Rush came in. [Sunday, September 24, 1775] He is an elegant, ingenious Body. Sprightly, pretty fellow. He is a Republican. He has been much in London. . . . Dilly sends him Books and Pamphletts, and Sawbridge and McCaulay correspond with him." Then Adams dismisses him by saying, "But Rush I think, is too much of a Talker to be a deep Thinker. Elegant not great."

This was a first impression. Rush was not yet thirty and certainly he was out of his depth with the seasoned politician from Boston. But as Rush matured, Adams changed his opinion.

A few days after General Washington had been appointed Commander-in-Chief of the American armies (June 15, 1775), a dinner was given for him at a tavern on the banks of the Schuylkill River by a group of delegates and several citizens of Philadelphia. Among the guests were Franklin and Jefferson, Samuel Ward, Governor of Rhode Island, William Livingston, Governor of New Jersey, John Langdon, later Governor of New Hampshire, and about a dozen others including Dr. Benjamin Rush. Except for

Jefferson, most of them were Rush's seniors by a wide margin. Rush was twenty-nine; Jefferson, thirty-two; John Adams was forty, while his kinsman Samuel was fifty-three and the venerable Franklin was about to turn seventy. George Washington had taken command at the age of forty-three.

After dinner the first toast was to the Commander-in-Chief of the American Armies. According to Rush, Washington, rising from his seat, thanked the company, but with some confusion, for the honor they did him. Whereupon everyone else rose to his feet and they drank the toast standing. Rush says that the scene was a solemn one and that a silence followed it "as if every heart was penetrated with the awful, but great events which were to follow the use of the sword of liberty which had just been put into General Washington's hands by the unanimous voice of his country."

At about this time, Rush saw Patrick Henry at his lodgings and Henry told him that General Washington had confessed to him that he felt unequal to the station to which his country had elevated him. Henry recollected that, with tears in his eyes, Washington added: "Remember, Mr. Henry, what I now tell you: From the day I enter upon the command of the American armies, I date my fall, and the ruin of my reputation."

*   *   *

On January 11, 1776, the day following the publication of Thomas Paine's *Common Sense*, Benjamin Rush was married to Julia Stockton at Morven, her father's country seat in Princeton. Appropriately enough, the Reverend Dr. John Witherspoon performed the marriage service.

Years before, on the day that Benjamin Rush had taken his degree at the College of New Jersey, he had come upon a small child who had lost her way in the commencement crowd. Taking her up in his arms he had carried her to her father's house, "listening with great pleasure to her prattling all the way." A dozen years were to pass before he saw her again and upon this later occasion she impressed him as "engaging in her manners and correct in her conversation." More important still, she professed a great admiration for the Reverend John Witherspoon, declaring him to be the finest preacher she had ever heard.

Benjamin Rush was impressed. Such a pronouncement he felt sure "could only proceed from a soundness of judgment and correctness of taste seldom to be met with in a person of her age." Julia Stockton was then seventeen and Benjamin Rush thirty. Upon his return to Philadelphia he wrote to her parents seeking permission to visit their daughter. In his autobiography the result is recorded in simple words—"After several visits my suit was blessed with success."

Their wedding marked the beginning of a confident and tender relationship that would end only with Rush's death thirty-seven years later. His choice of a wife was a happy one. Julia Stockton had been linked with his past. When at college in Princeton as a boy he had come to know her parents and to admire their home. Later at Edinburgh he had been associated with her father in the successful endeavor to persuade the Reverend Witherspoon to come out to the Colonies and assume the presidency of the future Princeton University. And Richard Stockton had been received with Rush by the Council of Edinburgh as a burgess and gild brother. Now, at the time of Rush's marriage to his daughter, they were, together with Witherspoon, fellow members of the Continental Congress, and six months later all three men would put their signatures to the Declaration of Independence.

Only the cynical could doubt the soundness of this marriage. In many places Rush bears testimony to her excellence. Through all his great trials, political and professional, he turned to her, not so much to look for comfort or solace as to share his almost unbearable burdens with his calm and steadfast partner. He acknowledges that had he listened to her advice on many occasions he would have known less distress in his life. Because of war and pestilence and childbearing, in itself then a hazardous undertaking, they were often separated, but throughout all these events there is a steady flow of letters from him to his wife. They form a running chronicle of his life. Although they begin with "My Dearest" or "My dearest Life" and gradually shift to "My dear Julia," the reader today feels no coolness in him.

Eight years after his marriage, in a letter written to his erstwhile Scottish love, now Lady Jane Belsches, Rush describes his Julia as having "brown hair, dark eyes, a complexion composed of white and red, a countenance at the same time soft and animated, a voice mild and musical. . . ." In the same letter he adds: "She knows that she owes her conquest in part to you, for it was by singing 'The Birks of Endermay' the first evening I was introduced to her, with the same air and lisp that I once heard your ladyship sing the same sweet song in Nicholson Square." A portrait painted by Charles Willson Peale shows Julia Rush as a patrician, pensive young lady with an oval face and hair piled high on her forehead, and seated, elegantly gowned, plucking the strings of a lute.

Anyone looking at Rush's portrait done by the same artist will at once be struck by the pronounced facial resemblance between them—a circumstance certainly not unheard of in many good marriages. Later portraits do not bear out his resemblance to Julia, however. He calls her friend, companion, wife, "in the full meaning of each of those words," and says that he "got a pretty little fortune with Mrs. Rush." Julia bore him thirteen children, of whom nine survived to maturity.

In a letter written to his wife in May 1776, Rush says he had not known till they were separated how much she had become a part of his life. He says that he feels some abatement of affection for his country when he reflects that it has deprived him of even an hour of his dear Julia's company. And he tells her how, on coming home from visiting his patients, he almost expects to find her waiting, but instead is oppressed by the melancholy silence that "reigns through every apartment of our house." The next letter, two days after this one, is addressed "My Dearest Life." It closes with the happy anticipation of their being alone together with "no third person to break in upon our sweet house . . ." and assuring her that he has a thousand things to say to her and that he thinks, writes, talks, works and lives only for her.

As is his custom, he keeps her informed of his doings. He tells her that General Mifflin relies chiefly on him and a few others for the salvation of the province. He is beginning to find that there is a great deal of difference between sporting a sentiment upon politics in a letter or over a glass of wine and properly discharging the duties of a senator, and he writes that his seat in Congress subjects him to cares he had not known when his whole business consisted in reading and writing, and feeling pulses. But he was too inept in the art of compromise and too impatient for the great game of politics.

Two weeks before this letter had been written to Julia, Congress passed a resolution (on May 15, 1776) recommending to each state "where no government sufficient to the exigencies of their affairs have hitherto been established, to adopt such governments as shall, in the opinion of the representatives of the people, best conduce to the happiness and safety of their constituents in particular, and America in general."

John Adams called this resolution the most important ever adopted in America. But when it was read aloud at the Coffee-house, only one man huzzaed. Feelings of indignation were strong, but it was necessary to remain mute. Peace seemed far off and it was predicted that it would probably be a terrible summer.

Adams had once written Benjamin Rush: "Patience! Patience! Patience! The first, the last and the middle virtue of a Politician." And now, although patience was not Rush's most conspicuous virtue, he soon found himself in the thick of the practical politics of his native Pennsylvania.

Five days after the Congressional Resolution of May 15, a Whig mass meeting was called. In spite of a downpour of rain, four or five thousand people gathered in the State House yard. It was decided to hold elections in June for deputies to a convention which would prepare to establish a state government. This convention was known as the Provincial Conference, and Benjamin Rush was elected a member of it.

On June 1 he wrote his wife that their cause continued to prosper in nine out of ten counties of the province, and he added in one of his extravagant and effulgent outbursts, designed, no doubt, in part to keep up his own morale:

"I hope, my dear, we shall see many happy days in Philadelphia together, notwithstanding we have precluded ourselves from the society of a few tory families. 'I should have blushed,' says Cato, 'if Cato's house had stood secure and flourished in a civil war.' I should have blushed much more to have heard it said at such times as these that I shook hands or drank madeira with men who would have sacrificed their country to ambition or avarice. . . . I trust the spirit of God himself moves me to declare that I will never desert the cause I am embarked in, till I see the monster tyranny gnash [his] impotent teeth in the dust in the Province of Pennsylvania. This I think will be the case on the 18th of next June, the day appointed for the provincial Convention." :

The Provincial Conference which Rush had helped create met on June 18. It issued a declaration proposing the annulment of the proprietary form of government. It took a strong stand in favor of independence and called for a convention to frame a new Constitution for Pennsylvania. The Conference also replaced the conservative members of the Pennsylvania delegation in the Continental Congress. One of the replacements was Benjamin Rush, who had unequivocally favored independence. On July 22 Rush took his seat in Congress.

The next day he writes, this time at night, to his dearest Jewel, telling her how happy he is that his appointment in Congress gives her so much pleasure. Meeting as a committee of the whole, Congress debated the proposed Articles of Confederation. Rush tells his wife that he spoke for about ten minutes on the subject, but that he had not thundered like Cato. Dr. Franklin's presence appears to have confounded him. He is delighted to find that his fellow Congressmen can talk nonsense now and then, and this, he says, reconciles him to himself. Rush's first recorded speech, on August 1, discussed the mode of representation in Congress. It ended with these ringing words: "When I entered that door, I considered myself an American."

*   *   *

To understand the situation in which Rush and his colleagues found themselves, it must be realized that in 1776 Pennsylvania was in the midst of a revolution within a revolution. The Scotch-Irish Presbyterians and the German Lutherans were beginning to throw over the autocratic rule of the English Episcopalians and Quakers. In addition to religious and ethnic differences, there were economic ones as well. While the interests of the East and Southeast were primarily mercantile and financial, the West's were exclusively agricultural. This made fair representation in the State Assembly a matter of pressing urgency. In this struggle, Philadelphia naturally took the lead, but here there were sharp conflicts between the landed aristocracy and the laborers and mechanics, who were denied the vote because of property qualifications. Rush supported the radical group in fighting the evils of the Proprietary Government and in trying to establish a democratic constitution.

The Whig party, to which Rush belonged, was itself divided between Right and Left wings. The Right, or conservative wing, included such men as Dickinson and Morris, who wanted the provincial charter preserved and, though in favor of independence, they
insisted that all means of conciliation should be exhausted before
independence should be proclaimed. Rush, along with Dr. Franklin, Thomas McKean, soon to be Chief Justice and later Governor
of Pennsylvania, and George Clymer, threw his weight on the opposite side. These men were the leaders of a party that included the
Irish and Scotch-Irish settlers of the western part of the State and
also the disfranchised inhabitants of Philadelphia and other parts of
the East. They demanded the overthrow of the charter because of
its undemocratic nature.

Under the prevailing Constitution, the state was possessed of
arbitrary powers which led to abuses both of property and persons. This Constitution also provided for a loyalty oath to the existing government that all white male inhabitants had to take or be
deprived of their civil rights. These included not only the right to
vote but also to hold office, transfer real estate, or engage in trade
and professions. Rush was outraged by this loyalty oath. Bitter
controversy over the Pennsylvania Constitution was to last for
more than another decade and he would play a large part in ex-
punging some of its evils and in its final dissolution.

Rush was quite aware that these activities—even though ultimately crowned with success—made him many enemies. Also they
subjected him to much abuse in the newspapers. For a man so inflexible in his aims and yet so sensitive and so much in need of ap-
proval, this must have cost him dearly. Both the die-hard Tories
and the new radical group turned against him. In time he found
himself in the position of many a political reformer: once a rebel
and a revolutionary, but now pushed into the middle conservative
position by the opposing forces at each end.

The new Constitution which the Pennsylvania radicals proposed
Rush at first supported wholeheartedly. But in time he shifted his
ground to the conservative position, joining Dickinson and Morris,
who had originally opposed independence and had been displaced
in Congress by Rush and others. Congress was concerned with the
problem of inflation; there was an increase in the quantity of
money and a scarcity of some articles of merchandise resulting in a

sharp rise in prices. The Committee of Inspection, to which Rush had been elected, for putting into effect the resolves of Congress, attempted to deal with this evil by fixing prices at their previous levels. Rush opposed this measure nearly alone, quoting from Hume's *History of England* in support of his stand. But the authority of Hume on the perils of price control had no weight and the measure was carried by a large vote over Rush's objections.

Although a neophyte in practical politics, he was learning through daily experience how people, with the best intentions, blunder on until they exhaust all the errors that have previously been made in other countries. He felt disgusted with the intolerance of his colleagues toward those who opposed the war and this attitude he thought lessened his influence as a Whig.

Rush made an interesting classification of his opponents: first, furious Tories, who had recourse to violence; second, writing and talking Tories; third, silent but busy Tories; and fourth, peaceable but conscientious Tories. As for his own party, he divides it into first, furious Whigs, who consider the tarring and feathering of a Tory as a greater duty and exploit than the extermination of a British army. These men, he adds, were generally cowards. Second, there were the speculating Whigs, who did the country great mischief; third, were the timid Whigs; and finally, fourth, came the staunch Whigs,—in which category Rush surely belonged—men moderate in their tempers, but firm, inflexible and persevering in their conduct. He recognized a third class of citizens which was neither Whig nor Tory. Although Rush describes them as without fixed principles, they had their uses because they protected each party from the rage of the other, and in their hands each found hospitable treatment. According to Rush, the Whigs constituted the largest class, who were soon to be reinforced by the unattached third class when the affairs of the new country appeared to be prospering, and he remarks that "many of the children of Tory parents were Whigs; and so were the Jews in all States."

On the 2nd of July 1776, the Congress passed a vote proclaiming the freedom and independence of the United States, and two days later came the publicly announced Declaration of Independence. Rush signed the Declaration on August 2, although he had not been able to vote for it.

"Human wisdom," wrote Rush retrospectively, "has derived

more honor from it [the Act] than it deserves. Most of the men who had been active in bringing it about were blind actors in the business. Not one man in a thousand contemplated or wished for the independence of our country in 1774, and but few of those who assented to it foresaw the immense influence, it would soon have upon the national and individual characters of the Americans."

Soon thereafter he joined forces with Adams and Witherspoon against a motion to appoint a Committee of Congress to meet with Lord Howe to discuss terms of peace. Rush was at his most oratorical. He saw no reason for humbling themselves at the feet of Great Britain. True, they had lost the battle of Long Island, but the City and State of New York were still free; and for his part he would resist until the last solitary state had been invaded, uttering the word Independence with her last breath. One hears the distant peal of Churchill's thunder on the beachheads.

But the motion was carried against Rush and his supporters, one speaker commenting that "he would much rather live with *dependence* than die with *independence* on his lips."

Three days after the visit to Lord Howe, Rush informed Julia that the commissioners had returned the day before, after a three-hour meeting. His Lordship had had no power to make peace except on condition that the Declaration of Independence be rescinded, and when the British Commander-in-Chief had asked the delegation in what capacity he was to receive them, Mr. Adams had replied, "In any capacity your Lordship pleases except in that of *British subjects.*" Lord Howe then declared that he would be mortified to witness the fall of America and that he would weep for her as for a brother. Franklin countered this with, "I hope your Lordship will be saved that mortification. America is able to take care of herself."

Rush's letter ends as always on a personal and lonely note. He was called out last night and now has to visit a family four miles in the country. William is gone. He has no horse and carriage. Betsey is out hunting a barber. His apprentices are irregular in their attendance. And then with a slight touch of bitterness, he adds: "The Romans educated slaves only to the profession of physic for 600 years. A wise nation! And a most suitable employment for slaves!" In the postscript he tells his wife that he borrowed Mrs. Walton's carriage but was obliged to wait three hours for it beyond the time he expected it. "Judge how I felt!"

After the American Army had retreated through New Jersey, General Howe made plans to pursue them across the Delaware and then to take possession of Philadelphia. Accordingly, on December 12, 1776, the Congress adjourned, to reconvene in Baltimore on Christmas Eve. With the adjournment Rush took pains to provide a safe retreat for his wife, who was pregnant with their first child. She was to stay with relations on the Susquehanna in Cecil County, Maryland, where her son John would be born the following July. Rush removed part of his furniture and all of his books and left them in a patient's house in Darby—a house which later became Howe's headquarters. The General wrote his dispatches to England on one of Rush's mahogany tea tables, leaving his ink marks but no other damage to the Doctor's property.

6

REVOLUTIONARY PHYSICIAN I

✿ BENJAMIN RUSH HAD LONG BEEN DETERMINED TO
join the Revolutionary Army as a doctor. During the fall of 1776
his letters to his wife, in which he bolsters up his courage, disclose
his increasing concern with the fate of the Colonies, whose affairs
then wore such a melancholy aspect. Canada had been lost, then
Staten Island, now Long Island and next New York. Rush not
only expected the evacuation of New York; he even hoped for it,
believing that General Howe would attract all the Tories in the
region to his Army, as molasses spread upon a board collects all the
flies in a house. Philadelphia he was sure would next be threatened
by British troops.

And so it came about that during the campaign culminating in
the battles of Trenton and Princeton in the month of December,
Rush saw active duty in the field as a surgeon with the Philadelphia
militia. At this time he was still a member of the Continental Congress, serving on its Medical Committee, which was responsible for
the supervision and conduct of the medical affairs of the Army.
This new experience gave him some familiarity with the problems
of administration in military medicine and surgery.

Shortly after the battle of Princeton, word reached Rush that
through the treachery of a Tory relative his father-in-law had been
taken prisoner and was being made to suffer indignities and hardships at the hands of the enemy. Richard Stockton was the leading

citizen of New Jersey. He had been a judge under British rule, was now Associate Justice of the Supreme Court of New Jersey, a trustee of the College of New Jersey and also a member of Congress. Rush promptly used his influence in Congress, urging a resolution of protest against this treatment of so distinguished a citizen. Congress did protest and Stockton was shortly after exchanged, but his health was ruined and so was his fortune.

Although the loss of men at Princeton had been relatively slight, the village looked deserted after the battle, as though the plague or an earthquake had devastated it. Both the College and church were badly damaged and the inhabitants were plundered. Mr. Stockton's furniture and clothing, even his valuable writings, had been burned, and his livestock, grain and forage carried away.

Rush was now about to play his part in one of the most dramatic engagements of the Revolution, and he would soon have his first taste of the horrors of war. On Christmas Eve he called upon General Washington at his headquarters near the Delaware River about ten miles above Bristol. He spent the night at a nearby farmhouse and the next morning passed nearly an hour in a private conference with the Commander-in-Chief. Rush reports him much depressed, lamenting "the ragged and dissolving state of his army in affecting terms." He tried to assure Washington that Congress would come to his support in his present difficulties and distress. While they were talking, the General was playing with his pen and ink and one of the pieces of paper on which he had been scribbling fell to the floor near Rush's feet. On it was written the phrase, "Victory or Death."

That same evening, Christmas night, Washington made his famous crossing of the Delaware. The Philadelphia militia under the command of General Cadwalader also attempted to cross and join forces with Washington, and Rush received his orders to proceed to Dunk's Ferry to attend the sick and wounded. However, masses of floating ice rendered the crossing impossible and Cadwalader's men returned to Bristol in the middle of the night in a heavy snowstorm. In the morning came the news of Washington's successful crossing, his silent descent upon Trenton and his capture of a thousand Hessian troops by surprise.

Directly Cadwalader's men crossed to the Jersey shore, slept that night in Burlington and marched the next day to Bordentown and

thence to Crosswicks, where Rush learned that at the surprise attack on Trenton the password for the troops had been "Victory or
Death." While the Philadelphia militia lay at Crosswicks, Rush
rode to Trenton and spent a day with some of the regular army
officers. He visited the headquarters of General St. Clair, a Scotsman who had done a medical apprenticeship under William Hunter
in London, and spent the afternoon and dined with another Scot,
General Hugh Mercer, also a one-time student of medicine. This
day was one that he always remembered with pleasure.

In the evening came a report that the British forces at Princeton
were about to attack the American posts at Trenton and Crosswicks. A council of war was held at Washington's headquarters to
decide what steps should be taken. There was some difference of
opinion about where the troops should best be stationed. Since
Rush was connected with General Cadwalader's brigade he was
sent for and asked to join the deliberations. Washington gave a
brief account of the controversy and asked Rush for his opinion.
Rush said he was no judge of what was proper in the business of
the council but he was certain that the Philadelphia militia would
be ready at a moment's notice to join Washington's troops at Trenton. He then retired from the meeting. A few minutes later he was
called back to be given a letter by the Commander-in-Chief to deliver to General Cadwalader.

Rush set out for Crosswicks at ten o'clock that night accompanied by a sergeant of the Philadelphia City Light Horse Troop. It
was dark, the road muddy, the weather damp and cold. When he
arrived, bearing Washington's letter, at about one o'clock in the
morning, General Cadwalader was in bed. He immediately got up,
ordered his brigade to move, and Rush accompanied them to Trenton, which they reached by seven in the morning. There he managed to catch a few hours' sleep in General St. Clair's bed. But he
was soon awakened by the news that the enemy was advancing.
General St. Clair, completely composed, buckled on his sword and
Rush followed him out of the room. Then Rush mounted his horse
and joined the Philadelphia militia a little below Trenton, riding
slowly toward the enemy. In the afternoon a cannonade began. In
the midst of the excitement, General Knox, who had been responsible for Rush's presence at the council of war, passed him and
shouted, "Your opinion last night was very fortunate for us." The

cannonade continued for several hours and then the American Army retired, leaving Trenton in possession of the British.

The scene that followed was a new and harrowing one for Rush. A house on the river had been appropriated as a hospital and here the wounded, about twenty in number, were being brought to be attended by Rush and a Dr. Cochran assisted by several young surgeons. Rush's experience lives retrospectively in his autobiography:

"It was now for the first time war appeared to me in its awful plenitude of horrors. I want words to describe the anguish of my soul, excited by the cries and groans and convulsions of the men who lay by my side."

After attending to the wounded, he and his fellow surgeons had lain down for rest on some straw in the same room with their patients. Rush slept for two or three hours, and when he awoke he and Cochran had lost track of their own army. Hearing that General Washington had met a part of the British Army and defeated it at Princeton, they proceeded there by way of Bordentown. Rush says that in many places the battlefield was still red with human blood. They found a number of the wounded of both armies there.

General Mercer had been badly wounded by seven separate bayonet thrusts in his belly, and the side of his head had been struck by the butt of a musket. He had had his horse shot from under him, and the British, thinking they had taken General Washington, called on the "rebel general" to surrender. But Mercer, a Scotsman, who had served as a regimental surgeon with the Highlanders at Culloden, was so incensed that he tried to strike his assailants down with his sword and it was then that he had received his several wounds.

He feigned death and the British left him. He was carried off the field to the house of Thomas Clark, a Quaker. Here the British gave him his parole. The next day Washington, hearing that he was still living, sent Dr. Rush and Captain George Lewis under a flag of truce to Lord Cornwallis to ask for permission to remain and attend Mercer. The permission was granted. Three days later Rush reported him much better and expected him to recover, writing that the General "is in good spirits, drinks plentifully, sleeps tolerably well, and talks cheerfully on all subjects," and that he had no intention of leaving him until he was out of danger. He did leave him on Saturday, January 10, when he considered him safe, although exceedingly weak from loss of so much blood that it had passed through the bed and stained the floor. A surgeon on Lord Cornwallis's staff agreed that Mercer's wounds were not dangerous; but Mercer, himself a physician of high reputation in Fredericksburg, Virginia, called Captain Lewis's attention to a small bayonet wound under his right arm, which he thought would surely cause his death. He suffered much pain and early the next morning died in the arms of this devoted companion.

Among the wounded was John McPherson, Captain of the British 17th Regiment of Foot. When Rush entered his room and was introduced to him, the Captain asked, "Are you Dr. Rush, Captain Leslie's friend?" When Rush told him that he was, McPherson exclaimed, "Oh! Sir, he loved you like a brother." The day before, Rush had learned from a prisoner the sad and affecting news that his dear friend of the Edinburgh days, the Honorable William Leslie, the brother of the Lady Jane Leslie, had fallen in battle near Princeton. His body had been thrown into his baggage wagon and carried along with the American Army to Pluckamin, a village some thirty miles north of Princeton. A letter from Rush had been found in his pocket which had requested that if the fortunes of war should throw Captain Leslie into the hands of the American Army the letter should be shown to General Washington or General Lee with the hope that they would grant him a parole to visit Philadelphia, where Rush was ready to receive him in his own house. This letter was shown to General Mifflin, who obtained an order to bury Captain Leslie with military honors in the churchyard at Pluckamin.

*   *   *

The following summer Rush visited Captain Leslie's grave and picked a blade of grass from it. When the war was over, he had a stone placed over the grave which can still be seen in the cemetery of the present Presbyterian Church in Pluckemin (as it is now spelled), New Jersey. This headstone reads:

> In memory of the Honorable
> Captain William Leslie
> of the 17th British Regiment
> Son of the Earl of Leven in
> Scotland, he fell January 3,

1777, aged 26 years, at the
Battle of Princeton.
His friend, Benjamin Rush, M.D.
hath caused this stone to be
erected as a mark of his esteem
for his worth and of his respect
for his noble family

After the war Rush wrote Captain Leslie's sister, by then Lady
Jane Wishart Belsches Stuart, addressing her as "Madam," to tell
her the facts of her brother's death as they had been recounted to
him by an American soldier. This man had seen Captain Leslie with
his arm extended at the head of his company attempting to flank a
party of the American Army, when the fatal bullet penetrated his
bowels. His death was sudden, for he lay on the ground with his
arm still extended.

Then Rush mentions his letter to her dead brother—the letter
which had accomplished his burial with the honors of war—a mark
of respect to an enemy, writes Rush, "at that time very uncommon
in our army." He tells her that he plucked a sprig of grass from
the grave and how he wept and grieved for all of the young Captain's family. In her reply the Lady Jane says, "Why did you not
send me the blade of grass? I would have preserved its verdure
forever with my tears."

Rush's next letter to her was written a little more than a year
later, on the 4th of July in 1785. In it he begs her to accept a small
picture on the back of a miniature portrait of his wife. The picture,
which is worked in hair, represents her ladyship having arrived in
America, visiting her brother's tomb and exclaiming, "Ah, Willie!"
while Rush himself is represented pointing to the monument which
supports an urn above which are the words, "My Redeemer
liveth." Over the whole device a large weeping willow drapes its
tresses. His letter says:

"The figures of the monument, the urn, the lady, the willow,
and all the letters are composed of your ladyship's hair. The figure
of the gentleman is composed of mine."

But these were sentimental fancies of peace time. At the moment
Rush had many grim duties to perform. He continued to attend the
wounded and comments tersely that Captain McPherson was
wounded in the lungs but recovered in consequence of the loss of

140 ounces of blood. Today this would hardly be thought of as having contributed to his recovery. On Rush's orders, four British soldiers had their legs amputated without benefit of anaesthetics, asepsis or antibiotics, and they all recovered. As soon as his wounded patients were out of danger, he set off to attend his duties in Congress, which was then sitting in Baltimore.

When he arrived, the streets were so muddy from yesterday's rain "that they are impassable to women. No ladies are seen abroad but in carriages." The cost of living was shockingly high, £100 a week for accommodations in a tavern. His wife must have twitted him when they parted, for she wished him a great deal of pleasure and frolicking in Baltimore. But poor Rush was in no frolicking mood. He was weary of public life and yearned for the sweets of domesticity. In fact, he confessed that his heart sickened "at the sound of what is commonly called pleasure." Even to listen to the music of Corelli would only serve to increase his melancholy in his present state of banishment from home and wife, and then he makes some very human husbandly comments:

"To exchange a *whole* house for a *single* room—to *request* instead of *commanding* when the most trifling favor is wanted—and above all to give up a most affectionate wife for the society of strangers—to lay aside freedom, ease, and unbounded confidence in conversation for constant restraint and formality, are circumstances that illy agree with a man of my age and disposition."

Again he complains of the high cost of living. Everything is three times as expensive in Baltimore as in Philadelphia—50 shillings a week for his board, 2/6 a day for his horse. This he cannot understand, since the markets abound not only with the ordinary provisions found in Philadelphia but with a great variety of fish and wild fowl. In his usual informative way he tells his wife that Baltimore contains about 1,000 houses, most of them large and built of brick, and that the first house was built not more than thirty years ago. Even so it vied with Philadelphia in commerce and for being the most wealthy spot on the continent.

Congress had now decided to adjourn to Philadelphia, and in the remaining weeks of February, while still sitting in Baltimore, addressed itself again to the matter of inflation. The motion to raise the interest rate to 6 per cent, which Rush supported, was once more lost. The vote was decided by seven members representing five states, whereas seventeen members were in favor of the motion. Rush believed that unless this unjust method of representation were altered it would be the ruination of the continent and that issuing more money would result in bankruptcy.

Rush remained in Congress until the end of February 1777. The Pennsylvania Assembly did not return him to his seat; in fact, all of its delegates were chosen from among the radicals with the exception of Robert Morris. Undoubtedly his public testimony against the Pennsylvania Constitution, in which John Dickinson and others of the more enlightened Whigs had joined him, had cost him his popularity. He seems not to have been offended by being dropped from the Pennsylvania delegation. He realized that he was far better qualified to serve in his professional capacity than as a politician, where his uncompromising attitudes—honest and energetic though they were—cost him popular support. A gadfly may have its uses, but most people do not like to be stung.

He felt that he could be of the greatest service to his country in the Army, where his brief medical experience had already convinced him of a lack of system and bad management of the military hospitals. On February 27, 1777 he quit Congress, after a year and seven months, and on April 11 he was commissioned Surgeon General of the Middle Department, which included the area between the Hudson and the Potomac. Three months later this appointment was changed to Physician General of the same territory.

In a letter dated April 14, 1777 he tells Julia that the appointment is perfectly agreeable to him and that tomorrow he starts his duties at a military hospital where there will be a hundred things of importance to do. The closing of his letters to his wife are always tender and never routine, and in this instance he signs himself "From, my very dear girl, your affectionate husband, B. Rush."

*   *   *

The medical affairs of the Continental Army were under the control of a relatively unimportant Congressional committee, one of the hundred committees in existence; its chairman, Samuel Adams, being a member of ninety and the chairman of twenty-four. The first Director of the Medical Department of the Army had been a Dr. Benjamin Church, who had modeled his administration upon the system then in use in the British Army. This system was characterized by a complete separation of responsibility for the procurement of supplies from the direction of medical administration. Dr. Church did not last long. He was soon accused of "holding criminal correspondence with the enemy" and court-martialed.

After Church had been cashiered, Congress did away with his system and combined the functions of the medical director and the purveyor—which would nowadays fall into the quartermaster's department—in the hands of the same person, the other system being rejected out of hand for no better reason than that it was British. Church was succeeded as Medical Director by the scholarly and elegant Dr. John Morgan, the aristocratic elder colleague of Benjamin Rush. He had been appointed Director General to the military hospitals and Physician-in-Chief to the American Army by Congress on October 17, 1775, and immediately joined Washington at Cambridge. There he found the hospital and the Army to be without medicines or appliances, and, to make matters worse, there were serious dissensions existing among the medical officers. Under Dr. Church disputes about their duties had already arisen between him and the regimental surgeons. They wanted to retain the sick of their battalions under their own care and draw what stores they needed from the Director. But he, in accordance with the provisions of Congress, required them to send the sick to the General Hospital, where they could be well taken care of, and he refused to furnish the battalions with anything beyond medicines and instruments.

This friction had led to great abuses and Dr. Morgan was quick to try to correct them. But he was powerless. Proper hospital establishment was at this time beyond the abilities of the country. The Army was a young one, composed partly of militia, unused to discipline and exposed to great hardships from lack of clothing and stores of all kinds which Congress was unable to provide. It was, moreover, an unsuccessful, dispirited, retreating Army, which met repeated disappointments and reverses. Dr. Morgan exerted every possible effort and sacrificed his private interests to relieve the sick and to correct the abuses he found, but the task was beyond his capacity or, indeed, beyond that of anyone.

It is clear why Morgan was at sword's points with the regimental surgeons. By and large, they were an unschooled and apprentice-trained lot, often drawn from the family physicians of the officers and selected by their colonels, who in turn were appointed, not by Congress, but by the Colonial legislatures. They defied the authority of the central hospital department and demanded that their requisitions be filled without giving any account of the use they made of the drugs they received. For example, in a period of six weeks, one regimental surgeon drew on the hospital for more than a hundred gallons of rum and a proportionate amount of wine and sugar. With this kind of waste and inefficiency Morgan would have no truck. He allowed the regimental doctors to treat sore throats and minor intestinal upsets, but the serious cases he removed to the central hospital. In addition, he lectured them on discipline and even insisted on the doctors of his own staff taking examinations to prove their competence. The result was that some resigned, and many who remained in service became his enemies, as did so many of the regimental surgeons.

There was much about Morgan that smacked of the arrogant Tory. This alone made them resent him and fear that he, too, would be caught in some treasonous act, as his predecessor had been. Although up to the outbreak of war he had sought a compromise with the monarchy, he had joined the cause of rebellion with courage, determination and self-sacrifice. After all, Morgan was an elegant, polished, sophisticated and highly placed city practitioner and professor of medicine, greatly honored abroad and at home.

In the field, conditions were deplorable. Rush's old companion of the Edinburgh days, now Dr. Jonathan Potts, on duty at Fort George in the North, writes to Dr. Morgan on August 10, 1776 describing the distressing situation among the sick soldiers under his care. He says there were upwards of a thousand crowded into sheds without clothing, bedding, or a shelter sufficient to screen them from the weather, and "labouring under the various and cruel disorders of Dysenteries, Bilious Putrid Fevers, & the effects of a confluent smallpox." To attend them there was only himself with four seniors and four mates, and the supplies of medicines were exhausted. Anthony Wayne had called the hospital at Ticonderoga a house of carnage.

In the Northern Army 5,000 men had suffered from smallpox between the 1st of April and the 8th of August. By February 1777, the disease had made such headway that Washington, finding it impossible to keep it from spreading throughout the whole Army, determined to inoculate all the troops in his command and all recruits as fast as they came in, despite the issuance of a general order prohibiting inoculation. The sufferings of the troops of New Jersey from camp fever were great. Rush describes how they were brought into Philadelphia in open wagons and how a thousand or more who perished from hunger and exposure were buried in Potter's Field. By September 7 nearly a quarter of Washington's army were in hospital.

The Committee of the Congress on Medical Affairs headed by Samuel Adams, who had little time and less energy to give to medical matters, was of no help. In point of fact, the Committee managed to interfere with everything Morgan tried to accomplish. Its members undermined his authority and forced political appointments on him, and when he wrote them for instructions his letters remained unanswered. The whole system was breaking down. There was no real hierarchy of command. There were no supplies to be had. And everybody blamed someone else.

Morgan, unlike Washington, was no diplomat. He did not conceal his contempt for regimental surgeons or officers, who, he said, were "men of the same mean, sordid, groveling disposition" as the troops, and these he claimed were full of "malingerers, public extortioners and cowards." Insisting on the respect of his subordinates and on the strictest military discipline, and all the while working night and day and with his own hands to save the sick and dying, he was too busy, too harassed and exhausted and, in addition, too proud to be conscious of the rising tide of feelings against him.

About this time Morgan discovered that Dr. William Shippen, his schoolmate, colleague and rival, whom he had once slighted in connection with the establishment of a medical faculty in Philadelphia, was plotting against him. Shippen was stationed in New Jersey. He had solicited Dr. Morgan's influence to have himself appointed Director of The Flying Camp there. The two men met and, although Shippen seldom showed his true feelings beneath a bland, well-fed smile, there was an angry exchange between them as to who was in authority. It turned out that Shippen was trying to get possession of all the supplies which Morgan had been at great pains to collect for the Army and to store in Newark. But this was not all. There was reason to believe that Shippen was using his influence in Philadelphia to unseat his hated rival. His two brothers-in-law were members of Congress. There is evidence, too, that he falsified his reports to Congress so as to make his own record appear much better than Morgan's. On all hands Morgan heard of Shippen's machinations against him. Finally in alarm he called on Washington at his headquarters near Trenton. Washington urged him to "lay the matter before Congress, that some steps may be taken to remedy this irregularity and inconvenience, and that I may know what I have to depend upon."

On November 28 Congress ruled that "Dr. Morgan take care of such sick and wounded of the army of the United States, as are on the east side of the Hudson river, and that Dr. Shippen take care of such of the said sick and wounded as are on the west side." Shippen had triumphed. Washington's army was now in New Jersey and the resolution of Congress made Shippen his principal medical officer. He lost no time in demanding Morgan's supplies, which Morgan, however, refused to surrender.

Morgan went to Philadelphia. In Independence Hall, outside the door of the chamber in which Congress was in session, he met Samuel Adams. Adams advised him to resign. At first he was dumbfounded. As soon as he could gather his thoughts, he asked to be heard by Congress, then and there. Demanding an inquiry and the opportunity to vindicate himself, he insisted on knowing the particulars of any charges against him and who his accusers were. Adams put him off, telling him that Congress was busily engaged, but he assured him that in due course it would grant him an investigation.

Morgan's dismissal occurred on January 9, 1777, while Rush was still sitting in Congress and a member of its Medical Committee. A few weeks later Morgan called on Rush, who gave him little comfort, saying only, "I would not for ten times the consideration go through the toils and difficulties of your station." But Dr. Shippen felt differently; he was delighted. Congress had taken his advice, and he wrote to his wife's brother, Richard Henry Lee, suggesting that he himself be made Inspector General of the whole Army. In fact, he was appointed to succeed Morgan on April 11, 1777, just three months after his rival's degradation.

*   *   *

Such was the shape of affairs in April 1777, when Rush assumed his administrative responsibilities as Physician General of the Middle Department of the Continental Army. The tragic feud between Doctors Morgan and Shippen, in which he was soon to become enmeshed, had consequences far beyond their personal fortunes and careers. The spread of communicable diseases in the Army of the North was attributable primarily to the breakdown in medical care and this was greatly abetted by the hostility between departmental directors, and by the division of authority, with its resulting inefficiency, confusion and chaos. It had turned the successful Canadian campaign into a rout and had contributed to the loss of Canada by the Revolutionary forces.

Benjamin Rush realized that the American Army had suffered severely in the campaign of 1776. In his view, its failures were attributable as much to the lack of system and the inept management of the Medical Department as to any other cause. And so at the very start of his new tour of duty he tried to introduce order and economy into the military hospitals. To this end he recommended that the British system be adopted—one in which direction and supplies were quite independent of each other. But his pleas for this reform were in vain.

Soon after he began his duties in the hospital he saw the evils of the Continental system at work. And scarcely a fortnight after he was commissioned he addressed a broadside "To the Officers in the Army of the United American States" containing "Directions for Preserving the Health of Soldiers." To the modern reader this still seems an eminently sensible document. And it is not surprising that it became a pattern of sound practice in military hygiene. Rush was asked to publish it in pamphlet form, which he did in 1778, after he had resigned from the Army. It was published again in 1808, at least twice during the Civil War, and a fifth time in *The Military Surgeon* in 1908. Its opening sentence, which has become a truism, was certainly not commonly accepted in his day.

"Fatal experience has taught the people of America . . . that a greater proportion of men have perished with sickness in our armies than have fallen by the sword."

His directions deal with dress, diet, cleanliness and encampments. Most of the diseases in military encampments are spread by insects or result from a contaminated water supply and faulty sewage disposal, or again from overcrowding. Since Rush was ignorant both of the cause and the means of transmission of the diseases that confronted him, we can only marvel at his astuteness. That insects could carry diseases was not discovered until 116 years after he wrote his directions, and it was yet another decade before it became known that mosquitoes were responsible for the spread of both malaria and yellow fever. In recommending the use of flannel shirts in place of the homespun linen ones worn by Washington's soldiers, Rush was convinced that flannel would protect them against fevers and keep the soldiers healthy. He offered as evidence Colonel Gage's experience in the French and Indian War, also observations in certain parts of Pennsylvania, where nothing else but the use of flannel shirts prevented "the yearly visits of the intermitting fever," and finally the good health of the Roman legionaries who wore flannel next to their skins. His observation may have been correct but his arguments were faulty. He thought and called it a well-known fact "that the perspiration of the body, by attaching itself to linen and afterwards by mixing with rain, is disposed to form miasmata which produce fevers." What he did not realize or even dream of was that the mosquito could easily insert its proboscis through loosely woven homespun linen but could not penetrate the thicker, closely woven flannel of the shirts.

Nor did he suspect that fleas, bedbugs and body lice were agents of disease. Even so he recommended that soldiers comb and dress their hair every day and, better still, wear it thin and short in the neck; wash their hands and faces at least once every day and the whole body twice or three times a week, especially in summer. More important still, he urged frequent changes of linen as indispensably necessary to the preservation of health. To these recommendations he added that the straw or hay of which a soldier's bed is made should be frequently changed and his blanket exposed to the sun every day, again, as he thought, to prevent the perspiration from becoming morbid and accumulating dangerously. He also had suggestions for the removal of wastes, for keeping camp sites clean, and for not making them near marshes and mill ponds or at a place where the prevailing wind blowing across a river would carry the seeds of bilious and remitting fevers to the Army, especially in the fall of the year.

What has been said of such insect-borne diseases as typhus, yellow fever and malaria holds as true for the enteric ones—typhoid, dysentery and cholera, for example—and for those spread by the respiratory tract—pulmonary tuberculosis, pneumonia, influenza and cerebro-spinal meningitis. For none of these did Rush know either their cause or the means of their transmission, yet he emphasized the importance of the removal of the offal of animals and of filth of all kinds. And he cautioned especially against allowing on any pretense whatever crowding too many soldiers into the same tent or quarter, thinking, to be sure erroneously, that "jail fever [typhus] is the offspring of the perspiration and respiration of human bodies brought into a compass too narrow to be diluted and rendered inert by a mixture with the atmosphere." The present regulations in the U.S. Army require 800 cubic feet per man.

Rush's recommendations for the diet of soldiers do not correspond with present-day knowledge. He thought that it "should consist *chiefly* of vegetables," well cooked, which he believed both the nature of the soldiers' duties and their former habits required. He was convinced that eating "two or three pounds of flesh in a day" would damage their health and that not all the Jesuit bark (quinine) in America could preserve or restore their health. He must have thought that eating meat was responsible for fevers, which he also attributed to damaged flour. Good flour could be rendered unwholesome by an error when making it into bread, and so he recommended in place of bread the use of whole wheat boiled, to which a little molasses was to be added and the whole to be eaten with a spoon. This was what Caesar had fed his troops on his expedition into Gaul.

Against the custom of drinking spirituous liquors Rush had much to say, though he was aware that to combat the prejudice in favor of it would require the arm of a Hercules. He had no patience with the argument that rum guarded the body against the effects of heat and cold. On the contrary, he believed that it left the body more susceptible to both. The use of rum, he stated, wears away the powers of the system and "lays the foundation of fevers, fluxes, jaundices" and most of the diseases which occur in a military hospital. He calls it "a vulgar error" to suppose that the fatigue caused by violent exercise or hard labor can be relieved by strong drink. Again he cites as an example the armies of ancient Rome, when every soldier's canteen was filled with nothing but vinegar, which was drunk in small quantities mixed with water. This Rush believed enabled the Roman soldier "to sustain tedious marches through scorching sands without being subject to sickness of any kind."

Benjamin Rush was always the crusader, always the champion who felt that the survival of his country and of all that he cherished and held most dear rested with him. It is no wonder that at times his zeal clouded his judgment and brought him into conflict with his superiors. He tried to introduce order and economy into the military hospitals and to this end pleaded in vain to have the British system adopted. Congress, however, had decided differently and his proposals were rejected. In his autobiography Rush records that he had accepted the commission of Physician General of the military hospitals only with reluctance, because of his disapproval of the system under which they operated.

At this time (May 1777) a fatal hospital fever broke out in a building next to the Philadelphia Alms House at Spruce and 11th Streets, being used for the care of sick soldiers. What this endemic disease was is not clear, but it probably was typhoid fever or typhus or perhaps some upper respiratory infection of the influenzal variety. In any case, several of the attending surgeons and mates died of it and most of them were infected. Believing that its spread was due to overcrowding, Rush appealed to the Director of the hospital for more room for the sick. But the request was denied, and the Director who denied it was Dr. William Shippen Jr. With this gentleman Rush was often to be at loggerheads. He found this, and other similar instances, an insufferable interference with the work of a responsible physician, whose duty and prerogative it was to prescribe for his patients. Any modern physician would agree, especially as the Director General seldom went inside the hospital and devoted most of his time and energy to procuring and distributing supplies. Rush continued to attend the sick during the summer months without complaining; but in August, in a letter to John Adams, he informs him, surprisingly enough, "that great order, cleanliness, and the most perfect contentment prevail in our hospitals," which he attributes to the humanity and zeal of the *Assistant* Director, Dr. Thomas Bond Jr., son of the distinguished founder of the Pennsylvania Hospital. It is fairly clear that he was trying to impress this influential member of Congress with the laxity of the Medical Director and with the competence of his assistant.

The next month, on September 11, while attending the wounded at the battle of the Brandywine, Rush nearly fell into the enemy's hands. Two days later Washington dispatched a letter to Lord Howe and sent Rush with several surgeons under a flag of truce to dress the wounded American soldiers who had been left on the battlefield. Rush was treated with great politeness by the British officers. Colonel Mawhood, whose men had been responsible for the wounding and capture of General Mercer during Washington's surprise attack on Princeton, now called on him to thank him in the name of the 17th Regiment for his care at that time of Captain McPherson. Rush was much impressed with the discipline and order of the British Army as contrasted with the American.

About a fortnight after this visit to General Howe's camp, Rush in his next letter to John Adams enlarges on his impressions of the enemy. He was struck with the vigilance of the sentries, saying that "they spoke, they stood, they looked like the safeguards of the whole army." He was examined by nine or ten inferior officers and then by one of distinction before a guard was ordered to conduct him to headquarters. The attention to secrecy he found extraordinary and also the "supreme regard to the cleanliness and health of their men." After the battle the British soldiers were forbidden to touch any of the blankets belonging to the American dead or wounded for fear of contracting and spreading "rebel distempers." Great pains were taken to provide the Army with fresh vegetables and he observed quantities of them about the soldiers' tents. Everywhere in the hospitals he found the utmost order and contentment and he attributed the excellent care of the American wounded not to the humanity of the British, who actually hated their opponents, but to the perfection of their medical establishment.

Rush's letter to Adams is datemarked Trenton. He had gone there from Howe's headquarters, which lay between Chadd's Ford on the Brandywine and the road to Chester. The American Army had reached Chester, where the Marquis de Lafayette, who had distinguished himself by his valor and was wounded in an attempt to rally troops, joined Washington. Washington had faced a superior force in an extensive, wooded and involved theater. Here the rapidly shifting strategy of General Howe had demanded all of Washington's presence of mind, readiness in emergencies, wisdom and steadiness. The battle ended in his retreat. Rush found the soldiers straggling from their lines in every quarter without an officer, and he observed "languor in all the branches and extremities of the army." He seems not to have understood the difference between a citizen's army, which to be sure he favored, and one composed of professionals and mercenaries. He bemoans the present management of the Army, tells his dear friend Adams that "we are on the brink of ruin" and he believes that hope lies with the militia under active and enterprising general officers. He says, "I should despair of our cause if our country contained 60,000 men abandoned enough to enlist for 3 years or during the war." This preference for the militia seems to have been shared by Congress but not by the Commander-in-Chief.

On October 10, 1777 Rush had written: "Dined with the commander in chief of American army—no wine—only grog—knives & forks eno' for only half the company—one half the company eat after the other had dined at the same table. The General gave the head of his table to one of his aids-de-camp, and sat 2^d or 3rd from him on his left side.

"The commander-in-chief at this time the *idol of America*—governed by Gen' Greene—Gen. Knox & Col. Hamilton, one of his aids, a young man 21 years of age.

"4 Major Generals,—Greene, Sullivan, Stirling & Stevens. The 1st a sychophant to the general, timid, speculative, without enterprise; the 2nd, weak, vain, without dignity, fond of scribling, in the field a madman. The 3^d, a proud, vain, lazy, ignorant, drunkard. The 4th, a sordid, boasting cowardly sot.

"The troops dirty, undisciplined, & ragged, guns fired 100 a day; pickets left 5 days & sentries 24 hours, without relief; bad bread; no order; universal disgust.

"Acc't of American army at Valley Forge March 1778.

"The encampment dirty & stinking, no forage for 7 days—1500 horses died from ye want of it. 3 ounces of meal & 3 pounds of flour in 7 days. Men dirty & ragged. The commander-in-chief and all ye Major Generals lived in houses out of ye Camp."

All the confusion and inefficiency of the Army he found again in the hospitals, which were conspicuous in their waste and peculation and in the number of unnecessary officers. Of the sick he said, "Upwards of 100 of them were drunk last night. We have no guards to prevent this evil," whereas in Howe's army there was a guard mounted over every 200 sick. And again Rush complains of the system which he claimed was designed for the benefit of the Director General rather than to help the sick and wounded.

7

REVOLUTIONARY
PHYSICIAN II

✿ AT THIS JUNCTURE BENJAMIN RUSH'S DEEP CONCERN over the inefficiency of the medical establishment of the Revolutionary Army becomes a constant preoccupation. And as always in such circumstances his first recourse is to his pen. So his polemical drive for reform, which had begun in his letters to John Adams, widens to include other influential figures, both political and military. His correspondence is now studded with letters to Major General Nathanael Greene, a greatly trusted member of Washington's staff, to William Duer, a delegate to Congress from New York and second only to Robert Morris as the financier of the period, to his superior, Dr. William Shippen, and finally to Patrick Henry and George Washington.

To Adams he writes (October 21, 1777):

"Our hospital affairs grow worse and worse. There are several hundred wounded soldiers in this place who would have perished had they not been supported by the voluntary and benevolent contributions of some pious whigs. The fault is both in the establishment and in the Director General. He is both *ignorant* and *negligent* of his duty."

Again Rush complains that Dr. Shippen never sets foot in a hospital. And now for the first time he threatens to resign if the system cannot soon be altered. The British system of administration, he is convinced, would save the country half a million dollars a year and produce general satisfaction instead of execration.

The burden of the other letters is much the same. There is a constant plea for introducing the British system and especially for a commanding officer attached to each hospital who could enforce discipline and prevent or punish the hundreds of irregularities of all kinds that were daily committed. To William Duer he writes:

"No man can suspect I wish for any alteration in the system from a desire of holding a higher or more lucrative office in it than the one I have received from the Congress. I would not accept of the directorship of our hospitals upon its present footing for the riches of India. On the contrary, I am resolved to retire as soon as the campaign is closed, since I cannot act agreeable to the dictates of my conscience and judgment."

And in the same letter there is this:

"Dr. Shippen has taken pains to represent my complaints of the sufferings of the sick as intended to displace him. This method of rising into importance I know has been practised with success in our department. But I despise it. And to show that I aimed only at the happiness of my distressed countrymen and the honor of my country, I shall seal my disapprobation of our medical establishment as well of its administration with my resignation."

But much was to happen before this would actually occur. Rush was deeply disturbed. He was casting about in all directions to find someone in authority who could help reform a medical system which he calls a mass of corruption and tyranny. At first his salvos were directed at the system, but gradually as his patience wore away he began to attack Shippen not only for negligence and callousness but also for downright dishonesty. On December 26, 1777 he addressed an important letter to General Washington. In this he sets forth his bill of particulars and goes over Shippen's head to the Commander-in-Chief himself, urging him to order the surgeons to billet such of the sick as are able to help themselves in farmhouses, where "the air and diet of a farmer's kitchen are the best physic in the world for a soldier worn down with the fatigues of a campaign." Rush had found this arrangement most beneficial instead of crowding twenty or more into a hospital room designed to house only six or eight. But his own influence, he says, is not great enough to make this practice universal. He assures Washington that if this measure can be immediately put into execution, it would add 3,000 men to the Army in the Spring, men who would otherwise perish in the hospitals.

Washington's reply to this letter was written on January 12, 1778. He assures Rush that he will do all in his power to remedy the situation, that he has "ordered a discreet Field Officer to visit the principal Hospitals" and endeavor to establish proper discipline, and that he has transmitted the substance of Rush's communication to Dr. Shippen. But Rush's concern is now at a fever pitch and he is not to be stopped. Dated the same day as Washington's reply and therefore written before this letter of his could have been received, there comes next a fateful letter to Patrick Henry, who was then Governor of Virginia. Rush says:

York town, January 12, 1778

Dear Sir,

The common danger of our country first brought you and me together. I recollect with pleasure the influence of your conversation and eloquence upon the opinions of this country in the beginning of the present controversy. You first taught us to shake off our idolatrous attachment to royalty, and to oppose its encroachments upon our liberties with our very lives. By these means you saved us from ruin. The independence of America is the offspring of that liberal spirit of thinking and acting which followed the destruction of the specters of kings and the mighty power of Great Britain.

But, sir, we have only passed the Red Sea. A dreary wilderness is still before us, and unless a Moses or a Joshua are raised up in our behalf, we must perish before we reach the promised land. We have nothing to fear from our enemies on the way. General Howe, it is true, has taken Philadelphia; but he has only changed his prison. His dominions are bounded on all sides by his outsentries. America can only be undone by herself. She looks up to her councils and arms for protection, but alas! what are they? Her representation in Congress dwindled to only twenty-one members. Her Adams, her Wilson, her Henry, are no more among them. Her counsels weak, and partial remedies applied constantly for universal diseases. Her army—what is it? A major general belonging to it called it a few days ago in my hearing a *mob*. Discipline unknown, or *wholly* neglected. The quartermaster's and commissaries' departments filled with idleness and ignorance and peculation. Our hospitals crowded with 6,000 sick but half provided with necessaries or accommodations, and more dying in them in one month than perished in the field during the whole of the last campaign.

The money depreciating without any effectual measures being taken to raise it. The country distracted with the Don Quixotte attempts to regulate the prices of provision; an *artificial* famine created by it and a *real* one dreaded from it. The spirit of the people failing through a more intimate acquaintance with the causes of our misfortunes—many submitting daily to General Howe, and more wishing to do it only to avoid the calamities which threaten our country.

But is our case desperate? By no means. We have wisdom, virtue, and strength *enough* to save us if they could be called into action. The northern army has shown us what Americans are capable of doing with a GENERAL at their head. The spirit of the southern army is no ways inferior to the spirit of the northern. A Gates, a Lee, or a Conway would in a few weeks render them an irresistible body of men. The last of the above officers has accepted of the new office of inspector general of our army in order to reform abuses. But the remedy is only a palliative one. In one of his letters to a friend he says, 'A great and good God hath decreed America to be free, or the —— and weak counselors would have ruined her long ago.' You may rest assured of each of the facts related in this letter. The author of it is one of your Philadelphia friends. A hint of his name, if found out by the handwriting, must not be mentioned to your most intimate friend. Even the letter *must* be thrown in the fire. But some of its contents ought to be made public in order to awaken, enlighten, and alarm our country. I rely upon your prudence and am, dear sir, with my usual attachment to *you* and to our beloved independence, yours sincerely.

What is very significant about this letter is the fact that it was unsigned.

In his covering letter to Washington enclosing this unsigned communication, Henry states: "I really cannot tell who is the writer of this letter, which not a little perplexes me. The handwriting is altogether strange to me. . . .

"To give you the trouble of this gives me pain. It would suit my inclination better to give you some assistance in the great business of the war."

But there is reason to believe that Rush counted on Henry to recognize his hand and style and sentiments, and that Henry, in forwarding Rush's letter to Washington, was acting disingenuously.

A month later comes Washington's reply, dated Valley Forge, 27 March 1778:

". . . Being intimately acquainted with the man I conceive to be the author of the letter transmitted and having always received from him the strongest professions of attachment and regard, I am constrained to consider him as not possessing, at least, a great degree of candor and sincerity, though his views in addressing you should have been the result of conviction and founded in motives of public good. This is not the only secret, insidious attempt that has been made to wound my reputation. There have been others equally base, cruel, and ungenerous, because conducted with as little frankness, and proceeding from views, perhaps, as personally interested."

The very next day another letter follows, and this time Washington names names.

"The anonymous letter, with which you were pleased to favor me, was written by Dr. Rush, so far as I can judge from a similitude of hands. This man has been elaborate and studied in his professions of regard for me; long since the letter to you. . . . I cannot precisely mark the extent of their views, but it appeared in general, that General Gates was to be exalted on the ruin of my reputation and influence. This I am authorized to say, from indeniable facts in my own possession, from publications, the evident scope of which could not be mistaken, and from private detractions industriously circulated. General Mifflin, it is commonly supposed, bore the second part in the cabal; and General Conway, I know, was a very active and malignant partisan; but I have good reason to believe, that their machinations have recoiled most sensibly upon themselves."

*   *   *

Benjamin Rush's curious communication to Patrick Henry deserves to be considered in the context of the time. In the first place a distinction exists between an anonymous and an unsigned letter. The purpose of the former is completely to conceal the identity of the writer; but that of the latter is merely to keep that knowledge from being seen by unauthorized eyes. In the days when letters were carried by messenger or courier they could easily become common property, and the absence of a signature protected the writer. It was a familiarity with the handwriting that was the key to the understanding, as in this instance, of the identity of the writer. Thus Benjamin Rush cannot be accused of the cowardice inherent in anonymity.

But why did he write it?

The rigors of the campaigns of 1776 and 1777 should be borne in mind. Except at Princeton and Trenton, Washington had suffered a series of costly defeats in Long Island, New York, the Brandywine, Germantown and Philadelphia. On the Hudson, where land batteries had been erected to prevent British men-of-war from running up the River and cutting the communications between New England and the middle and southern Colonies, the Commander-in-Chief had had to abandon his most important battery at Fort Washington. It had been necessary for him to shift most of his troops to the interior in order to protect Westchester County and Connecticut, and the result was that Howe fell upon the Fort and captured it, inflicting heavy losses. Washington lost nearly 3,000 of his best troops, together with forty-three guns, large stores of ammunition, and other valuable material. Four days later Fort Lee, across the River from Fort Washington, had had to be abandoned with further severe losses; and thereupon the British had overrun central New Jersey and had occupied Newport, Rhode Island, the second most important town and port in New England.

Such was the news that had been assailing Rush's ears and oppressing his heart and it is this background of events that supplies the setting for the tenor of his letter to Patrick Henry on January 12, 1778. It begins with a cry for help. Oh, for a Moses or a Joshua to deliver his people! Ten days later in a letter to John Adams he used the following significant words:

"I am daily looking out for some *great* military character to start up, perhaps from the plow, to save this country."

He goes on to mention Gustavus of Sweden, Prince Maurice of Holland, Braganza of Portugal or Pompey as exemplars of the kind of leader he is hoping for. But his anxiety and agitation are such that he could not recognize those very qualities in Washington.

If Rush was endeavoring to shame Washington into doing something about the lamentable medical situation, hoping that thereby Shippen would be dismissed, the letter went way wide of its mark and failed utterly to accomplish its purpose. It had reached Washington at a fateful hour, when he was at Valley Forge in the deep winter of his discontent. Its timing, moreover, was most unfortunate in a more particular connection. For it came to the Commander-in-Chief's attention at the height of the machinations, fancied or real, of what is known to history as the Conway Cabal. With the particulars of this curious affair, this account cannot be concerned. If such a plot actually existed, to supplant General Washington by General Horatio Gates, and it has been doubted by many authorities, it was nevertheless very real in the minds of the Commander-in-Chief and his entourage. Gates, who had triumphed over Gentleman Johnny Burgoyne at Saratoga, was much in the public eye, and so it was natural to see him as an ambitious rival. Indeed, Washington had heard many statements and received considerable private correspondence, including Rush's unsigned letter, to support him in his suspicions.

Washington was a just man, meticulous, deliberate and slow to move. Nonetheless, Rush's letter alienated him from the Commander-in-Chief and placed him in his mind among his enemies. Gates, whom Washington mistrusted, had been made president of the War Board and thus, in a sense, he was Washington's superior. Moreover, Conway, whom Washington described as a "secret enemy" and a "dangerous incendiary," had been appointed by Congress to be Inspector General of the Army. Much of this Washington bore with silence for the good of the service and because of a certain magnificence of style—he had even sent General Burgoyne a letter condoling with him for the ill fate that had overtaken him and wishing him restored health.

As for Benjamin Rush it may safely be claimed that conspiracy and intrigue would have been wholly out of character. If he was opinionated and impetuous, he was also incorruptible. But it was by no means out of character for him to scold and to be importunate. And so he later came to rue the day when his volatile nature had driven him to write so indiscreetly and incautiously. The episode is not mentioned in his autobiography. Years later he pleaded with both Judge Bushrod Washington, the first President's nephew, and Chief Justice Marshall, who was preparing his third volume of *The Life of George Washington*, to delete his name from among the harsh and stinging words that Washington had written about him in his correspondence with Patrick Henry. And in this, at least, he was successful.

*   *   *

Rush paid heavily for his indiscretion. The scars from these wounds were to smart for the rest of his life. Because he had been openly critical of Washington, he was naturally classed with his opponents—with Mifflin, Conway and Lee, all now banished from Headquarters, and Lee ordered by the Commander-in-Chief to stand court-martial for disobeying orders and retreating before General Clinton's forces at the battle of Monmouth Court House. Though, in this sense, Rush was never suspect, his was guilt by association because he had singled out these three men and General Gates among those officers whose characters and abilities he most admired.

If Rush felt remorse for his bad judgment, his remorse did not silence him. He was incapable of silence. When he saw what he conceived to be an evil, he had to shout it down from the house-tops, always with the hope—even the expectation—of its being immediately eradicated. The evil that confronted him was the tragic plight of the common soldiers. His heart was almost broken at seeing their distress without the power to remedy it. This was his urgent and honest lament. He was powerless because he lacked the authority and the facilities to administer the kind of care that his medical knowledge and his conscience dictated. And in Shippen, the Director General, he saw a chief obstacle to the successful performance of his own clear duty.

In January 1778, shortly after writing the ill-fated letter to Patrick Henry, Rush had gone to Yorktown to lay down his commission. In consequence of his earlier letter to Washington making charges against Shippen, he had been ordered by Congress to appear there on the 26th. On the 15th he had written his dear Julia:

"It will be a disagreeable task to accuse him [Shippen] publicly of ignorance and negligence of his duty. But the obligations I owe my country preclude all other ties. I shall act strictly agreeable to the dictates of my conscience, and if the system is altered and Dr. Shippen can be restrained by proper checks from plundering th sick, I shall not resign my commission but shall serve another ca paign. This resolution is taken not only from a sense of duty a love of my country, but in consequence of the advice of some very worthy members of Congress, who assure me that a contrary step will be ascribed to want of perseverance or to downright disaffection."

Shippen contradicted the charges which Rush had preferred against him in his communication to Washington of December 26 in a public letter addressed to the whole body of Congress. In a letter to the President of Congress Rush now appealed for a public hearing. Although his letter of complaint was read to Congress, no public hearing was granted. Instead, the two doctors appeared before a Committee of Congress of which his old friend Dr. Witherspoon was the chairman. The findings of this Committee were sent to Rush a few days later, in a letter signed by Witherspoon.

His resignation "was accepted without a word said by any Person on the Subject. I am sorry for the Necessity of the Measure," Witherspoon goes on to say, "and yet I question whether you could have done anything more proper for Dr. Shippen was fully determined to bring the Matter to a Contest between you, refusing positively to serve with you which would have occasioned an Examination and Judgement troublesome to us, hurtful probably to both of you and uncertain in its Issue." Witherspoon then closes his message on a personal note, saying that he supposes he will see Rush at Princeton in a short time and sending his compliments to Mrs. Rush and her parents.

What had happened was that Shippen had succeeded in turning the tables on him and had accused him before Congress of being derelict of his duty and of having abandoned his post in New Jersey without leave. Rush had anticipated this turn of events, for in his previous letter to Julia he had said that if Congress should support Shippen in his folly and negligence he would see her as a private citizen in a few weeks. And again a week later he talks of retiring to a small farm in the neighborhood of Princeton until he can get back to Philadelphia. So when the axe fell, although the blow was staggering, it came as no surprise.

Rush went down fighting. Up to this point his attack had been aimed principally at the system, but now his charges of ignorance, negligence and dishonesty were forced from him in self-defense. With respect to Shippen's sanguine account of the numbers who had died in the hospitals, Rush says sarcastically that he himself must have been mistaken because he had supposed that the number of coffins daily put underground was a fairly accurate tally of the number of dead. In a letter to his adversary he gives Shippen the lie for asserting in a letter to Congress that "No fatal disease prevails in the hospitals, very few die and the hospitals are in very *good* order."

Some of Shippen's misconduct he spells out in a letter to Adams, who unfortunately was no longer in Congress and so was unable to see that the alleged abuses were corrected. He accuses Shippen of having bought six casks of wine at £150 each and storing them with hospital stores but afterward selling them on his own account for £500 apiece. There are bills for poultry and other delicacies bought for the hospitals "which no *sick* man ever tasted." A few weeks later Rush provides Washington with a statement signed by four military surgeons who had been associated with him. They too claimed that it was a common practice of Shippen, as Commissary General, to deduct about a third from orders of wine, sugar and molasses, that Director General Shippen ordered large quantities of venison, poultry and wild fowl but that none of the patients ever got them, and that he never entered the hospital during a six weeks' residence in the village of Bethlehem, in spite of the utmost distress and a high rate of mortality from putrid fever that had been greatly intensified by overcrowding.

This hospital in Bethlehem was established in the Moravian Brethren House. There the sick were crowded together—over 700 of them—in a space suitable for about one-third of that number. The hospital was filthy; sanitation was non-existent. Several patients were piled together on one straw mat. Four to five were permitted to lie on the same straw before it was changed, a practice providing an ideal setting for the outbreak of disease, especially typhus fever, which was spread from one man to another by the bite of the body louse. When it is realized that many of the soldiers were admitted to the hospital for minor complaints, only to succumb to the endemic infections prevalent there, Rush's sense of outrage is entirely understandable. Nine of eleven surgeons came down with the disease. Two hundred soldiers died of it within a period of four months. And four-fifths of this number caught the infection while in the hospital.

Rush came to the conclusion that "hospitals are the sinks of human life in an army." He recommended that they should be abolished and that sick soldiers should be cared for in private families except for those laboring under "the calamities of madness," or suffering from venereal disease, or those who were the subjects of some surgical operation.

In another letter to Washington, Rush says that since his resignation he no longer feels it necessary to try to live in harmony with Shippen, and that it is now incumbent on him to tell the truth because of his regard for the honor of the Army and his sense of duty to His Excellency. This was the letter that had reached Washington after the Patrick Henry epistle and had made him question the candor and sincerity of Rush.

Washington's mistrust of Rush may well have influenced his judgment in this ugly controversy. But he was a just man and he transmitted Rush's letters of accusation to Congress, which ordered an inquiry into the Director General's conduct. But this failed to satisfy Rush. He urged a court-martial and expressed his willingness to furnish full evidence of all his charges. His request was based on the fact that the matter under consideration was a military one, and also on a resolution adopted by Congress a year earlier which laid down the terms of court-martial procedures. Congress, wishing to avoid an open scandal, tabled the request.

Rush was defeated. His adversary, a skilled politician, was a man of position, wealth and influence, with two brothers-in-law in Congress and much patronage to dispense. He was lazy and self-indulgent and, as Rush said of him, "absorbed for the last 15 years of his life wholly in pleasure," spending "whole nights and days in reveling and debauchery." Benjamin's brother Jacob described Shippen as a man of cool malice and treachery. Shippen met these attacks with disdain and ridicule, charging Rush in turn with desertion of his proper military post.

Now Rush too had played the political game and had tried to influence members of Congress and of the high command by his barrage of letters, but there is no reason to believe that he ever falsified medical facts or lied to Congress as Shippen had done. His effort throughout had been to try to have the system changed wherein the Chief Medical Officer was also the purveyor. When Witherspoon had told Rush that either he or Shippen must go, he had at first refused and replied that he was quite indifferent to the number of enemies he had made in Congress by his complaints against Dr. Shippen. He then said, "Do not think to terrify me into a resignation by the fear of being dismissed by the Congress. You have suffered enough in the opinion of the public by dismissing Dr. Morgan without a trial. I dare you to dismiss me in the same manner." Witherspoon then informed him that only very trifling alterations would be made in the system and it was this that decided him to give up. Under these circumstances he knew that it was hopeless to go on.

*   *   *

These events occurred in early February of 1778 and for several months thereafter Rush retired to a small farm in Princeton. There he smouldered and if the fires of his indignation were banked they would soon burst into flame again. He was not a man to be worsted nor to suffer injustice at the hands of corruption, and certainly not one to be deprived of his accustomed occupation. In these troubled days he was heartened to learn that Congress had acted to amend the system in the military hospitals, and the new regulations contained every improvement he had so long wished for—indeed, had clamored after.

And then, to cap the climax, there came, a year later, on June 12, 1779, the exoneration of Dr. John Morgan. The Resolution of the Congress stated that that body was "satisfied with the conduct of Dr. John Morgan, while acting as Director General and Physician-in-Chief in the General Hospitals of the United States, and that this resolution be published."

Morgan wasted no time in proceeding against Shippen—the man who had schemed against him and had accomplished his downfall —and he succeeded where Rush had failed. Congress notified Washington to investigate the charges. Morgan enlisted Rush's willing help. He wrote Morgan, giving in detail the motives and reasons for his resignation, and later he specified for him all the charges to which he would be willing to testify. There was much delay, during which Morgan and Rush both tried to muster their evidence. Witnesses were hard to locate and Shippen, since he was still in command, had plenty of time to intimidate them, or to send them away. But Morgan was relentless and insistent.

The trial was held in Morristown, New Jersey. Shippen had been charged with "Scandalous and infamous practices such as are unbecoming the Character of an Officer & Gentleman." The proceedings were conducted in an atmosphere of great excitement and personal bitterness during March, April and May of 1780. Rush testified to all the accusations already mentioned, and he wrote his wife from Morristown:

"Dr. Shippen appeared sanguine and insolent. The next day Dr. Morgan opened his evidences. This produced a *total* change in Dr. S's behavior. He appears agitated and distressed. All will end well. The trial will probably last a good while, as S's hopes now are only for delay and embarrassment. One thing is certain. Provisions of all kinds are so scarce here that a month's confinement to low diet will do more to ruining Dr. S than the disgrace that can be heaped upon him."

Rush's testimony against Shippen was supported in full by the sworn statements of Dr. James Tilton which were printed in the *Pennsylvania Packet* for October 14, 1780. But the court, although it was of the opinion "that doctor Shippen did speculate in and sell hospital stores, THAT IS, stores proper for hospitals whilst he was purveyor general: which conduct they consider highly improper, and justly reprehensible," found that the charges had not been clearly established. He was acquitted by a single vote and thus was finally cleared, but without honor, of the criminal charges against him. Congress voted that he be discharged from arrest but shortly thereafter through some political maneuvering he had himself reappointed as Director General. Many members of Congress opposed this move, but Pennsylvania supported its son successfully and carried the nomination.

This was too much for Rush. He let fly his literary salvos in the press and in an open letter to Shippen. He seems to have quite lost his head in rage and indignation.

"Your injured country," he wrote, "which you have robbed above a thousand of its citizens by your negligence and inhumanity; the parents and children of those brave men whom you suffered to perish without honor or benefit to their country in your hospitals; and the graveyards of Bethlehem, Reading, Lancaster, Leditz, Prince-Town, and Philadelphia, all of which you have crowded with the bodies of your countrymen, cry aloud for your dismission from office. You have become the butt of the camp, the jest of taverns, and the contempt of the coffeehouse. Women bedew the papers that contain the tales of your cruelties to the sick with their tears; and children who hear them read ask if you are made and look like other men.

"Your crimes, I believe, have been equaled in other countries. . . . But your reappointment to your present high and important office, after the crimes you have committed, is a new phenomenon in the history of mankind. It will serve like a high-water mark to show posterity the degrees of corruption that marked the present stage of the American Revolution."

In spite of Rush's high-flown language, his acrimonious pen, and his stubborn and undiplomatic tactics, the conviction is inescapable that he was driven, not by personal ambition and rivalry, but by an honest desire to right the egregious wrongs that he had seen with his own eyes. Within less than two weeks Shippen resigned his commission, and thereupon Morgan issued a statement which read:

"I am happy to inform my fellow-citizens that Dr. Shippen, at length unable to bear further investigation of his conduct, has been compelled to quit the station of director general of hospitals by a forced resignation."

Washington, a peace-loving man, gave Shippen a certificate of good conduct in which he asserted that, as far as he was capable of judging, no hospitals could have been better administered. He had also even written to Rush inviting him to dine at Headquarters. This was while Rush was attending the court-martial. The General was reported to have been in good cheer and to have discoursed on affairs in Ireland. What Rush talked about is unreported, but undoubtedly it was not about the things in his mind at that moment. Later the two men gave up their rancor. They managed to become reconciled, at least on the surface, and established pleasanter relations with each other.

As for John Morgan, ten years after his official vindication by the Congress he died a broken, lonely, unhappy man. Rush had seen him at a public meeting only a week before. Under the date of October 15, 1789 there is a touching entry in Rush's *Commonplace Book:*

"This afternoon I was called to visit Dr. Morgan, but found him dead in a small hovel, surrounded with books and papers, and on a light dirty bed. He was attended only by a washerwoman, one of his tenants. His niece, Polly Gordon, came in time enough to see him draw his last breath. His disorder was the Influenza, but he had been previously debilitated by many other disorders. What a change from his former rank and prospects in Life! The man who once filled half the world with his name, had now scarcely friends enough left to bury him."

8

RETURN TO
PHILADELPHIA

✿ BENJAMIN RUSH'S ACRIMONIOUS CONTROVERSY WITH his former teacher and colleague, Dr. William Shippen, continued for over two years. Before its culmination, first in Shippen's trial and ultimately in his resignation as Director General, Rush had returned with his family to Philadelphia in July 1778. The six-month interlude following his own resignation in the preceding January as a medical officer in the Revolutionary Army had been spent with his wife and small son at his father-in-law's house in Princeton.

There he had looked back upon what he calls his "indiscreet zeal for justice and humanity" without repentance, even though its consequences were so injurious and distressing to him. What, he asks, would be the mass of human misery if there were no public advocates for the oppressed?

In Princeton he had been forced to lead an inactive and, to him, a disagreeable life. A small village, greatly devastated by war, afforded no prospects for the practice of his profession. He did not wish to engage in a country practice. Rush was troubled and discouraged by the turn of events, and in this situation he had characteristically resolved to study law, thus returning in fantasy at least to his earlier love.

It will be recalled that on graduating from the College of New Jersey he had been told by its president, Samuel Davies, that he would "make a better figure at the bar than in the walks of a hospital." But his steps had then been deflected toward medicine by his uncle and former schoolmaster, the Reverend Dr. Samuel Finley. Again, when still in his early twenties on his return from England on board the ship *Edward*, Rush had occupied himself by reading the first three volumes of Blackstone's *Commentaries* and Foster's *Crown Law*. Now he seemed once more to have been flirting with the same notion. But it was more serious this time. Although he was a mature man of thirty-two, Rush appears to have entertained without misgivings the plan of acquiring a new profession and of gaining admittance to the bar of New Jersey. His father-in-law, Richard Stockton, a member of the Executive Council of New Jersey and Associate Justice of its Supreme Court, had encouraged him in this venture and promised to use his influence so that within a year or two Rush could be admitted to practice.

Then, just as he was preparing to embark on this new enterprise, he learned that the British were about to evacuate Philadelphia. They left the city a few weeks later in such a filthy state that there was an abnormal number of sick persons. Rush and his family returned and, thereupon, with his accustomed vigor, he immediately began to rebuild his practice. It soon became both extensive and profitable. He had many new patients and for a time he devoted himself exclusively to his profession and turned his back upon public pursuits. His wife must have returned to Princeton, because in August he writes to her, anxiously hoping that she continues to mend and asking her why she is "so silent upon the subject of our dear boy's health? Is he fallen away? . . . How many teeth has he got? Does he run alone?" and, "Did he know you?" He claimed to have detached himself wholly from public business and would now "live only for the benefit of an amiable wife, a promising boy, and my circle of patients." He reassured himself by saying that this was from choice, not necessity. Philadelphia he found had undergone some purification but still too much resembled the ark, which had preserved from the deluge not only the clean animals, but also the unclean. There were plenty of Tories about.

As Rush was trying to reestablish himself in practice, he was seized, on September 12, 1778, "with a most malignant bilious fever (caught from one of my patients)." Presumably this was typhoid. Whether the worry and anguish and partially suppressed rage of the past year had lowered his resistance to make him more susceptible must remain unanswered. He tells us that this "reduced me to the brink of the grave;" that his physicians—Redman, Kuhn and Morgan—shook their heads as they went out of his room and that his friends wept at his bedside. "I made my will and took leave of life. But in the extremity of my danger it pleased God (on the 11th day) to break the violence of my disease, and I am now through divine goodness so perfectly recovered as to be able to do business as usual."

Business as usual for Rush was more than a full day's work. First came his patients, with endless visits, night calls, emergencies and consultations, both in person and by letter, and then the training and supervision of his apprentices, who numbered at one time as many as six. Applications for this privileged post came to him from all over the country so that he had to stick to his fee of £100 cash in order to control their numbers.

During the British occupation his formal lectures had been interrupted. Now he was back and his lectures began again, but only for a short time, since because of political strife the Legislature suspended the charter of the College and set up instead a new institution, the University of Pennsylvania, which took over all the property of the College. The professors of the College were invited to continue their work in the new University. All except Shippen declined as a protest against the action of the Legislature. In Rush's case, as in Morgan's, the ancient animosity against Shippen played a major part in their refusing the invitation. In fact, they notified the trustees of their unwillingness to accept their appointments if Shippen were also elected, thinking that the board would rather lose one man than two. But the trustees did not act as anticipated; they elected Shippen rather than Morgan and Rush. Finally Rush relented and resumed his course in chemistry in November 1780. Whether he was more forgiving than Morgan and held a grudge less tenaciously, or more practical and ambitious, realizing the value of a professorship both in terms of prestige and in financial gain, who can say? Morgan, however, never again served.

At this time in his life Rush was suffering much worry and strain—inevitable in so intense, ambitious, idealistic and impatient a man. This was compounded by the financial stringency always attendant upon war. The new nation was nearly bankrupt; in fact, it was going through its most critical period.

A new baby was added to the family, Anne Emily, born January 1, 1779. Knowing his seriousness and his solicitude for his wife and the real dangers that then attended both childbirth and infancy, his concern can be imagined. He addresses his wife as "My loveliest Girl," telling her that he will try to visit her on *Wednesday* evening and hopes to hear "all the pretty stories you can collect of our dear little ones," and he begs her to bring Jack along with her as far as the creek or the lane beyond Mr. Paul's.

He continues his restless correspondence, praising, felicitating, cautioning and condemning. Two subjects constantly occupy his mind, the Shippen court-martial and the Constitution of Pennsylvania, which he declares provides neither "restraints against the tyranny of rulers" nor against "the licentiousness of the people." During the next ten years Rush was to do his share to have the Constitution of Pennsylvania rescinded and revised. But now he was leading what he called "a most unrepublican life," wholly devoted to his family and his patients—except for his presence at Morristown to testify in the Shippen trial. In August of 1780 Mrs. Rush gave birth to her third child and second son, Richard, who was to become the most distinguished of all their offspring.

That autumn Rush was attacked by the prevailing epidemic of the season, known and described by the name breakbone fever, which he says "yielded in a few days to an emetic and the Bark." Since this is a self-limiting disease, almost never fatal, it would probably have yielded without these medicines. But perhaps they made him feel more comfortable. Rush was the first to describe this disease clinically and to call it in print by its popular name. It was also known as dengue fever. The origin of this name is not without interest. It came from a West Indies Negro corruption of the word dandy, which was thought to describe the stilted, high-stepping, dandified gait of its victims, whose leg pains caused them to walk in this fashion.

Rush's description appeared in 1789 in the first volume of his *Medical Inquiries and Observations*, dedicated to his former teacher, John Redman, under the title "An account of the bilious remitting fever, as it appeared in Philadelphia in the summer and autumn of the year 1780." This remains a medical classic. Although ignorant of the cause and means of transmission of the fever,

Rush made some pretty shrewd observations about both. He says:

"All ages and both sexes were affected by this fever. Seven of the practitioners of physic were confined by it nearly at the same time. . . . The pains which accompanied this fever were exquisitely severe in the head, back and limbs. The pains in the head were sometimes in the back parts of it, and at other times they occupied only the eyeballs. In some people, the pains were so acute in their backs and hips, that they could not lie in bed." He speaks of the flesh being sore to the touch and the resemblance of the disease to rheumatism, but he says "its more general name among all classes of people was the *Break-bone fever*."

There were other incidental clinical descriptions of its manifestations—important, when one considers that a physician of that day had to differentiate between typhoid, typhus, various kinds of malaria, cholera, dysentery, yellow fever and now dengue, all by means of their symptoms and signs without the benefit of any information about causative agents. Even though there was, from our point of view, no specific treatment for any of these ailments, each category bore its own prognosis. In the case of dengue, one could predict recovery after a week or two of suffering, but in some instances there were recurrences, stretching the illness to a period of approximately three weeks.

Of its climatic antecedents, Rush says that July and August of 1780 were uncommonly warm. The mercury on August 6 stood at 94½° and again on the 15th at 95°. It was then that the remitting fever had first made its appearance. On the 19th of August the weather suddenly turned cool and the next day many hundreds of people complained of different degrees of indisposition and suffered from a sense of lassitude and from a fever of the remitting type. He observed that the winds during these months blew chiefly from the south and southwest and passed over the land that lies between the city and the point where the Delaware and Schuylkill Rivers meet. He was convinced that unwholesome exhalations drifted from the streets and from the docks and that "the muschetoes were uncommonly numerous during the autumn."

In the previous chapter of his *Medical Inquiries and Observations* Rush deals at length with the climate of Pennsylvania and its influence upon the human body. In the year 1779 he had begun a book in which he recorded an account of the diseases of every season, often of every month of the year, together with a history of the weather and the state of vegetation. He continued this every year thereafter and declares that it helped him greatly in both his studies and his practice.

Rush observed that intermitting and bilious fevers increased in Pennsylvania in proportion as the country had been cleared of its woods. After the year 1778, Philadelphia was unusually sickly and this he attributed to the cutting down of the trees by the British and to the flooding of the surrounding meadows. He observed that winds which pass over mill dams and marshes in August and September generally carry with them the seeds of fevers. And he states that it is unsafe to sleep with open windows. When the banks of the meadows were repaired to exclude the tides and when ground formerly covered with filth and stagnant waters was cultivated, the health of Philadelphia improved, as it did with regular cleaning of its streets and the enclosure of a large and offensive dock area which crossed two of the principal streets near the center of town. In a letter to his revered master, Dr. Cullen, Rush enunciated two important propositions in sanitation: First, clearing a country makes it sickly and, second, cultivation makes it healthy. This was succinctly put somewhat later in the statement that American fevers result from neglecting to follow the axe with the plow.

But another century would pass before it became known that insects are the carriers of disease and the cause of such epidemics as malaria, yellow fever and dengue. In the last two, the carrier is the same mosquito, known as the *stegomyia* or *Aëdes aegypti*. Breakbone fever was first reported in Egypt the year before Rush came down with it. It was then and still is endemic in various parts of the world, mostly in the tropics. Sometimes it reaches epidemic proportions and every individual in a community will be afflicted. The mosquito which transmits it, unless blown by winds, does not travel far; its larvae live mostly in rain barrels or in small pools of stagnant water. Hence in Rush's time, when the disease was for a while confined to one street only, it was called by some Front-Street fever. The fact that dengue was caused by a filterable virus was unknown for another century and a half.

Rush's treatment of this disease corresponded to many of his other medical practices except that he did not resort to bloodletting because the pulse though *full* was never *hard*. He depended mostly on tartar emetic or gentle doses of salts and cream of tartar or on the butternut pill made from an extract of a strong decoction of the inner bark of the white walnut tree. He also resorted to opium and to blisters applied to the wrists. Mostly, however, his therapy was supportive: bed-rest when the patient's pains could tolerate it, and later gentle exercise in the fresh air. This was particularly valuable in relieving the convalescent of the uncommon dejection of spirits which accompanied the disease, and which led a young lady patient to propose to Rush that he change its name to *break-heart* fever. For the depressed phase of the ailment, he recommended the plentiful use of ripe fruits and temperate meals, of oysters washed down with liberal draughts of porter. "The quickest and most effectual way of conquering a fever, in most cases," he wrote, "is, by an early submission to it."

*   *   *

When he recovered from his own fever but was still confined to his room, Rush had a curious dream which made a deep and lasting impression on his mind. He says of it that it increased his disposition to attend the poor and, when he could not serve them, never to treat them in an uncivil manner. This is the dream as he reported it.

"I dreamed that a poor woman came to me just as I was getting into my chair in Penn Street, and begged me to visit her husband. I told her hastily, that I was worn out in attending poor people and requested her to apply to another Doctor. 'O! Sir (said she, lifting up her hands) you don't know how much you owe to your poor patients. It was decreed that you should die by the fever which lately attacked you, but the prayers of your poor patients ascended to heaven in your behalf, and your life is prolonged only upon their account.' "

This answer affected him so much that he awoke in tears. He assures us that he had been little disposed to superstition and had, indeed, often exposed the folly of being influenced by dreams, explaining their cause by obvious physical principles.

It is tempting to try to analyze a dream to which the dreamer himself attaches so much importance. But while we lack some essential data for such an analysis, namely the dreamer's own associations, Rush does furnish some of them. It is possible, therefore, to venture a few reasonable guesses.

Dr. Rush is still confined to his room, but he dreams that he is up and about and doing business as usual, actually getting into his chair, by which he means chaise, on Penn Street. Knowing his restless disposition, one can be pretty sure that he wishes he were back at work and this perhaps is the immediate instigation for the dream. Although he states that he has often explained the cause of dreams by obvious physical principles, we know that such principles alone do not disclose the content of dreams and their meaning. As for his being little disposed to superstition, much of Rush's religiosity sounds a good deal like superstition to us and, furthermore, many men who have been critically ill easily return to a more primitive kind of thinking, of which superstition is an example. One must recall that two years earlier his life had been despaired of, but, as he had said, in the extremity of his danger it had pleased God on the eleventh day to break the violence of his disease, which had probably been typhoid fever. His present illness was not only painful and prostrating, but highly inconvenient. He had just re-established himself in practice in spite of the opposition of many of the people who called themselves great in the city, including, of course, the well-to-do Tories.

Just before recounting the dream, Rush gives a clue as to its significance. He says, "My business from this time was extensive, but less profitable than it should have been, from being obliged to receive the payment of my bills in paper money which frequently depreciated 200 and 300 per cent below their value at the time they were delivered to my patients." There seems little doubt that the Doctor was hard pressed financially. We know how greatly concerned he was over the depreciation of the currency. His family had grown; there were now three children, and he was about to move into a spacious three-story house with a fine garden on Second Street, between Chestnut and Walnut.

Before his military service, Rush had practiced chiefly among the poor, whom he frequently visited on foot; prescribing sometimes for as many as sixteen on a morning's walk, he would charge only one of them. He tells us in his autobiography that his disposition made this mode of getting into business agreeable because he had a natural sympathy with distress of every kind. And he cites the examples of Dr. Cullen in Scotland and Dr. Fothergill in London, who had established themselves in their professions by practicing among the poor. Even the great Dr. Boerhaave in Leyden had said that the poor were his best patients, because God was their paymaster.

Now Rush is older, perhaps less resilient, tired from his strenuous exertions and bitter altercations, worn out in attending poor people, as he says, and just recovered from a painful illness. He wants to be taken care of himself, or at least to have some well-to-do patients who might help support him. Because of his weakness, his own dependent needs assert themselves. When the poor woman approaches him, he waves her aside and gets into his carriage; he is no longer on foot. But he cannot deny his tender, altruistic nature and his idealistic concern for the poor, and so the woman tells him that it was their prayers which saved him. Thus the dream tries to reconcile a conflict. He awakens in tears—tears of guilt—because the dream reveals to him, even as it tries to conceal from him, the struggle he is experiencing between his self-interest and his high-minded dedication to the poor. And so, in order to deny what he would regard as his baser nature, he resolves more than ever to attend the sick poor.

But there is more to the dream than this. As all dreams do, this one, too, has a foot in childhood. It is not too remote a conjecture to think that the poor woman in the dream represents the dreamer's mother. She was then sixty-three years old, a widow, either living in the Rush household or soon to be. As is to be expected, he was kindness itself to her. At a later time, when she protested that she was being too troublesome and should quit his home to relieve his wife and him from the care of nursing her, Rush said to her, "No . . . , my dear madam, should you continue to lie on this bed till you are an hundred years old, you will never tire my family. I shall chearfully and thankfully nurse you here if it were only for the pleasure of your conversation."

We need not doubt his filial devotion, but all such feelings have their darker sides and here in the dream, by turning his back on the poor woman (his mother), he seems to be admitting this shadowy side of himself. The picture brings tears to his eyes because of his love for her and his guilt at denying her. In the dream the poor woman begged Dr. Rush to visit her husband; that is, to take care of him. Now, what of his mother's husbands? She had made three marriages. The first marriage he had called "unfortunate," but happily for her it "terminated in three or four years by the extravagance and intemperance of her young husband." Her second marriage was to John Rush, the husband of her warmest affections, who left her with but a small fortune and six young children. And then some years after Benjamin's father's death she was married for sixteen years to a distiller, Richard Morris, an uncouth and unfriendly man. During this marriage Rush had left home to embark on his studies, but who can doubt how grievously he must have suffered for his mother because of this unhappy marriage? Now she appears in a dream in the guise of a poor woman asking him to visit her husband, perhaps to intercede for her. But Rush will have none of it; indeed, he suggests to her that she apply to another doctor. What the dream signifies about his relations with his father, we can only conjecture. We know, however, that Benjamin was five years old when his father died—a time when the hostility of a small boy toward his father is at its height. It is not surprising that the dreamer has no interest in visiting the poor woman's husband.

Just about this time he engaged the services of one of his former students, Dr. James Hall, to relieve himself of the pressure of too much work and to assist him in the care of the poor. Although his mother's maiden name was Hall, this James Hall was not a blood relative of hers. Perhaps he was the other doctor to whom Rush was recommending the poor woman of the dream. Although Dr. Hall had spent fifteen months in London attending lectures and studying at St. Thomas' Hospital, the partnership, instead of increasing Dr. Rush's business, lessened it. Apparently Rush's medical colleagues gave it out that he was gradually retiring from practice to devote himself exclusively to public pursuits. This was far from the case, but frequent attacks of a pulmonary infection made it unsafe for him to go out at night or in bad weather. Hall remained with Rush for eight years, until he married and moved to York, Pennsylvania. Their parting was touchingly described in a letter to Julia dated June 27, 1787. He writes:

"He took me by the hand at 4 o'clock—but was unable to bid me farewell. His eyes filled with tears and he attempted in vain to give utterance. . . . He has left a blank in every part of the house. I feel without him as if I had lost my right arm." Fourteen years later, in his *Commonplace Book*, he made the following entry:

"September 17, 1801. Dr. James Hall, my former pupil and partner. He lived 8 years in my family, during which time I never
knew him to equivocate, much less to lye. He was amiable in his
temper, and elegant in his manner. By marrying into an intemperate family he learned to drink. It was continued by habit, until it
destroyed him." Rush calls him "my old and once valued pupil Dr.
Hall."

                    *   *   *

If Rush's practice did not continue to prosper in spite of the relief of his overburdened days which Dr. Hall brought him, this was
no fault of his young assistant. There were other circumstances in
his life, besides the time he had to give to his lectures in chemistry,
that interfered with the growth of his practice. He had become not
only a public figure but a very contentious one, expressing his opinions on many different topics in the public press, sometimes over
his own name, sometimes over an assumed one—always outspoken,
often dogmatic and seldom conciliatory. His style of writing was
easily recognizable. The American public has never felt comfortable with a physician who meddles in politics or, indeed, in public
affairs. Rush, however, was convinced that if they had agreed with
his political views, they would have been more tolerant of his public activities. The republican principles which he had adopted in
Edinburgh and the rejection of those principles in which he had
been educated now acted as a ferment in his mind, and he addressed
himself to such subjects as education, penal laws and capital punishment, always the staunch supporter of what would nowadays be
called the "liberal," but often the unpopular, side. On all these subjects he published essays and in the early '80's his letters ring out
the news like a town crier.

Using the pseudonyms "Retaliation" and the more frequent one
"Leonidas," Rush wrote and published extensively. In the *Pennsylvania Journal* he put forth in 1782 a strong plea for the necessity
and importance of a navy to the young nation. He was opposed
not only to dependence on Great Britain but even to "alliance with
her upon terms of the most perfect equality." And, as in the
past, he was in correspondence with many of the notable figures of
the period, including three Revolutionary generals in the field—

Horatio Gates, Nathanael Greene and Anthony Wayne. To the latter he wrote on October 30, 1781:

"Beware, my friend—not of bullets, for they do you no harm—but of a bilious fever. Avoid the evening air, drink wine moderately, wear flannel next to your skin, and take a dose of bark every day. Death from a fever or a flux may be natural for a citizen, but a soldier can only die naturally and professionally of a ball or a bayonet."

One of Rush's more interesting letters, written on July 16, 1782, was addressed to a lady whose identity is uncertain—she was either Elizabeth Graeme Ferguson, a famous and influential Philadelphia hostess whose house was the center of a literary circle, or his mother-in-law, Mrs. Stockton. This letter describes an elaborate fête arranged by the French Minister, the Chevalier de la Luzerne, to celebrate the birth of a Dauphin of France. Pierre-Charles L'Enfant, who a decade later would plan the city of Washington, was responsible for the architectural and landscaping arrangements, which displayed all the symmetry and subtlety of 18th-century neoclassicism. A large dance hall had been built, supported by painted pillars and open all around. The ceiling, Rush tells us, was decorated "with several pieces of neat paintings emblematical of the design of the entertainment." And the adjoining garden, traversed by walks, was divided into artificial groves with cedar and pine branches. Thirty cooks borrowed from the French Army provided the supper, which was served at midnight in three large connected marquees. What with numerous lights in the garden, music, dancing, a cold collation ("simple, frugal, and elegant, and handsomely set off with a dessert consisting of cakes and all the fruits of the season"), and an assemblage numbering about 700 persons distinguished by "the brilliancy and variety of their dresses," Rush describes the scene as resembling enchantment itself.

Although the great and the near-great were there, Rush assures us that it is a truly republican mixture: merchants and gentlemen of fortune, respectable and opulent tradesmen, lawyers, doctors, professors and members of the clergy, Whigs and erstwhile Tories, members of Congress, governors, generals, ministers of state and judges with their secretaries and clerks. Here, General Washington is engaged in earnest conversation with John Dickinson; there,

Mifflin and Reed, though political rivals, "accosted each other with all the kindness of ancient friends;" and the Count Rochambeau, in his expensive and splendid uniform, stands talking with an Indian chief in his savage habits, as if they had been subjects of the same government. Even the celebrated author of *Common Sense*, Tom Paine, is among the company, keeping his own counsel and enjoying "the repast of his own original ideas." And ladies beautifully attired, many of whom had had their heads dressed between four and six o'clock that morning because "the gentlemen of comb" were completely booked up, are greeted in person by the Chevalier "with all the splendor of the minister and all the politeness of a gentleman," who had thought of everything—a "neat palisado fence" so that the crowds outside could look on, money distributed to prisoners in the jails and patients in the hospitals of the city, and "a private room where several Quaker ladies, whose dress would not permit them to join the assembly, were indulged with a sight of the company through a gauze curtain."

With Julia on his arm, accompanied by her sister, Sukey Stockton, there was Rush, who would not have been himself without some *arrière pensées:* To think of an American celebrating the birth of a Dauphin, who one day as a Prince must inevitably support monarchy and slavery. Rush commented on the decorum and the good breeding exhibited by all. Although "Everybody felt pleasure, . . . it was of too tranquil a nature;" there was a lack of gaiety. Several gentlemen remarked that the "company looked and behaved more as if they were *worshiping* than *eating*." The Ode, written for the occasion, was not read, nor set to music. This in Rush's view was a pity because it would have "formed a most delightful and rational part of the entertainment" and a suitable climax to it.

Actually he was not one for formal festivities of this sort, nor one to crow over victories. There was always more to be done, more wrongs to right, more evil to conquer, more ignorance to dispel, more light to shed if we were to fulfill our hopes of liberty and of perfect republicanism. He writes to General Greene, now settled in South Carolina on a plantation granted him by that state, urging him to use his great influence to do away with the importation of slaves. This would indeed be a new spectacle in the world, to follow a war fought for liberty by importing fellow creatures from Africa, only to reduce them to slavery. He does not urge the emancipation of slaves now, since he considers them unfit for freedom by their habits of vice. "Make their situation comfortable by good treatment" and "time may unfold a method hereafter of repairing to their posterity the injustice that has been done to the present generation."

Rush was now to engage in three interests which would occupy him intermittently for many years. One was his war against the Pennsylvania Constitution and the Radical Party which supported it; the second was his relentless crusade against the use of what he called "Ardent Spirits;" and the third was his participation, a principal one, in the founding of Dickinson College. These three apparently discrepant interests were in fact closely interrelated. Each of them won him a few friends and admirers, but these were more than outnumbered by new arrays of enemies. When Rush's feelings and enthusiasms were aroused, his way had to be the right way, his side God's side, and any opposition came from the Devil himself.

*   *   *

Soon after the British Army left Philadelphia, a number of citizens allied themselves to form a conservative "Republican Society." These moderate Whigs, men of property or of commercial interests, who had played a leading part in the beginnings of the Revolution, had lost their political power and been supplanted by a more radical group, which consisted mostly of the city proletariat, of Scotch-Irish and German immigrants, and of farmers. The latter were intent on bringing Pennsylvania into the Revolution and their first step was to do away with the old forms of provincial government. This they accomplished in the Constitutional Convention of July 1776, which took over the function of the State's assembly. Gradually, the moderate Republicans, including with Rush such men as John Dickinson, Robert Morris and James Wilson, regained their power, and in 1790 they drew up a new State Constitution.

The plan to accomplish this originated at an evening meeting at Rush's house in the spring of 1789. In the reform of the Constitution two principal targets drew his fire. One was the fact that all legislative power was lodged in a single body of men who administered the law in an arbitrary fashion, and the other was the so-called Test Laws. These had come into being in June 1777, when an Act of Assembly had been passed requiring all white male inhabitants to take an oath of loyalty to Pennsylvania as an independent State and to renounce allegiance to the British Crown. It also provided that officers of the peace should be informed of all traitorous conspiracies against the united colonies. Whoever refused to swear to this loyalty oath was deprived of many of his civil rights, including the right to vote, to hold office and to transfer real property. Within a year the law was extended to forbid those who would not swear to the oath, or non-jurors as they were called, to engage in trades and professions.

Rush would have none of this. He fought the oath fiercely, not so much as a champion of civil rights but for partisan political reasons. He pamphleteered against it and took much credit for its final repeal, ten years after it had been enacted. By this time Franklin had succeeded John Dickinson as President of the State, and he added the weight of his name to remove this stain from the American Revolution. He had just returned from France and was surprised to learn of the continuance of such a law in peace time. Franklin, then in his eightieth year, enjoyed, according to Rush, "the full exercise of all faculties of his mind," as well as "clearness of perception on the great affairs of government." Because of his presence Rush expected "a revolution in favor of reason, justice, and humanity."

Shortly after Rush wrote these words he dined with his venerable friend, Dr. Franklin, "in a most agreeable circle, where he appeared as cheerful and gay as a young man of five-and-twenty. But his conversation was full of the wisdom and experience of mellow old age. He has destroyed party rage in our state, or to borrow an allusion from one of his discoveries, his presence and advice, like oil upon troubled waters, have composed the contending waves of faction which for so many years agitated the State of Pennsylvania."

9

THE DOCTOR AS EDUCATOR

THE FOUNDING OF DICKINSON COLLEGE WAS CLOSELY related to the existing political and social situation. Pennsylvania had a population of some 350,000, composed chiefly of English, Scotch-Irish and German immigrants and their descendants. Of these, the English, who were both the most numerous and the wealthiest, were chiefly Quakers and Episcopalians. The Germans were Lutherans, Baptists and Roman Catholics, and the Scotch-Irish, mostly Presbyterians, comprised but one-sixth of the population and possessed not more than one-twentieth of the wealth of the State. These figures are Rush's, and according to him the Presbyterians were divided among themselves into splinter groups because of serious doctrinal disputes. Nonetheless, the passive conduct of the Quakers and the moderate conduct of the Episcopalians threw the government during the Revolutionary movement into the hands of the four Presbyterian sects. These were supported by the Germans, who were politically unsophisticated and easily dominated.

The first act of power of this radical group had been to impose on the people the hated Constitution of 1776 and to keep it in force by "means of the most disgraceful test laws." The Quakers would not swear to the oath and many upper-class Episcopalians refused as well. According to Rush, this disenfranchised approximately two-thirds of the population. Furthermore, the Constitution could be altered only by the concurrence of seven-eighths of the voters.

Rush, being by temperament always partisan, says that "The op-
pressions of this party were so great, and their private and public
characters so infamous, that they were deposed in the year 1780 by
their former adherents." His own party, he assures us, consisted of
the ancient inhabitants of the State, "distinguished for their wealth,
virtue, learning, and liberality of manners," and it included those
patriots who had been most active in bringing about the Revolution. It was this party, and especially the Episcopalians among
them, who had founded the College of Philadelphia and had supported it for twenty-two years without any aid from the government. Now in 1778 the College, with all its funds, was seized by
the Constitutional Party, contrary, says Rush, "to justice and
policy and even contrary to their own Constitution."

The leaders in this nefarious business were Dr. John Ewing,
George Bryan and Joseph Reed. Rush made himself their implacable enemy. Ewing was rewarded by being made provost of the
new University. He was also pastor of the First Presbyterian
Church, from which Rush now resigned. To a trusted friend Rush
wrote that if he lived at Carlisle nothing could induce him to
change his mode of worship.

"But in Philadelphia, where it is equally pious to renounce the
devil and Dr. Rush among the Presbyterians, I cannot think it my
duty to continue among them. I disturb their devotion every Sunday, and they will neither accept of forgivenesses nor of services
from me. There are not more than 10 Presbyterian families that employ me, and most of them pass me without speaking to me in the
streets."

George Bryan was the leader of this Scotch-Irish Presbyterian
faction in Pennsylvania politics. The third member of the tri-
umvirate, Joseph Reed, had been General Washington's military
secretary and aide-de-camp and later Adjutant General of the Continental Army. After the war, he became a leader of the radical
party and eventually President of Pennsylvania, preceding Dickinson and Franklin in that office.

Rush would never forget his ride with Reed on Christmas Eve in
1776, when they visited General Washington at his headquarters
four miles from the Delaware River. Reed had been discouraged
about the war and had talked despondently about its outcome.

Later at election time in 1782, Reed's loyalty came into question and Rush, being of the other party, did not hesitate to testify to his defeatist attitude during the war. The quarrel between them lasted into the third generation. Among Rush's many talents, the art of making enemies was certainly not the least.

When the charter of the College was revoked, Rush grew anxious with others "to provide a seminary for the better education of our youth." The idea of Dickinson College had been conceived at a meeting of several gentlemen on Mr. William Bingham's porch sometime in 1781 or 1782. Bingham, a wealthy Episcopalian, became a trustee of the College and one of its benefactors. There were many advantages in having it placed beyond the Susquehanna, in the western part of the State, where the rural population of quarreling Presbyterians and materialistic Germans might be brought into line.

Rush hoped that the new College would ". . . soften the tempers of our turbulent brethren, to inspire them with liberal sentiments in government and religion, to teach them moderation in their conduct to other sects, and to rescue them from the charges of bigotry and persecution that are so often brought against them. It was intended further to reform and civilize our German citizens, too many of whom imagine the whole business of life to consist in *labor*, and all its happiness in *gold and silver* and fine *plantations*."

He protested that the only principles which actuated him in promoting the establishment of a college at Carlisle were "The extension of the Kingdom of Christ and of the empire of reason and science in our country." Despite his protestations, in this, as in other of his activities, Rush's motives had indubitably been mixed —partly altruistic, partly political, partly animated by love for his fellow man, partly by hatred of his adversaries.

The friends of the College of Philadelphia viewed the whole enterprise with suspicion, if not indignation. They recognized the trustees of the new College as their political foes, and they made every attempt to deny it a charter. Its sponsors were calumniated in the public press, and Rush himself came in for much abuse—most of it stemming, he claimed, from Dr. Ewing. Rush describes the latter as having few equals in the vices of his heart. "Revenge, envy, malice, and falsehood rankle forever in his bosom." Deficient in outward morality, he had been seen "reeling in our streets," and he even permitted his servant to drive his wagon on the Sabbath day! In Rush's whole gamut of hated men, Dr. Ewing took the lead.

In the fracas Rush got as good as he gave; Ewing charged him with double dealing and with dishonesty in attributing religious bigotry to him. By a contemporary newspaper Rush was portrayed as "changeable as the wind, fickle as the water, unstable as the ocean. . . . He is contemptible in every point of view but one. *He is a mischievous and implacable enemy*. Tho' he contradicts himself ten times in a minute, yet if anyone also contradict him, he is sure to attempt some mean revenge. A LIE is generally his instrument. The press or private conversation are alike the vehicles of his poison."

Because of his quick temper and his fluttering rages, Rush earned for himself the sobriquet of "Dr. Froth." He was notorious, it was said of him, for his "sprightly imagination," often "leaping before the judgment."

With all his many gifts, and at the height of his intellectual powers, Benjamin Rush lacked the talent for what we call insight. This has been true of many great men—especially of men with sensitive introversive natures who hide what they wrongly consider their weaknesses behind restless and aggressive outward activity.

In Rush's energetic sponsorship of the new College there was an opportunity to spread the republican idea in education and to do some much-needed missionary work among the radical immigrant classes. If the establishment of a nursery of religion and learning on the west side of the Susquehanna made him enemies, it also won him friends, two in particular: John Dickinson, for whom Rush named the College, and John Montgomery, one of its charter trustees.

Rush's relations with John Dickinson were good, with one exception, and this had to do with the invitation which Rush extended to Charles Nisbet, a Scottish divine, to leave his parish and come to America as principal of the new College. He had met Nisbet fifteen years earlier when he was trying to persuade Witherspoon to leave Paisley and come to Princeton. On that occasion he thought of Nisbet as a possible second choice, or at least for a professorship; and he said then that he loved the man's character, was charmed with his disinterestedness and praised his "pregnant genius." Thus it was natural for him to think of Nisbet for the position at

Carlisle. Perhaps he was especially disposed toward him because of his outspoken support of the American cause during the war. Nisbet had been described by a fellow Scot as a moving library, whose reading was extensive, his memory vigorous, his discernment quick and his judgment wise. "In theology he is a sound Calvinist, in politics a thorough whig, in heart—an American." What more could Dr. Rush ask for to train the uncouth youth of America in the ways of gentility and virtue?

So in December of 1783 Rush wrote to Nisbet in his most persuasive, even crafty, style, telling him that the trustees of the College were to meet next April to choose a principal and that he had taken great pains to direct their attention and votes to him. "Come, sir," he writes, "and share with us in that liberty and independence which you have loved." And then he paints a glowing picture of a land of plenty, where reason, justice and common sense prevail and where there is ample scope for the activity of a benevolent mind. When Rush wanted something, nothing could stop the flow of his rhetoric.

But he had two opponents to his scheme. One was Ewing, not only a political adversary but a man who, Rush believed, regarded himself as the arbiter of education in Pennsylvania. The other was Dickinson himself. Dickinson had written Nisbet dissuading him from coming because of the parlous political situation in the State. This was too much for Rush to bear. He was infuriated and suffered a degree of anxiety he had never before experienced at what he considered Dickinson's treachery. Finally he faced up to him. To Dickinson's counsel of prudence, he countered by saying that where honor is concerned prudence is a rascally virtue. Dickinson relented and Rush won the day.

With Colonel Montgomery, Rush enjoyed an unblemished friendship for thirty-three years. He gives him much credit for the existence of the College, and on his friend's death he refers to him in his *Commonplace Book* as a "Blest Saint." An untutored man, Montgomery has been described as a man of passionate honesty, representing the finest qualities of the Scotch-Irish character plus those of the American frontier. Together these two men built the College. But Rush assumed all the onerous burdens that fall on the shoulders of any college president: choosing a board of trustees sufficiently conservative to be safe, and yet politically varied enough to be representative of the inhabitants of western Pennsylvania; inducing a reluctant faculty to come to an intellectually unsophisticated community in relatively primitive surroundings; making sure that the several Christian denominations were included; raising funds when money was tight and many of the rich had lost their fortunes; planning a building program and arranging the curriculum; and, above all, doing the necessary log-rolling and politicking to keep the enemies of the College at bay.

In all this Rush showed much skill. He won over a leading opponent in Carlisle. This was General John Armstrong, a power in Pennsylvania politics, who had objected to any institution that might compete with the College of New Jersey. Montgomery advised Rush to flatter Armstrong, a wealthy landowner, by appointing him to the board of trustees. This worked; the hook that finally landed him was Rush's suggestion that values in Carlisle real estate would undoubtedly go up just as they had in Princeton after the founding of the College there.

In the end, Rush's labors were rewarded. On September 9, 1783, six days after the peace treaty with England went into effect, the Legislature passed an act to establish the College at Carlisle in Cumberland County.

*   *   *

Now the "great and solemn 6th of April" was about to arrive—the day of the first meeting of the trustees of Dickinson College. With a servant and two horses, Rush leaves Philadelphia at ten in the morning of April 2. On his way to Carlisle he stops at various taverns—the Buck, the Sign of Admiral Warren, the Ship, the Sign of the Bear and the Sign of General Washington. At the Ship, after an agreeable dish of tea, he alternately walks, reads and writes. He feels "now & then an inclination for a pinch of Snuff—but was restrained from taking it by recollecting how many pathetic—animated—and affectionate remonstrances I had received Against it from my dear Mrs. Rush."

He arrives at Lancaster at about six o'clock on the evening of the 3rd. There, at the Sign of the Bear, he encounters the President of the State, John Dickinson. Several callers come to pay their respects. There is enthusiastic talk about the College and the usual complaints against the Constitution and the evils of paper money which Rush has been hearing from innkeepers and travelers alike. The next day, riding along the bank of the Susquehanna, he is struck by the effects of the great freshet which had inundated the surrounding countryside. The farms on the river were owned chiefly by Germans, whose neatness, orderliness and great industry impress him. A few miles from the river the Irish settlers live in houses without windows, their poor lean cattle restrained by broken fences. This contrast is a theme to which Rush recurs in his writings; it was certainly related to his feelings about strong drink. The English inhabitants of Pennsylvania drank mostly wine and Madeira, the Germans drank beer, but the Scotch-Irish drank whiskey.

Rush arrived at Carlisle on the 5th, where he was greeted by his friend Montgomery, who lived in a stone house, still standing, called *Happy Retreat*. The next morning the trustees assembled in the Episcopal Church to listen to a sermon on the utility of seminaries, and then they dined elegantly at Colonel Montgomery's. After dinner they proceeded to the courthouse to conduct their business meeting. It was then that Dr. Nisbet was elected principal. Rush lost no time in informing him and congratulating him upon the event.

Nisbet was a sensitive, thin-skinned scholar who bore transplantation poorly. Two years later, on the 4th of July, the Reverend Doctor and his party were met on the road from Yellow-Breeches Creek to Boiling Springs by a Carlisle troop of light horse, which conducted him to the College to hear an address of welcome. Apparently poor Dr. Nisbet was so excited he was unable to respond. Like Rush, he was stubborn, opinionated and sensitive, and the two men were bound to come into conflict. Nisbet was full of complaints and soon at loggerheads with the trustees. He clung to his ancient Scottish academic traditions and failed to profit by the experiences of other American institutions of learning. Rush soon grew tired of the constant whining of the new principal and of the undisguised hostility of his wife and son. He was having difficulty enough in finding cash to meet operating expenses; and Nisbet, on his side, felt that Rush had lacked candor and had held out false promises to him. In addition, he was offended when he learned that Rush had spent several days in Carlisle without even calling on him. Shortly thereafter he resigned, with the intention of returning to Scotland; but when the beautiful fall weather came, he changed his mind. With great difficulty he was reappointed. Gradually the College prospered, funds began to accumulate and buildings were erected. On April 5, 1787, Rush wrote to Dickinson, saying:

"I have great pleasure in informing you that your College is in a very flourishing condition. Pupils are coming and expected in great numbers from Maryland, Virginia, and even North Carolina. Twenty young men will graduate there in May. . . . Thus, sir, after all our difficulties and disappointments, heaven has at last crowned our labors and wishes with success."

But this sanguine outburst told only part of the story. A conflict had arisen between the teaching staff and the trustees over the proper administration of discipline. There was no faculty representative on the board of trustees, and Rush, the most forceful and influential member of the board, was loath to relinquish authority over the affairs of the students. He should have known better. When his personal interests were involved, however, his judgment sometimes went astray. He was afraid that the republican Constitution of the College would lose its character and that it would degenerate into the despotic organization of a private school.

However personal or political Rush's motives may have been in the founding of Dickinson College, there can be no doubt of his idealistic, if not Messianic, concern with the spreading of republican education. Although the peace treaty had been signed, he was convinced that the Revolution was not over. He saw the struggle as the unfolding of a great drama, of which only the first act had been performed. This act consisted of the war itself and the subsequent establishment of independent governments. In the second act, these governments would be perfected, or new and still more perfect forms would be devised. Act three was commencing, and Rush was stepping onto the stage to play his part. Now the people would be prepared to live under the improved governments, and education would be concerned with their morals and manners in order to make good citizens of them. He proposed to establish a federal university for the training of governmental leaders, and a national postal system to diffuse knowledge and formulate public opinion in favor of free government.

". . . Every state—city—country—village—and township in the union, should be tied together by means of the post-office. . . .

It should be a constant injunction to the postmasters to convey newspapers free of all charge for postage.—They are not only the vehicles of knowledge and intelligence, but the sentinels of the liberties of our country."

Rush conceived of republican education as a process of social evolution. His importance as a political thinker lies in the fact that he was the first to spell out this idea.

* * *

But Rush was not yet through with his promotion of education. He now began the preparation of an article published in the *Pennsylvania Gazette*, for August 31, 1785, in which he urged his fellow citizens to establish a college for the education of German youth. Two years later this campaign too was crowned with success by the establishment of Franklin College at Lancaster. Rush was a charter trustee of this college, later to be called Franklin and Marshall.

Even though Rush found the Germans of Pennsylvania too materialistic, there was much about them that he admired. As compared with the Scotch-Irish, he valued their freedom from bickering and strife and their preference for cider, beer and wine over hard liquor. He appreciated the cleanliness of their houses, their punctuality and responsibility in business, their piety and love of music and the way they accustomed their children early to habits of hard work. This latter especially appealed to him. Indeed, all the traits of the Germans that he prized so highly throw a light upon his own character.

In sponsoring this new college, Rush anticipated the objections to such a separatist institution. Far from rendering the Germans a people distinct from other citizens of the state, his argument was that ignorance and prejudice alone kept men of different countries and religions apart. Education, by removing these barriers, would prepare the way for the Germans to unite with their fellow citizens of British and Irish origins into a "homogeneous mass of people." It would preserve the purity of their own tongue and at the same time teach them the use of correct English. He was interested not only in blending people of different national backgrounds together, but also the farmer and the scholar. For such an amalgam he thought the Germans happily suited.

No one would call Rush a man without prejudices. Yet in relation to people of origins alien to his own he was without bias and remarkably tolerant. He treated the native Indian with respect. On the few occasions when he came face to face with Orthodox Judaism, his interest and admiration were aroused. From his early life he had embraced the cause of abolition and had favored the education of Negroes. Through the influence of Dickinson College he hoped to bring culture and understanding and harmony to the dissident Scotch-Irish Presbyterians of the western frontier of Pennsylvania. He was the first wholehearted friend of the Germans, realizing how much they had to contribute to the welfare of the state. Through education he hoped to help them achieve positions of leadership, not only in Pennsylvania but also in the country at large. In addition, he wanted to rescue them for the Republican Party, that is to say, the early conservative party in Pennsylvania.

Benjamin Rush's educational proposals went even farther. He favored free tax-supported schools for the children of the poor. And since education without religion was anathema to him, he also favored sectarian supervision of public schools, believing that the morals of the members of society are of more consequence than their health or even their lives. The religion that he recommended was that of the New Testament, for he was persuaded that "A Christian cannot fail of being a republican." :

Although in New England there were already many free, non-sectarian schools—600 in Connecticut alone—a parochial view of education had prevailed in Pennsylvania and the middle Colonies from the beginning. Rush fell in with its philosophy. In other respects, however, he was a progressive. He advocated the phonetic method of teaching English; he insisted that less time be devoted to the study of Greek and Latin; he suggested relieving the tedium of study by athletics. Manly exercise, he thought, would impart health, strength and elegance to the human body. He even proposed practical work in manual occupations in the intervals of study, as was instituted more than a century later at Antioch College. Students should not live in dormitories—"the gloomy remains of monkish ignorance"—but, in order to improve their manners, with adults. He conceded that while housing them together in seclusion might make scholars of them, in his opinion the first business of a school was to make students into men, citizens and Christians.

Rush felt strongly that the cultivation of the English language was a matter of great consequence, especially as the models provided at the bar, on the stage, and in the pulpits of Great Britain would soon be lost to Americans. With prophetic foresight he realized that within two or three centuries more people would be speaking English than had ever before spoken any one language. He believed that a sound knowledge of English was essential for young women, with due attention paid to speaking correctly and writing a legible hand. He also favored the inclusion of music and dancing in the curriculum.

At a time when the rod was the principal instrument for governing school children, Rush was as opposed to its use as he was to the tyranny of teachers. Corporal punishment, he held, is never necessary except in children under four or five years of age. Teachers he ranked second only to mothers as the most important members of civil society. In fact, he believed that there have been few great or good men who have not been blessed with wise and prudent mothers. In view of these opinions, it is natural to find him one of a group which established the Young Ladies' Academy in Philadelphia, where he delivered the commencement address, "Thoughts upon Female Education."

Being a feminist at heart, Rush wanted to remove "the present immense disparity which subsists between the sexes, in the degrees of their education and knowledge." He knew that the elevation of the female mind was "considered by some men as unfriendly to the domestic character of a woman," but this attitude he thought was simply an expression of "the prejudice of little minds." He was sure that the cultivation of reason in women would contribute both to private and to public happiness. In fact, he believed that education alone, for all citizens, could save mankind.

Rush's zeal for education was at its peak in teaching his medical colleagues and future doctors. In 1786, for a second time, the Philosophical Society invited him to give its annual oration. The title of his address was "An inquiry into the influence of physical causes upon the moral faculty." This essay was immediately recognized as an important philosophical contribution, and attracted much attention. It was printed in pamphlet form and later was included in the second volume of his *Medical Inquiries and Observations.*

By the moral faculty, Rush meant the capacity of the human mind to distinguish and choose between good and evil. This capacity he believed is inborn, although capable of improvement by experience and reflection. It is not to be confounded with *conscience*, which is a distinct and independent capacity of the mind and which confines its operations only to its own actions, whereas the moral faculty exercises itself upon the behavior of others. Rush considered virtue and vice to consist in action and not in opinion. He was dealing with the distinction between morality and ethics, moral rules of conduct being based on law and convention reinforced by the threat of punishment, whereas ethical rules have their being in some definition of perfection and hope of self-realization. Perhaps he was foreshadowing that evolving element in the personality described as the *super-ego*, which functions partly consciously and partly unconsciously, and is responsible for socially adaptive behavior. When this is defective in development, we are confronted with the sociopath—the pathological liar, the cheat, and the chronic criminal.

Rush recognized that this moral faculty, and thus man's behavior, was dependent on the integrity of memory, imagination and judgment. These, in turn, can be affected by various bodily and mental states or by environmental conditions, such as climate and diet. Not only madness but also hysteria and hypochondriasis can dispose to vice. "It is in vain," he stated, "to attack these vices with lectures upon morality. They are only to be cured by medicine. . . ." In adopting this clinical point of view toward man's deviant behavior, he was indeed in advance of his time, even though the cures he recommended—exercise, the cold bath, or a cold or warm atmosphere—sound naïve and have in them perhaps a suggestion of the punitive.

What was true for individuals, he thought, was also true for nations. In fact, with extraordinary prescience he declared:

"Should the same industry and ingenuity, which have produced these triumphs of medicine over diseases and death, be applied to the moral science, it is highly probable that most of those baneful vices, which deform the human breast, and convulse the nations of the earth, might be banished from the world."

The intervening decades have not as yet revealed this sovereign remedy for man's cosmic ills, but he still labors with them, as Rush did, with hope and perseverance.

Rush's clinical concern with man's moral faculty naturally inclined him against all excesses in punishment. With his accustomed fluency and persuasiveness, he spoke against public punishments, believing that they increase the propensity to crime. "A man," he said, "who has lost his character at a whipping-post, has nothing valuable left to lose in society." He was opposed to all jails, and wanted in their stead a house of repentance, where punishments would be moderate, just and private, and where useful work could be done under sanitary conditions. Rush was inalterably against the death penalty on any account. When he first took this position, he met with but three persons in Philadelphia who agreed with him; but within two years, he tells us, many hundreds had come over to his side.

* * *

It is clear that Rush regarded himself as a doctor not only to sick men and women but also to the ills of society. Already he had come out strongly in many public communications against the use of strong drink, but his often reprinted major treatment of the subject was not published until some years later. In 1787, largely because of his influence, the College of Physicians of Philadelphia placed itself on record in favor of temperance, setting forth the pernicious effects of spirituous liquors upon the human body, and praying that such laws be passed as would diminish their consumption.

This College of Physicians had been instituted the year before. John Redman, Rush's venerable preceptor, was its first president, and there were twelve senior fellows, of whom Rush was one. Monthly meetings were held in a little house belonging to the University, known as Surgeon's Hall. There the fellows gathered for their deliberations or to listen to an address by one of the members. Some were in Quaker dress; others wore knee breeches, as did Rush, with silk stockings and low buckled shoes. Many carried gold-headed canes and were equipped as well with snuffboxes. Powdered wigs were beginning to go out of fashion with the younger group of physicians, but many of these still wore their hair in queues. Rush himself had no patience with singularities in manners, dress or general conduct. "The formal and pompous manner, whether accompanied by a wig, a cane, or a ring," he thought, "should be all avoided as incompatible with the simplicity of science and the real dignity of physic."

Perhaps Rush's most radical medical undertaking was his promotion of the Philadelphia Dispensary for the medical relief of the poor. This was the first of its kind in the United States, and from its beginning in 1786 Rush continued for many years to serve it without recompense, although doing so reduced the number of his patients by one-fourth. During its first five years, nearly 8,000 patients received treatment there. Patients too ill to come to the Dispensary were advised to leave their names with the apothecary and they would then be called upon in their own houses by one of the staff physicians. These two institutions—the College of Physicians and the Dispensary—were closest to Rush's heart, and to them he gave much thought and effort.

Rush had long resolved and repeatedly declared that he would close his political labors when a safe and efficient general government was established. This was slow in coming and was marked by bitter and acrimonious debate. The controversies and enmities in which he had been embroiled led him to entreat his sons "to take no public or active part in the disputes of their country beyond a vote at an election. If no scruples of conscience forbid them to bear arms, I would recommend to them rather to be soldiers than politicians, should they ever be so unfortunate as to live in a country distracted by civil war. In battle men kill, without hating each other; in political contests men hate without killing, but in that hatred they commit murder every hour of their lives."

For most of the decade of the 1780's Rush worked for the repeal of the Test Laws and for the revocation and reform of the State Constitution. In these political activities he was, of course, motivated by partisan considerations. Because of the weakness of the Articles of Confederation and the enforced circulation of paper money, the situation in the country was distressful and perilous. Commerce was greatly restricted. There was massive unemployment. Rush tells us that bricklayers, house carpenters, mechanics and common laborers were out of work and that 1,000 houses in

Philadelphia were standing vacant. The value of property had fallen by 75 per cent in a dozen years. Bankruptcies were frequent and beggars were to be seen on every street. Taxes were steadily mounting and subscriptions for the relief of the poor were additionally burdensome.

Together with other thoughtful and concerned patriots, Rush realized that these egregious social ills stemmed from the weakness of the general government. He was not one to stand idly by in the face of so much misery. Because of his political publications and his fervid speeches at town meetings, the citizens of Philadelphia elected him a member of the Convention that met in Pennsylvania to adopt or reject the proposed Federal Constitution. While this State Convention was sitting in the early winter of 1787, he received a letter from John Dickinson, a member of the Federal Constitutional Convention, calling upon him to come forward in support of the proposed Constitution of the United States. Rush had heard enough of its form and principles to be satisfied with it and he immediately rose to defend it and urge its adoption. The Constitution went into effect in 1789, and within two years the last of the laggard states had adopted it. Rush now felt that his long-cherished purpose had been accomplished. Not only had he helped his fellow countrymen achieve freedom, he had also helped them acquire the means of preserving their freedom. Yet he was far from finished with political controversy.

Despite all these varied and manifold preoccupations, Rush's principal job was the care of the sick. This he put first among his duties. He was the harassed servant of countless suffering, frightened men and women, and he never failed them.

His growing family naturally made demands on him, but he seems not to have resented them. In 1787 his son James was born, his fifth surviving child, and one of the two sons who followed his footsteps into medicine. His letters to his wife, often at Morven, the Stockton country seat near Princeton, continue to be affectionate, expressive, and full of thoughts he wanted to share with her. "To a mind like mine," he writes, "which so soon (perhaps from its slender size) becomes plethoric with ideas and which delights so much in communicating them, it is a new and peculiar hardship to lose at once a domestic friend, a wife, and five children, to most of whom I had been in the habits of imparting every thought as soon as it rose in my mind." He tells her that he needs people to dispute and contradict him, as this is not only "the life of conversation but steel to the flint of genius."

Even his books lose their relish without her company. Not a day goes by without his hearing and seeing many things which perish in his bosom without being communicated. He longs to put Paley's *Moral Philosophy* into her hands, since he enjoys it only by halves from not reading it with her. He wants her to become mistress of it in order to qualify her to educate their children properly. This task must of necessity devolve upon her because of his own professional and public obligations. He closes a letter to his Julia with "Adieu, thou dear right side of my heart," and with the comforting thought that he knows she believes in him, in spite of all his "passions, infirmities and enemies." Previously he had written her, after telling her about the meeting at which the plan for free schools was adopted, "Methinks I hear you cry out. . . . Alas! my poor husband! he is as crazy as ever."

10

AN 18TH-CENTURY
PRACTITIONER

❀ FROM 1787 ON, DR. RUSH HAD EXCLUSIVE CARE OF
the "maniacal patients" in the wards of the Pennsylvania Hospital. There he began to gather the facts and to draw the conclusions
which twenty-five years later he would bring together in the most
famous of his writings—his *Medical Inquiries and Observations
upon the Diseases of the Mind*. In 1787 there were thirty-four such
patients in the Hospital. He refers to their care as a desperate undertaking. In treating them his chief reliance was on warm and cold
baths, alternating them as the Indians did.

It was natural that his interest should have taken this direction.
His wide clinical experience had included work with the sick, the
wounded and the dying in the Army, visits to the homes of all kinds
and conditions of people, perhaps especially the poor, who knew
mostly hardship and deprivation, and now work in the city dispensary and in the jails. In addition to this, his inordinate curiosity
and his eagerness to acquire and store new facts brought him in
contact with a great variety of people. He was always questioning,
conversing and exploring, either face-to-face or by letter.

In May 1787 the Philadelphia Society for Alleviating the Miseries of Public Prisons was organized. Rush lost no time in joining it.
He was elected one of its physicians whose duty it was to visit the
prisons and to make recommendations on matters concerning the
health of the inmates. The unwholesome and insanitary conditions

that prevailed were heightened by the fact that the warden of the Walnut Street jail managed it for his own profit. Even if the Society did not accomplish the good for which it was designed, Rush felt that "men grow *good* by attempting it."

His medical experiences exposed him constantly to the whole panoply of human distress, misery and tragedy. For a man as sensitive as Rush and endowed with his restless, questing, acquisitive mind, and, moreover, with a nature so full of contradictions and conflicts, it is small wonder that to account for what he saw he looked to forces behind the obvious. It was perhaps this that led him into his studies of deranged minds. But what is more likely is that it was part of his need to identify himself with the oppressed and the unfortunate—his reformer's zeal, which made him always do battle with the wrongs he encountered. It was lucky for him that he found an active outlet for his energies, else his anger and sense of outrage might have consumed him and rendered him a neurotic malcontent instead of a vigorous and dauntless pioneer, and reformer.

Although the study of mental illness was to engage much of Rush's apparently inexhaustible energy in his mature years, his practice was never confined to that alone. He was no specialist in the modern sense and his writings at this time of his life show how widespread his medical concerns were, and also how shrewd some of his observations. Among other clinical subjects, he had written on breakbone fever, pulmonary consumptions, scarlatina and tetanus.

During the late war he had been called to visit a Colonel John Stone, who had been shot through the foot at the battle of Germantown, and he described the Colonel's illness and treatment thus:

"He was in the third day of a tetanus. His spasms were violent, and his pains so exquisite, that his cries were heard near a hundred yards from his quarters. His head was thrown a little backwards, and his jaw had become stiff and contracted. He was under the care of a skilful regimental surgeon, who was pouring down opium in large quantities without effect.

"Duty and friendship both led me to do my utmost to save the life of this valuable officer. I immediately dismissed the opium, and gave him large quantities of wine and bark, to the amount of two or three ounces of the latter, and from a bottle to three pints of the former in the day. In a few hours I was delighted with their effects. His spasms and pains were less frequent and violent, and he slept for several hours, which he had not done for several days and nights before."

Dr. Rush had made two sound empirical observations: one, that in some individuals opium in large doses will excite rather than relax, and the other, that quinine (bark) diminishes neuro-muscular excitability. His procedure seems to have been effective, although the theoretical basis for it does not accord with later knowledge. He thought, in fact, that tetanus was occasioned by relaxation.

As for consumption, Rush observed that it was unknown among the Indians of North America and rarely seen in the first settlers or in people who led vigorous, laborious lives and were exposed to hardships in all kinds of weather, whereas it was far more common among indoor workers and those with sedentary occupations. He believed that lawyers, actors, town criers and city watchmen—all of whom exercised their lungs by long or loud speaking—were less susceptible to consumption than people who did other kinds of work. Ministers of the Gospel, however, take the disease; perhaps they do not use their voices with such stentorian effects. They are also, it seems, susceptible to "pulpit sweats."

According to Dr. Rush, the most sovereign remedy for consumption was physical exercise—the preferred form being horseback-riding. In this opinion he was supported "by the venerable Doctor Franklin, whose conversation at all times conveys instruction and not less in medicine than upon other subjects," and by the great Sydenham. Rush could hardly have found two observers more astute than these to corroborate his views. Later he was to say: "The first question . . . to be asked by a physician who visits a patient in this disease should be, not what is the state of his lungs, but, is he able to ride on horseback." And he closes his thoughts on the subject with the rather disarming comment that he was confident of the certainty of the facts but somewhat doubtful of the truth of his reasoning—an unaccustomed expression of skepticism and modesty for a man usually so cocksure.

In the case of scarlatina, he believed that camphor suspended in a little bag from the neck as a preservative against disease possessed little virtue as compared with washing the hands and face and rinsing the mouth and throat with vinegar and water. His fondness for emetics and purges was much in evidence; ipecacuanha, tartar emetic, calomel and jalap he used freely. He doubted that cholera infantum or summer diarrhea was produced by teething or worms or eating fruits, as was then commonly held. He recognized this as a seasonal disease, beginning generally in the middle of June and lasting until mid-September. His description of the afflicted child is a medical classic. Of all the remedies he prescribed for this often-fatal disorder, the one he favored most was country air.

Two more of Rush's studies from this period of his life call for mention. One concerned the influence of the military and political events of the American Revolution on the human body. The other was a kind of homily addressed to his students on their future conduct in the practice of their profession.

In the first of these, Rush was concerned with how the events of the war could affect the human body *through the medium of the mind*. As an example of this, he mentions the fact that the Philadelphia Militia, which had joined the remains of Washington's Army in 1776 and had shared with him the surprise attack on the Hessians at Trenton, remained in excellent health. Out of 1,500 men previously accustomed to the habits of city life, only two cases of sickness developed and one death, in spite of exposure to bitter cold and of sleeping in the open air under insufficient shelter. He ascribed this remarkable record to the vigor infused into the human body by the victory at Trenton. This *post hoc* reasoning was characteristic of Rush and of 18th-century medicine in general, but the possible value of such observations should not be discounted just because critical proof of their soundness was lacking. After furnishing several other examples, he states that an inquirer after philosophical truth should consider the passions of men in the same light that he does the laws of matter or motion. This represented a scientific attitude toward human emotions and behavior which would later prove to be prerequisite for the study of both.

In another lecture, published at the request of his students, Rush has other salient comments on the effects of the mind on the body. He thinks that the influence of the will has not yet been fully explored, and he rejects the futile pretensions of Mesmer to the cure of diseases by what he had absurdly called animal magnetism. But he is ready to concede that the facts which Mesmer established clearly prove the influence of the imagination and the will upon diseases. Rush believed that these relationships, if fully explored, could lead to some very important discoveries in the cure of diseases. He was obviously at the threshold of what a later generation would call psychosomatic medicine. He enjoins his students "to open all the dead bodies you can, without doing violence to the feelings of your patients, or the prejudices of the common people." And he recommends that they keep careful written records on their patients, including reports on the weather, on the prevailing epidemics, an accurate description of the disease and the effects of the drugs prescribed upon it. Physicians, he asserts, seldom remember more than the last two or three years of their practice. Such records would supply this deficiency of memory.

He urges his listeners to study the anatomy of the human mind, if, as he says, "I may be allowed the expression"—an expression made familiar generations later through the writings of Freud. And he wrote: "The reciprocal influence of the body and mind upon each other, can only be ascertained by an acurate knowledge of the faculties of the mind, and of their various modes of combination and action." It is the duty of physicians, he believes, to assert their prerogative and to rescue mental science from "the usurpations of schoolmen and divines," and this, he says, can only be accomplished through the discoveries of medicine.

In the next paragraph Rush goes on to say that improvement in medicine is not to be derived only from colleges and universities. Systems of physic are the productions of genius and learning; but those facts which constitute real knowledge are to be met with in every walk of life. Remember, he says, how many of our most useful remedies have been discovered by quacks. And therefore, he urges his students not to be afraid of conversing with them nor with nurses and old women, who "will often suggest facts in the history and cure of diseases which have escaped the most sagacious observers of nature. Even Negroes and Indians have sometimes stumbled upon discoveries in medicine. Be not ashamed to inquire into them."

Rush could have given no better example than the bark he was so fond of using. It was Indians in Peru who found that the water of a certain lake cured them of chills and fever. Around its banks grew cinchona trees. Their shedding bark was extracted by the

lake water, which became thereby a crude decoction of quinine.
The medicinal properties of this bark had been recognized for
more than a century before Rush's time. It was known also as
Jesuit bark because it was carried by the members of that order
throughout Europe. But its active ingredient, the alkaloid quinine,
was not chemically isolated until long after Rush's death.

Rush favored simplicity in the preparation of medicines. He was
opposed to too many mixtures because, when mixed, medicines frequently vitiate each other. Furthermore, in a simple state one can
obtain exact knowledge of the virtues and dosage of each ingredient. He was opposed to sacrificing too much to taste, fearing that
the nature of medicine might be wholly changed by being mixed
with sweet substances. In fact, he believed that "The author of
nature seems to have had a design, in rendering medicines un-
palatable." If they had been more agreeable to taste, they might
have become articles of diet or condiments and thus have lost their
efficacy in diseases. He taught his students to give as few medicines
as possible in tinctures made with distilled spirits for fear of inno-
cently seducing people into a love of strong drink.

Then his closing paragraphs reveal the teacher in a transport of
optimistic idealism, which echoed vibrantly in the hearts of the
aspiring young men before him. This is what he says:

"Human misery of every kind is evidently on the decline. Happiness, like truth, is an unit. While the world, from the progress of
intellectual, moral and political truth, is becoming a more safe and
agreeable abode for man, the votaries of medicine should not be idle.
All the doors and windows of the temple of nature have been
thrown open by the convulsions of the late American revolution.
This is the time, therefore, to press upon her altars. We have already drawn from them discoveries in morals, philosophy and government, all of which have human happiness for their object. Let
us preserve the unity of truth and happiness, by drawing from the
same source, in the present critical moment a knowledge of anti-
dotes to those diseases which are supposed to be incurable."

*   *   *

Imagine oneself in the lecture room listening to this colorful,
vivid and emphatic man. Possessed of a quick perception, a tenacious memory, persistent industry and an eminent facility in the

use of language, he must have captured his students completely. Apparently it was his habit to remain seated and to read his lectures from manuscript, meanwhile making notes on the reverse blank page. Occasionally he would rise, take off his spectacles and drive home a point with special emphasis. A member of one of Dr. Rush's classes, Dr. Charles Caldwell, says this of him:

". . . he was one of the best public readers I have ever heard. As a mere colloquist, moreover, having cultivated, with great attention and care, the art of conversation, he was uncommonly eloquent, correct, and interesting."

Caldwell said of him that Rush had taught him very little, but in the next breath admitted that he had taught him to teach himself. What better can be said of a teacher? When Rush expressed his strong sentiments for America and the American people, he drew a spontaneous burst of applause from the whole audience, and it caused young Caldwell to rise from his seat.

Dr. Rush valued this gifted student who was learned in literature and the classics and had studied with John Hunter in London. Rush was always quick to single out the most promising young men in his class and he spared no pains to win them over to his opinions. But Caldwell did not want to be, as he said, molded into a retainer. He was ambitious and he had an eye on a professorship for himself. A coolness developed between the two men which ultimately led to a breach, because Caldwell implied that Dr. Rush had borrowed from him and passed off as his own the discovery that cold water can put an end to attacks of fever. This occurred in May 1796. Rush was incensed. He showed himself at his worst by bullying the student who was trying to defend his thesis and by finally refusing to sign his diploma. Caldwell stood his ground. He said:

"As the Professor of the Institutes of Medicine and Clinical Practice has refused me his name, I shall in a short time convince him that I can do without it. I have been anxious, and even ambitious to remain on good terms with him, and have faithfully and strenuously exerted myself to that effect. But, for the accomplishment of neither that, nor any other earthly purpose, will I ever surrender my independence of mind."

This language Rush should have understood. But at this moment he was a hot-headed, vain prima donna whose self-love had been seriously offended—and by a student! Later, he relented; he signed Caldwell's diploma, but the occasion was conspicuously lacking in warmth on both sides.

Of the many careers which Benjamin Rush pursued, in none was he more pre-eminently successful than in that of a teacher. The number of his students steadily increased, with minor fluctuations, from forty-five in 1790 to 332 in 1812. There were 2,872 students registered in his medical classes between 1779 and 1812, and the fees they paid totaled slightly more than $69,000.

In addition to these students, Dr. Rush had his private apprentices, whose training he supervised. In the year 1790 he maintained as many as six of these at one time. They also increased in number, reaching as many as fifteen to thirty at the time when his practice was most extensive and lucrative. Toward his students and apprentices, other than in the brush with young Caldwell, he seldom displayed the stubbornness, egocentricity and irritability which often crept into his relations with professional colleagues or with political opponents. When he was on surer ground and in contact with young men who looked up to him as a master, he could lay aside his overbearing pride.

The same was true with his patients. The more they suffered, the more that life had buffeted and battered them, the more was Rush their solicitous protector, ready to sacrifice his own comfort and safety and even his life on their behalf. He was as renowned for his faithful attention to the sick as he was for his sympathy and kindness and his gentleness of manner. Here again he was not threatened by any element of competition, and none of his dogmatic self-assertiveness showed itself, nor his often unreasonable resentment, nor yet his impatience at contradiction. In those days, when medicine was based more on opinion than on hard-won fact, a doctor of medicine was a revered authority and no patient would have dared to contradict him.

Dr. Rush's students and apprentices came to him from all of the thirteen states. Many of his former pupils, after entering the practice of medicine, naturally turned to him for advice about their own patients. They also often consulted him about their personal lives. From all parts of the country sick people wrote him about their headaches and backaches and swellings and tumors, begging for medicine or for some plan of treatment. He found himself carrying on a kind of medical mail-order business or correspondence course. His answers to their often importunate demands were written far into the night, after he had already done a hard day's work.

His cousin and former apprentice, Dr. Elisha Hall, of Fredericksburg, Virginia, wrote for advice about the care of Mrs. Mary Washington, George Washington's mother, who was suffering from a cancer of the breast. Rush answered on July 6, 1787:

"The respectable age & character of your venerable patient, lead me to regret that it is not in my power to suggest a remedy for the cure of the disorder you have described in her breast. . . . I am disposed to believe that there do not exist in the vegetable kingdom an antidote to cancers."

He rather favored the use of arsenic in the form of Dr. Martin's powder applied externally to the cancer, which he said had been successful in some cases, but had failed in others. "Give anodynes when necessary," he advised, "& support the system with bark & wine. Under this treatment she may live comfortably many years, & finally die of old age."

Other letters begged his advice on the treatment of uterine hemorrhage, hydrophobia, mental derangement, inflammatory rheumatism, gout, persistent headache and giddiness, to mention only a few. One of his former students wrote him:

"I am now in a most dreadfull dilemma, will you be so favourable as to give me your ingenious observations on the passion of love, it will tend to extricate me from the dreadfull situation—To love & be disappointed most unhappy dreadfull state! advise how to forget a lady whom for years (think it not recent for it has subsisted four years) I had the most ardent passion, & enjoyed every promise and privilege, save only I can say we were not united.— Teach me the noble science to forget? Teach me how to conduct myself when frequently in her company, she appearing to triumph at my mortification."

Alas! We do not know his advice to this unhappy young man.

Most of the writers referred to Rush's pre-eminence, calling him the greatest physician in the United States. Perhaps his greatness lay in his limitless energy and his capacity for empathy with all suffering people. In spite of his therapeutic procedures, which often seem medieval and even preposterous, he had a grasp of the importance of the environment in relation to the organism and the

organism's adaptation to the extraneous conditions of life. This
was in advance of his time. In fact, one of the most striking qualities of this versatile man is that he lived simultaneously in several
centuries. Rush was an 18th-century man, but he lived as well in
the 16th century and even in the 20th.

In addition to his private practice, which was at its height between 1780 and 1790, Dr. Rush served as one of the Senior Physicians of the Pennsylvania Hospital from 1783 to the end of his life.
His ward rounds were formal and punctilious, and he lost no opportunity in using them for the purposes of instruction of the
younger physicians who accompanied him.

In 1786 the Legislature revived its revoked charter to the old
College of Philadelphia, and three years later the Board of Directors met at the home of Benjamin Franklin to appoint a faculty.
Rush was elected to the Chair of the Theory and Practice of
Physic which Morgan had occupied. He was now forty-three
years old. Within three years the College of Physicians would
merge with the University to form one medical school, under the
name of the University of Pennsylvania. Rush was then elected to
the Professorship of the Institutes of Medicine, which dealt with
physiology, pathology and therapeutics. The Chair got its name
from *Institutiones Medicae*, the title of a book by Hermann
Boerhaave published in Leyden in 1708, which dealt for the first
time with bodily functions as a separate subject for study. Rush
occupied two Chairs and he also supervised the work of the medical clinics. In these posts his duties were arduous ones, but it was
not his work alone that exhausted him.

*   *   *

Benjamin Rush now regarded himself as a mere spectator of public affairs. Nonetheless he continued to play a minor part as a
vicarious politician, as is evidenced by his correspondence with
John Adams. These letters are distinguished for their tone of simplicity, candor, forthrightness and affection. Neither Adams' elevation to the second highest position in the land nor the fact that the
two men had some sharp differences of opinion seemed to interfere
with the free flow of feelings and ideas between them. The subjects
on which they differed were the value of the study of the classics,
which Rush dismissed as not only useless but harmful, and which

Adams extolled, and the notion of there being any good in an hereditary monarchy or a titled aristocracy, to which Adams apparently clung, but which Rush looked upon with abhorrence. "Although we hold different principles upon some subjects, yet I cannot help loving and respecting you," Rush wrote. To continue to love someone with whom he differed—especially on matters of principle—this was surely unusual for Benjamin Rush.

He tried to persuade Adams of the importance of placing the seat of government in Philadelphia rather than in New York, spelling out for him its many civic, cultural, moral and political advantages. Rush was afraid of exposing the members of Congress to a community largely composed of Antifederalists and British-hearted citizens, a city "contaminated by having been for seven years a garrison town to a corrupted British army," where even at this late date a lady had been heard to inquire at a large gathering, "What news from *our* poor king?" At a public dinner given sometime later at the St. Andrew's Club of New York, two toasts were offered, the first to "The President of the United States" and the next to "George the Third." According to Jefferson, although the first "was drunk without any particular approbation" at the next "Hamilton started up on his feet, and insisted on a bumper and three cheers. The whole company accordingly rose and gave the three cheers. . . ."

Rush compared New York with the New England states, where virtue, order, and liberty prevailed to a degree not found in the other states. It was this influence that he hoped to see revived and perpetuated. But because of the geographical position of Pennsylvania, lying between New England and Virginia, or perhaps because of his own chauvinism, he continued to urge Philadelphia as his first choice for the seat of government. By delaying to remove Congress to Philadelphia, the country would run the risk of being "dragged in a few years to the banks of the Potowmac, where Negro slaves will be your servants by day, mosquitoes your sentinels by night, and bilious fevers your companions every summer and fall, and pleurisies every spring." So he warned Adams.

Convinced that republicanism had never had a fair trial, Rush hoped that in America, at last, it would prove to be safe and durable. But like a child once burned, he could not expose himself again to the suspicions and persecutions he had earned, simply by trying to do good. If he had ever been popular for as much as a week or a day, he was convinced, it would have been at the expense of his own integrity. His effort to reform the State Constitution and to have the Test Laws repealed had lost him favor with Governor Mifflin; and now his fellow Presbyterians avoided him on the street as if he had been bitten by a mad dog. He who once had been considered "one of the firebrands of independence" could now see nothing before him but labor and self-denial in the pursuit of his profession.

Adams had wished to see him restored to public life, and Rush could have accepted an appointment abroad, where his knowledge of European languages, his acquaintance with eminent literary men and his great interest in agriculture and manufacture would have served his country well. But the time, he thought, was now past to accept an appointment in the government of the United States. He was too sensitive and too idealistic to risk being smeared with the mud of corruption which he saw on all sides. In fact, his apathy was such that he often passed whole weeks without reading a newspaper.

Was Rush, perhaps, going through the kind of depression that comes to some active and driven men in their middle forties? Clearly he had retreated into what he called his little bower. There he was happy, at least so he claimed; he envied and blamed no man. Heaven had showered blessings on him—a wife that was everything a wife should be to any man, and children affectionate, dutiful and promising. What more could a man ask for? Nineteen out of twenty evenings were spent in their society.

On July 3, 1789, Mrs. Rush had given birth to their fourth boy. They now had six living children: John, who was twelve; Emily, ten; Richard, eight; Mary, five; James, three. But little Benjamin, just born, lived only three weeks. They had previously lost two girls and a boy, all in their infancy.

Rush describes an evening at home at this period of his life when he was in his forty-fourth year. He has been writing a letter to his friend, John Adams. At the table where he sits his wife is deeply engaged in reading Millot's *Account of the Manners and Laws of the Ancient Egyptians*. John is plodding through Rollin's *History of Cyrus*, and Richard has just begun to read Goldsmith's *History of England*. The boys frequently turn to their father for ex-

planations of difficult words. One of them, who has just finished
Ovid at school, unhappily asks him whether there is such a river as
the Nile or such a country as Egypt. Having answered the question, Dr. Rush seizes the opportunity to express his strong disapproval of a system of education that acquaints a boy first with
fables and with the gross errors and fictions of the ancient poets,
leading him only to reject the truth.

Emily is also present. She is busy with her sewing and, though
only ten years old, by no means out of the conversation. She is all a
parent could ask for—loving, generous and open-hearted. She
often makes tea for her father when her mother is away, and she
entertains him and soothes him with little anecdotes picked up at
school. To complete the family picture, Rush adds that his venerable mother, then seventy-five years old, occupies a room in their
Walnut Street house. Though often in poor bodily health, the
powers of her mind were in full vigor and of her he writes, "Such
is my veneration for this excellent parent that I never look forward
to that hour which must perhaps soon part us without feeling
an anguish which I cannot describe."

Perhaps Rush was not so much depressed as he was disillusioned
and exhausted from long years of constant labor, from inner conflicts and recurrent illnesses. In any case, his customary industry
and alert curiosity showed no impairment. Epidemics of measles
and influenza had assailed Philadelphia from the spring of 1789
through the winter of 1791. These kept him greatly occupied,
though he found time to write careful clinical descriptions of each.
The account of the influenza would sound familiar enough to anyone who has experienced similar epidemics a century or more later.
The one that Rush described in Philadelphia lasted for about six
weeks. It spread from there and from New York in all directions
to every state in the Union, not avoiding the West Indies or the
Spanish settlements in South America.

"Many thousand people had the disease who were not confined
to their houses, but transacted business as usual out of doors. A
perpetual coughing was heard in every street of the city. Buying
and selling were rendered tedious by the coughing of the farmer
and the citizen who met in market places. It even rendered divine
service scarcely intelligible in the churches." Rush adds that
convalescence from the disease was very slow and that "a general

languor appeared to pervade the citizens for several weeks after it left the city."

By comparing contemporary accounts of the influenza with those handed down by ancient physicians, Rush could find that no material change had occurred in it.

In spite of these epidemics, and his night calls and enfeebled health, he continued to make entries in his *Commonplace Book*, which throw interesting sidelights on the man and his times:

[1789]

"*May 31.* A ditcher at Kensington who has worked up to his knees in water occasionally for 25 years, and is now 51 years of age, never eats warm victuals. He drank Rum when at work, by taking a spoonful of it in his mouth, and washing it down by cold water. He is now in good health. . . .

"*June 19.* There is now a horse alive and good health in the Pennsylvania hospital which was in Braddock's defeat, July 9th, 1755, at which time he was supposed to be 3 or 4 years old. Of course, he is now either 37 or 38 years of age.

"*July 2.* Mrs. Patten informed me she had delivered between 9990 and 10,000 women, inclusive of seven months' children, and lost only one. Mrs. Patten is 58 years of age.

"*August 16.* I met James Pemberton, Jno. Parrish, and Jer. Parker in the street, and proposed to them to get on foot an association to purchase 500 barrels of maple sugar every year in order to encourage the manufacturing of that article in Pennsylvania, and thereby to lessen or destroy the consumption of West India sugar, and thus indirectly destroy negro slavery. They were pleased with the proposal and agreed to meet on the Tuesday following at James Pemberton's at 6 o'clock.

"*Sept. 18.* Mr. Holt of Virginia wondered at General Washington's military fame, for he was a very dull young man. As a proof of it, he mentioned that he was unable to count some change he once saw him receive in a store."

[1790]

"*March 17.* Visited Mr. Jefferson on his way to New York. It was the first time I saw him since his return from France. He was plain in dress and unchanged in his manners. He still professed himself attached to republican forms of government, and deplored the change of opinion upon this subject in John Adams, of whom he spoke with respect and affection as a great and upright man.

"*April 18*. Last evening at 11 o'clock died the venerable Dr. Franklin. He had been reduced by the stone in his bladder, but died finally of a pleurisy which terminated in an abscess in his lungs from which he discharged matter a few days before his death. The pleurisy was caught by lying with his windows open. He possessed his reason to the last day of his life, but spoke nothing of his future existence or expectation beyond the grave.

"*Wednesday, 21st April*. Attended the funeral of Dr. Franklin. The concourse of spectators and followers were supposed to amount to 20,000 people. On the Monday preceding I visited at the Doctor's old mansion house, and was introduced by Mr. Bache, his son-in-law, to view his corpse. It was much reduced but not changed. . . . I obtained a promise, while viewing him, from Mr. Bache, of a lock of his hair, which I afterward procured, and sent some of it to Dr. Price and some of it to the Marquis of Fayette."

[1792]

"*June 18*. This day I attended the funeral of Wm. Gray's wife, a black woman, with about 50 more white persons and two Episcopal Clergymen. The white attendants were chiefly the neighbours of the deceased. The sight was a new one in Philadelphia, for hitherto (a few cases excepted) the negroes alone attended each other's funerals. By this event it is to be hoped the partition wall which divided the Blacks from the Whites will be still further broken down and a way prepared for their union as brethren and members of one great family."

They were of one great family, Rush thought, because all were descended from the same pair in the Garden of Eden. He was, of course, ignorant of genetics and the laws of heredity. He believed that the normal color of the human race was white and that the dark skin of Negroes and the shapes of their noses were the result of leprosy. If their color is actually the effect of disease, it should entitle them to a double portion of our humanity. He was sure that a remedy would be found and this would destroy the last argument in favor of slavery. The claims of superiority of whites over blacks were founded, he thought, on ignorance and inhumanity.

During the next two years Rush's *Commonplace Book* contained many entries of interest to him—odd bits of information about natural history and agriculture passed on to him by acquaintances; bits of travelogue gleaned from others; commentaries on some of his contemporaries, by no means all flattering; conversations with Jefferson; thoughts on solitude, on war, on the origin of evil, on monarchy and aristocracy. There were many entries on the disastrous effects of the funding system and the scrip mania, with tales of bankruptcy, ruin and the debtors' jail.

In the epidemic of influenza that prevailed in Philadelphia in the autumn of 1789, the spring of 1790, and in the winter of 1791, there seems to have been fairly general susceptibility to the disease. It affected adults of both sexes alike, and of all professions and occupations. In Rush's experience a few old people escaped it and it usually passed by children under eight years of age. Only three of the thirty-five "maniacs" in the Pennsylvania Hospital came down with it. Persons who worked in the open air, such as sailors and longshoremen or surveyors, had it much more severely than tradesmen who worked indoors. The Indians of Niagara were especially hard hit; indeed, they thought they had been bewitched, so continuous and irritating were their fits of coughing.

Rush observed that neither the smell of tar nor of tobacco served as a preventive, nor did smoking, chewing tobacco, nor the use of snuff. All these measures had once been thought effective against the plague. There was, to be sure, a less violent and more local form of influenza commonly encountered in the winter months. The source of this, as well as of colds, he thought could be traced to "morbid matter, generated in crowded and heated churches, and other assemblies of the people."

Just such an assembly had taken place in the open air on January 9, 1793, when all of Philadelphia was on hand to watch François Blanchard, the French aeronaut, make his first American balloon ascension. He took off from the yard of the Walnut Street jail and after forty-six minutes in the air came down in Woodbury, New Jersey. The city was jammed with thousands of spectators. People had come from as far away as Baltimore and New York to witness the spectacle. The day was fair but hazy, and the temperature fluctuated between 33° Fahrenheit in the morning and 48° in the afternoon. While watching the balloon go up, crowds of people sat on the damp ground for hours, and, according to Dr. Rush, this resulted in many cases of catarrh, which spread throughout the city.

Being the man of genius that he was, Rush missed none of the important implications of the flight. The day before, he had called on M. Blanchard, bringing him a pulse glass and asking him to make some observations on the state of his pulse during the voyage. These were to be America's first contribution to aviation physiology. They must have been recorded with difficulty. Shortly after the flight, Blanchard, who had come to drink a cup of tea with Dr. Rush, told him that the temperature had fallen to 40° below zero Fahrenheit and that his ink had suddenly frozen.

In a letter to his friend Elizabeth Graeme Ferguson, a few days later, Rush called the ascension a sublime sight and allowed his fantasy to take flight with the balloon. He could not believe that such an invention, in which so much ingenuity and fortitude had been displayed, was intended only to amuse. All inventions, he thought, are progressive by nature, even if they appear to have been asleep for centuries. God's command to "subdue the earth" included water and air as well as dry land, and that command must be fulfilled. Rush anticipated that "immense discoveries of the nature and number of the heavenly bodies" would result from improved methods of flying and also increased connections between distant countries by means of commerce. In the period of the millenium he could foresee the inhabitants of the western world converging by air in Jerusalem "to pay their annual homage to the Savior of the World." But he did not picture to himself some of the dire and devastating consequences of man's subjugation of the atmosphere.

* * *

"During the last winter and part of this spring," Rush confided to his good friend, John Montgomery, in 1788, "it has pleased God to visit my family with several afflictions. In the month of January we buried our youngest son with a pleurisy." Within two months of this unhappy event Rush himself was seized with the same disorder and for nine days his recovery was despaired of. Thus for the second time within this decade Rush prepared for death and, he tells us, was ready to quit life with perfect composure. He not only settled all of his worldly affairs, but gave the most minute directions for his funeral. Throughout all of his trials he was sustained by the religion of Jesus Christ, which was indeed a reality to him, a comfort in life and of inestimable value when the last enemy was close at hand.

A just understanding of Rush and the part he played, both in medicine and in the birth and growth of his new country, is possible only when his faith in the Gospel and his belief in man's salvation are kept constantly in mind. He had a reverence for life in all its manifestations. From a philosophical point of view Rush, with some propriety, might be labeled a behaviorist and also a pragmatist, although these designations are far removed from his teleological and theological views. The human body, he believed, was not an automaton or self-governing machine, but was kept alive and in motion by the constant action of stimuli upon it. The characteristics of life are motion, sensation and thought, and each of these exists only as a response to a stimulus.

In Rush's lexicon there are no such things as innate ideas. They derive from impressions acting upon an innate capacity to receive ideas. This innate capacity is God-given. God alone is the author of "that peculiar organization of matter, which enables it to emit life, when acted upon by stimuli." Without these there would be no life. Stimuli are of many kinds—outer ones, such as light and heat and wholesome nourishment, and inner ones, which spring from the faculties and operations of the mind, its emotions and passions. Among them he included the desire for life itself, love of money, love of dress, of fame, of country, of liberty and, above all, love of religion. He speaks of the invigorating influence of the Christian religion on animal life. Man is as naturally a religious animal as he is a social and domestic one. He was persuaded that the Christian religion, more than any other in the world, is friendly to animal life because it elevates the understanding and acts upon the passions of love and hope.

Nowhere, according to Rush, is animal life in a more perfect state than in the inhabitants of Great Britain and the United States of America. This is because of the invigorating influence of liberty, in addition to all the other natural stimuli they are exposed to. He believed there is an indissoluble union between moral, political and physical happiness. Since elective, representative governments are most favorable to individual and national prosperity, it follows they are also most favorable to animal life. Of all the states of the Union, Connecticut was supreme, because here republican liberty had existed for more than 150 years.

Contrast its inhabitants with those of the Turkish Empire, Rush suggests, where life is in its most feeble state because of a general deficiency of aliment and also of stimulants from the operation of the mental faculties. The despotism of the government weakens the understanding. A Turk lives wholly to himself, and only in the moment. Fear, devoid of joy and hope, is the reigning principle in his life. Rush quotes a traveler who observed that the Turks are slow in motion, that their bodies are small and that they have small evacuations. "They speak . . . with a slow feeble voice, as if the lungs wanted strength to propel air enough through the glottis to form distinct articulate sounds." Not so, however, in the fair and free State of Connecticut.

Although Rush's speculations refer mostly to human beings, what is true of them, he thought, is true of other animals as well and of the seeds of plants. They grow and function only as a consequence of stimuli acting upon a capacity for life. The Deity alone possesses life within Himself and this divine prerogative was imparted only to His Son. "For as the Father hath life in himself; so hath he given to the Son to have life in himself." The best criterion of the truth of a philosophical opinion, according to Rush—and here he speaks like a pragmatist—is its tendency to produce exalted ideas of the Divine Being and humble views of ourselves.

Although at heart Rush was an idealistic Whig, his view of his fellow man was in some respects a mechanistic one. He saw human beings in terms of reflex behavior—that is, of stimulus and response. In this area his biological-medical principles cannot be separated from his social-political ones. For both, sickness and health depended upon the number and intensity of stimuli and upon the quality of the reaction. Although striving always to be a democrat and abjuring all bias and bigotry, he recognized "that the people are as much disposed to vice as their rulers, and that nothing but a vigorous and efficient government can prevent their degenerating into savages or devouring each other like beasts of prey." In fact, he mistrusted a simple democracy and advocated a government composed of three legislative branches as the most likely to establish justice, to insure order, cherish virtue, secure property and protect man from every sort of violence. Such a government, he thought, was essential to health and to the expansion and dignity of the American mind. He agreed with Locke that "where there is no law there can be no liberty; and nothing deserves the name of law but that which is certain and universal in its operation upon all the members of a community."

Rush tried to withdraw from public duties and public life—not because he had been hurt by slander and ingratitude, he says, but because his health could no longer stand labors beyond those of his profession. He felt, too, that his sons were now entitled to some of those evenings which he formerly gave to his country. Besides, he considered "the federal ship as nearly moored. Let the proper officers now repair her rigging and stop her leaks. I am only a passenger."

But he could not let go. To caution and to exhort was his peculiar function. Only by such stimuli would America fulfill its destiny and become "the theater on which human nature will reach its greatest civil, literary, and religious honors." He believed that much good could be done by individuals, and, moreover, in a short time. He looked forward with certainty toward a blessed day when knowledge would triumph over ignorance, virtue over vice, and liberty over slavery, and when human nature would be forever saved from "the disgraces and desolations of war." Political joy, he held, was one of the strongest emotions of the human mind. It is to Rush's credit that he recognized, before his day, the potent force of thoughts and emotions on human destiny and human disease.

Just as life was a manifestation of the response to stimuli, so death resulted from the abstraction of all such stimuli, or from excessive stimulation, or, again, from too much relaxation because the texture of the matter which composed the human body was too weak. This thought he illustrated by comparing the body to a violin. Too much pressure on the strings prevents the instrument from emitting musical tones. When the strings are slack, they do not vibrate, nor do they when they lie on the body of the violin instead of being elevated on a bridge. This rather elaborate figure of speech is of interest because it reveals Rush's notions about the rôle of structure and function in the cause of disease. The system of pathology here outlined naturally suggested to him what a proper therapy consisted of. It depended on removing excessive stimuli, or on reinforcing them when insufficient or when they operate in the presence of too much relaxation. This he believed to be true both for the body politic and for the human body. In each case his aim was to promote a perfect balance between stimulus and response, and thus achieve peace and harmony.

*   *   *

There were two subjects that continued to plague Rush and to give him no rest. One was the existence of slavery in the United States, with the mistreatment of Negroes; the other was the abuse of spirituous liquors and widespread drunkenness. To both he applied the point of his sharp quill. By the spring of 1788 he felt encouraged because of the agitation in Britain for the abolition of the slave trade. The combined efforts of Wilberforce and Pitt were beginning to make headway in Commons, but it would take another forty-five years before the Emancipation Bill was passed, twenty years after Rush's death. He was concerned, as he naturally would have been, with the effects of slavery on the health and lives of the Negroes. Lockjaw or "jaw-fall," as it was called among the planters, was a very common disease among the children of slaves. Rush did not understand its cause. He attributed it to the heat and smoke of the cabins in which the children were born, whereas it was almost certainly caused by the insanitary methods of dressing the umbilical cord. Childbearing among slaves was also attended by a high mortality, and this he thought was due to the injury to the women's bodies from carrying heavy burdens when young, or from the kicks they received from their masters. In addition, he described a state of hypochondriasis among slaves—a condition often coming on shortly after importation and "ignorantly ascribed to the effects of slow poison," but actually, "with all its terrible consequences . . . occasioned wholly by grief" and therefore "justly chargeable upon slavery." To Jeremy Belknap he wrote, "I love even the name of Africa, and never see a Negro slave or freeman without emotions which I seldom feel in the same degree towards my unfortunate fellow creatures of a fairer complexion."

Showing his awareness of social forces on health, Dr. Rush believed that the various chronic diseases prevalent among slaves in the West Indies resulted from their inadequate diets. He realized that this evil could not be corrected because very accurate calculations proved that the whole profit of a sugar estate derived from savings made on the necessary food and clothing of slaves. Further-more, with remarkable psychological perceptiveness, Rush realized that the claim that slaves are the happiest people in the world, just because they are merry, is a false one. He distinguished between happiness and mirth. Mirth and a heavy heart often go together. The songs and dances of slaves were not marks of happiness, but the physical symptoms of melancholy and a certain proof of their misery.

Benjamin Rush's concern with that other social evil—the en-slavement of many of his countrymen by alcohol—had long before caused him to publish a lecture bearing the title "Sermons to Gen-tlemen Upon Temperance and Exercise." His conviction that strong drink was harmful never left him. A decade after this lec-ture he had addressed a letter to the editor of the *Pennsylvania Journal* against the use of spirituous liquors. These two communi-cations were part of a persistent campaign that he carried on for the rest of his life. Its high point came with a famous tract grandiloquently called "An Enquiry into the Effects of Spirituous Liquors upon the Human Body, and Their Influence upon the Happiness of Society." This was probably published as early as 1784, and for many years thereafter was frequently reprinted in newspapers and magazines.

He would circulate this tract for two or three weeks before every harvest, because that was the time of greatest abuse. He counted very much on the support of the Quakers and the Meth-odists in this war against strong drink. But his principal support came from his own uncompromising convictions. He could find no extenuation for strong drink, recognizing it as physiologically harmful, morally degrading and aesthetically abhorrent. Never the pure scientist who could look at human folly with cool detach-ment, he was a Savonarola rather than a Leonardo. In a letter to Jeremy Belknap, written in May of 1788, Rush referred, with rather unusual simplicity of spirit, to his efforts to abolish slavery and to his next objective—"the extirpation of the *abuse* of spir-ituous liquors"—as among "my romantic schemes." ·

Even before the war, Colonists who lived in the interior had begun to make whiskey by distilling alcohol from fermented grain. The importation of rum from Jamaica was interrupted by the Brit-ish Navy and by privateers. The interruption helped promote this new industry which flourished in the country west of the Alleghenies. Indeed, one of the principal motives that had prompted Rush to sponsor the new College at Carlisle was his hope that, through education, the social standards of the whiskey-drinking Scotch-Irish farmers of western Pennsylvania would be raised. The same habits existed among the settlers of Kentucky, whose rich farm lands yielded almost unlimited quantities of Indian corn. Their bourbon whiskey became a valuable article for export, both over the mountains to the east and down the Mississippi to New Orleans. In fact, for a time whiskey took the place of money and became a valuable medium of exchange. It was consumed in large quantities, neat or diluted with a little water, and drunk on an empty stomach both before and between meals.

Drunkenness had become a national vice. Cotton Mather had inveighed against it as early as 1711, and Benjamin Franklin, certainly no spoilsport, acting thirty years later as the foreman of a grand jury, declared that an increasing number of the shiftless poor in Philadelphia owed their lamentable lot to strong drink. He was in favor of restricting the number of licensed taverns. Other men of influence and weight joined in the battle, but the consumption of spirits grew at the expense of milder beverages.

Rush had no notion that the abuse could be legislated out of existence. But it was an integral part of his faith that knowledge of the facts and an appeal to reason could change men's behavior. Moreover, he had the advantage of being a man of science, endowed with great authority, and one of the first to refute the commonly held belief that alcohol served as a dependable mental and physical stimulant. On the contrary, he had learned from his observations of soldiers that alcohol neither protects against cold nor provides fuel for physical exertion, and in civilian life he had ample opportunity to recognize the part the excessive use of strong drink played in mental deterioration as well as in moral degradation.

But Dr. Rush was no fanatic. He was never in favor of renouncing the pleasures and benefits of drinking light wines and beers—only the consumption of ardent spirits. By this term he meant those liquors which are obtained by distillation from fermented substances of any kind. His treatise begins with a brief but graphic description of a fit of drunkenness, which he names an odious disease.

Nor did the familial aspects of this disorder escape him. He believed that it bore a close resemblance to certain hereditary and contagious diseases.

Of the more chronic effects of strong drink, Rush was persuaded that no part of the body was immune to its baleful influence and that most diseases terminated more speedily in death because of it. As for the mind, ardent spirits "impair the memory, debilitate the understanding, and pervert the moral faculties. . . . They produce not only falsehood but fraud, theft, uncleanliness, and murder. . . . Thus we see," Rush goes on, "poverty and misery, crimes and infamy, diseases and death, are all the natural and usual consequences of the intemperate use of ardent spirits." In their place he recommended simple water, cider, malt liquor and wines, which generally inspire cheerfulness and good humor. He regretted that the grape had not yet been sufficiently cultivated in the United States, but he said that there were many excellent substitutes. For example, if two barrels of fresh cider are boiled into one and afterward are allowed to ferment and kept for two or three years in a dry cellar, a liquor results which has the taste of Malaga or Rhenish wine. When mixed with water, it makes a most agreeable summer drink. Other warm weather drinks could be made from molasses and water or vinegar and water, sweetened with sugar, or again from the thin juice of the sugar maple. This last concoction had long been used by the farmers of Connecticut as a cool and refreshing drink at harvest time. He had only good to say of coffee and tea, especially for men who follow professions which require constant exercise of the faculties of the mind.

To drive his point home, he presented his facts graphically in the form of *A Moral and Physical Thermometer*. At the top of the scale is temperance, which leads to health and wealth. This is compatible with drinking water, milk and small beer. Cheerfulness, strength and nourishment can also be had with cider and perry, wine, porter and strong beer when taken only in small quantities, and at meals. Then the scale descends rapidly to a freezing 70° below zero, beginning with punch and passing through toddy and egg rum, grog, flip and shrub, bitters infused in spirits and cordials, gin, brandy and rum in the morning, and even worse when taken day and night. The attendant vices run from idleness to burglary and murder; the resulting diseases, from tremors of the hands with puking, to melancholy, palsy, apoplexy, madness and despair; and the list of punishments begins with the debtors' jail and ends with the gallows.

It is to his credit that, in spite of his moral outrage, Rush recognized addiction to strong drink as a medical and public health problem of the first magnitude, which it still unfortunately remains. To be sure, his *Enquiry* often reads more like a temperance tract than a scientific document, and his "cures" seem naïve in the extreme, but he hoped with his pen to gain adherents and to rouse the nation. He had already won the support of the College of Physicians. Now he appealed to the clergy for their help. To Jeremy Belknap he wrote, "In the year 1915 a drunkard I hope will be as infamous in society as a liar or a thief, and the use of spirits as uncommon in families as a drink made of a solution of arsenic or a decoction of hemlock."

Now Rush also turned his reformer's zeal against the habitual use of tobacco, which he thought led to a desire for strong drink and was injurious both to health and morals. He found smokers generally offensive. What reception would the Apostles have met, he asked, if they had carried into the houses to which they were sent "snuff-boxes, pipes, segars, and bundles of cut, or rolls of hog, or pigtail Tobacco?" Snuff, at the height of its popularity in the 18th century, he condemned because it obstructed the nose and thus impaired the voice. To use it, moreover, meant to waste precious time. He calculated that a man who takes a pinch of snuff every twenty minutes, assuming that each time he opens his snuff-box he spends half a minute doing so, wastes five whole days a year! The notion that it might afford him both pleasure and relaxation did not enter into his calculations, though it will be recalled that on his trip to Carlisle to attend the founding of Dickinson College he had apparently himself almost yielded to the temptation of its use. Rush's campaign against tobacco never gained momentum nor won many adherents, and he abandoned it for more important goals.

With the close of this decade of the 1780's Rush was coming into his own. He now felt the power of his authority and the weight of his words. He signaled this maturity in a eulogy on Dr. William Cullen, his former teacher of Edinburgh days.

"While we celebrate the praises of Dr. Cullen, let us take care lest we check a spirit of free inquiry, by too great a regard for his authority in medicine. I well remember an observation suited to our present purpose which he delivered in his introduction to a course of lectures on the Institutes of Medicine in the year 1766. After speaking of the long continued and extensive empire of Galen in the schools of physic, he said, 'It is a great disadvantage to any science to have been improved by a great man. His authority imposes indolence, timidity, or idolatry upon all who come after him.' Let us avoid these evils in our veneration for Dr. Cullen. To believe in great men, is often as great an obstacle to the progress of knowledge, as to believe in witches and conjurers."

Rush himself had always been a believer in great men and had acknowledged his own strong inclination toward hero worship, which later he called a kind of perversion of Christian piety. Now this phase of his life was past. And what Cullen had said of Galen and what Rush now said of Cullen, soon succeeding generations would be saying of Rush.

11

YELLOW FEVER

❀ TOWARD THE END OF JULY AND AT THE BEGINNING of August in the year 1793 a number of distressed inhabitants from the island of Santo Domingo, who had escaped from the desolation of three years of war and the insurrection of incendiary slaves, arrived in the port of Philadelphia. Beginning with only a shipload or two, their numbers increased until by the end of August more than 2,000 homeless and destitute French-speaking aliens, both black and white, were crowded into this city of 55,000, which was already suffering a housing shortage. They brought disease with them. Rush reports that soon after their arrival the influenza made its appearance and spread rapidly.

On August 5 Dr. Rush was asked to visit the child of Dr. Hugh Hodge, who lived at the foot of Drinker's Alley on Water Street. The little girl was ill with fever of a bilious kind and she had a yellow skin. Two days later she died. The very next day his friend Thomas Bradford, the printer, sent for him to see his wife. She was the former Polly Fisher, for whom Benjamin Rush's heart had raced faster in his Edinburgh days. She, too, had "all the symptoms of a bilious remittent"—so acute, in fact, that she required two bleedings and several successive doses of physic, including calomel. For several days after her recovery her eyes and face were yellow. Within the next twelve days he saw five more such patients. Of these, three recovered and two died.

None of these events "excited the least apprehension . . . of a yellow fever in our city." This is strange, indeed, for yellow fever was not new to Rush. He had treated many patients suffering from it during the days of his apprenticeship under Dr. Redman. His failure to recognize the disease should not be attributed wholly to his persuasion that only one epidemic could prevail at a time and that influenza, which the émigrés from Santo Domingo had also brought with them, then still appeared to be dominant. Nor can he be charged with reluctance to call the Devil by name, for, when he finally came out with it, he was ready to stand up to a storm of abuse from his colleagues. Rush tells us rather that he "had frequently seen sporadic cases in which the common bilious fever of Philadelphia, had put on symptoms of great malignity, and terminated fatally in a few days, and now and then with a yellow color on the skin, before, or immediately after death."

One must realize that without immunological tests, unknown in the days of Rush, the clinical diagnosis of yellow fever, except during an epidemic, and even then, presented great difficulties. The disease was not always associated with yellowing of the skin, whereas some other common febrile illnesses, such as dengue and malaria, were sometimes complicated by jaundice. Perhaps the most ready source of confusion was infectious hepatitis, in which fever, prostration, jaundice and a tendency to hemorrhages are all present, as they are in yellow fever. Still other causes of error could have been both typhus and typhoid fever and the various relapsing fevers of spirochetal origin, which are conveyed by tick bites.

Two weeks after he had seen the Hodge child, Dr. Rush was called in consultation with Dr. Foulke and Dr. Hodge to visit the wife of a Mr. Peter Le Maigre, a merchant from the West Indies. She lived in the very same district as the other patients—on Water Street between Arch and Race Streets, near Ball's Wharf, where a load of coffee had been dumped on July 24 and now lay putrifying in the August heat. The next evening, August 20, Mrs. Le Maigre died. Upon coming out of her room, Dr. Rush remarked to the two other doctors that he had seen an unusual number of cases of bilious fever "with symptoms of uncommon malignity," and that he suspected all was not right in the city. Dr. Hodge had similar misgivings. He said that four or five persons had just died within a stone's throw of the Le Maigre house, one of them twelve hours after coming down with the disorder. Dr. Foulke, a former pupil of Dr. Rush's, spoke of the putrifying coffee and of what a great annoyance it had been to the whole neighborhood. He said it had been brought on the sloop *Amelia* from Santo Domingo—the same ship that had carried the hapless crowd of refugees.

Dr. Rush took thought. He was able to trace all of his cases of fever to the same source, and he enumerated them—the Hodge child, Mrs. Bradford, her sister, Mrs. Leaming, young Mr. McNair, Mrs. Palmer's two sons, Mr. Aston. All of them lived in this same neighborhood or had visited there. Many had complained of having been made sick by the offensive smell. At this point, Dr. Rush, recognizing the disease to be both highly contagious and mortal, did not hesitate to call it the "Bilious remitting Yellow Fever." After all, he had seen an epidemic of it during his apprenticeship in the year 1762, when he had kept an account of it in his notebook.

Soon the report of there being a serious contagious fever at large spread through the city. But it was quickly denied and discredited by many citizens and especially by those physicians who had not yet seen a case. In fact, Rush says he was treated with ridicule and contempt by some of his indignant colleagues. But he recognized this as the lot of anyone who first spreads the word of danger in a community.

Late that night Rush, exhausted from work and worry, sat down at last to write to Julia. She was in Princeton with their younger children. He told her the disturbing news of the epidemic and the fact that twelve persons had already been carried off by it, all in the neighborhood of one of the wharves. Fortunately, it had not spread "beyond the reach of the putrid exhalations which first produced it." He would warn her if it did, and she was to stay in Princeton until he advised her. Most of the cases he attended were "acute and alarming, and require an uncommon degree of vigilance and attention." He assured her that Richard and Ben and all the rest of the family were in good health, but that his devoted Negro servant Marcus was down with influenza.

The tidal wave which Rush saw coming had not yet broken over him. He was still able to write of other things. The very next day he told his wife that he had attended a dinner to celebrate the raising of the roof of the African Church. About 100 white persons, chiefly carpenters, dined at a long table. They were waited on by the Negroes. Then about fifty blacks sat down at the same table and "Six of the most respectable of the white company" waited on them.

"Never did I see people more happy," Rush says in his *Commonplace Book*. "Some of them shed tears of joy." And to Julia he adds, "They forced me to take the head of the table much against my inclinations. . . . I gave them the two following toasts: 'Peace on earth and good will to men,' and 'May African churches everywhere soon succeed to African bondage.' Billy Grey in attempting to express his feelings to us was checked by a flood of tears. . . . To me it will be a day to be remembered with pleasure as long as I live."

Billy Grey, whose wife's funeral Rush had attended, was one of the leaders of the Negroes in Philadelphia. He was soon to distinguish himself by his courageous services in the yellow fever epidemic, in which he joined Richard Allen and Absalom Jones—both freed slaves and both friends of Dr. Rush's—in their heroic, self-sacrificing efforts to nurse the sick and bury the dead.

Three days later Rush acknowledges to Julia that the fever has assumed a most alarming appearance. It has begun to spread through several parts of the city remote from the spot where it had originated. The night before he had lost two patients, a respectable merchant and his only child, and he describes the wife as frantic with grief. And then he addresses his wife with these words:

"After this detail of the state of the fever I need hardly request you to remain for a while with all the children where you are. Many people are flying from the city, and some by my advice. Continue to commit me by your prayers to the protection of that Being who has so often manifested his goodness to our family by the preservation of my life, and I hope I shall do well. I endeavor to have no will of my own. I enjoy good health and uncommon tranquillity of mind. While I depend upon divine protection and feel that at present I live, move, and have my being in a more especial manner in God alone, I do not neglect to use every precaution that experience has discovered to prevent taking the infection. I even strive to subdue my sympathy for my patients; otherwise I should sink under the accumulated load of misery I am obliged to contemplate. You can recollect how much the loss of a single patient used to affect me. Judge then how I must feel in hearing every morning of the death of three or four!"

Thus, to Julia. From late August until mid-November he sends her almost daily bulletins. They reveal him, as nothing else does, with all his anguish and anxiety, all his fear and faith, all his obstinate prejudice, his embattled errors, his brilliance coupled with an egregious lack of common sense, his almost paranoid suspiciousness, his deep kindness, his selfless devotion to the task in hand and, above all, his superlative courage. A picture of him comes into view— sitting alone by candlelight late at night or in the early morning hours, writing, writing, writing, not only letters to his wife, but to his colleagues as well and to the press, and making full notes of the day's observations and experiences for publication.

* * *

At this juncture Rush's writing reveals a mounting realization of the coming tragedy. On August 24 Dr. Hutchinson, the inspector of sickly vessels, wrote to Dr. Rush, at Governor Mifflin's direction, to inquire about the existence and nature of the infectious disorder in the city. Rush replied the same day. The fever, he said, was first confined to Water Street between Race and Arch Streets, but by now it had spread to Second Street and to the village of Kensington. Rush was no longer certain whether it was propagated by contagion or by the original exhalation. Dr. Hutchinson estimated that about forty persons had already died of yellow fever, but Rush amended the number to 150. Both men held the view that the disease was of domestic origin, in spite of the traditional opinion of the citizens and most of the physicians of Philadelphia that yellow fever was imported from the West Indies.

Immediately this became a major cause of controversy. Before long the public grew confounded and bewildered by the clamorous disputations among the medical doctors, which naturally aggravated their mistrust and their growing fears. Even Dr. Rush's own boys, Richard, then thirteen, and Benjamin, seven, were afraid of being infected by his clothes (with some justice, he thought), and so he packed the boys off to his uncle's in Trenton. Others avoided him and, when they passed him on the street, managed to keep to windward. They sniffed rags dipped in vinegar, or smelled pieces of camphor or of tarred rope, or they used snuff freely or smoked cigars—even women did, sometimes to their discomfiture—and they chewed garlic. This was the only precautionary measure he

favored, hoping perhaps that people would keep their distance.
Some even put garlic in their shoes. They lighted fires, burned
gunpowder, whitewashed walls, discharged muskets from their
windows, and the militia rolled out its cannon and let fly several
salvos in the streets. Thus, as the people tried to keep the enemy at
bay, did terror replace reason.

On August 26 the College of Physicians issued a series of recommendations to their fellow citizens. All unnecessary contact with
infected persons should be avoided. The doors of houses containing infected persons should be marked. The strictest cleanliness
must be observed. A stop must be put to the tolling of bells. Burials
should be as private as possible. The streets and wharves were to be
kept as clean as they could be. The members of the College believed that the contagion could pass into and out of the body without producing the fever, and therefore all the occasional causes
should be avoided "to prevent the contagion being excited into action in the body." Among these causes, the College listed fatigue,
exposure to the sun or currents of air, and intemperance. Fires they
thought ineffectual and dangerous; they placed more dependence
upon the burning of gunpowder. Vinegar and camphor were
chiefly of use in infected rooms. This order of the College was
signed by Rush's old adversary, William Shippen Jr.

Three days later, Rush published his own statement in the *American Daily Advertiser*, addressed to the citizens of Philadelphia. He
wanted to leave them in no doubt whatever about the place of
origin of the fever. He boldly espoused and supported its domestic
origin and thus exposed himself to much abuse. Among the secondary causes which introduced what Rush called *"indirect* debility" were not only fatigue, heat, cold and intemperance, but
also fear and grief. In fact, he thought that in many people a
paroxysm of fear brought on the disease and in others death by the
final extinction of hope. Since he was surrounded by terrified and
grieving human beings, it would have been difficult for him to give
these major emotions their proper place among the contributing
causes. In fact, he seems to have seized upon all kinds of coinciden-
tal events as of determining importance—a hard-trotting horse,
gunning, a fall, a blow on the head, or the exertions of manning the
pumps to extinguish a fire; to each of these he ascribed the onset of
the disease. Since people were attacked at night, Rush concluded

that sleep induced direct debility and so disposed the contagion, which floated in the blood, to act with such force upon the system as to destroy its equilibrium and thus excite a fever. Rush obviously had some notions of physiological equilibrium or what, at a later period, would be called "homeostasis," but he had little idea of controlled observations or of statistical evidence.

Rush made many incidental epidemiological notations. There was great mortality in wooden houses, which he attributed to their small size and want of cleanliness; the contagion, he thought, adhered to the wood. The disease was especially prevalent in the crowded parts of the city and could easily travel across narrow streets and alleys. In fact, the morbid exhalations could traverse a distance of two or three miles, unless opposed by houses, woods, or hilly country. Any farmer who lived near a millpond knew this. Rush thought that cases of reinfection were very common—a belief which later evidence was to disprove. At first he thought that Negroes were immune, but before long he changed his mind about this.

* * *

A 20th-century physician, reading Rush's accounts of this melancholy year, can hardly refrain from calling to him across the intervening 170 years and saying:

"Don't you see, Dr. Rush, that what you called morbid exhalations were really nothing but infected mosquitoes? The danger you attributed to putrid coffee or stagnant pools and dank millponds—how nearly right you were. But it wasn't from corrupt material in the atmosphere. It was only from a particular variety of mosquito whose larvae float in these dangerous still waters. How did the mosquito become infected, you might ask. By sucking the blood of a yellow fever patient in the first three febrile days of his illness, during the period of what we now call *viraemia*—that is, while the virus of yellow fever is circulating in the patient's blood. After that it enters his body and works great damage to his internal organs or to his brain and brings on all the symptoms that you were so familiar with.

"Sometimes 80 per cent of all those bitten will die, sometimes only 10 per cent. You can understand how hard it was for you to be sure that what you prescribed for your patients really helped them, without the most careful kind of counting and comparison with other methods of treatment. But you had no time for that and, besides, such an approach to epidemic disease had not yet been heard of. And you never heard of a virus, either. How could you have? Viruses weren't discovered until you had been dead many years, and this is true also of the part the mosquito played. Many heroic men would have to give their lives first to establish these two basic facts.

"Why does a mosquito bite a sufferer from yellow fever, you want to know? It doesn't seek him out especially. It needs blood, or its eggs won't develop. If, by chance, it sucks in the virus with the blood, then, after a period of about nine to twelve days, its bite will become infectious and it will transmit the disease to a non-immune person—to someone who has not already had the disease. Perhaps the reason you thought Negroes were immune is because so many from the West Indies had already had yellow fever. One attack establishes immunity. You were mistaken in thinking that people can have it several times. It is fortunate that they cannot; otherwise preventive inoculation, which was to become so effective, probably would not have worked.

"Of course, the disease was imported from the West Indies. It probably came there originally from Africa, perhaps on slave ships. But you were right. Once it was brought to your native city, it became a domestic disease, spreading by the only agent that can transmit it—the *Aëdes* mosquito. How shrewd you were to have decided finally that the infection wasn't carried from person to person—not by his breath nor his clothing nor his bedding, although it must surely have looked very much as if it were. No one can criticize you for what you could not have known—only for being more certain than you had a right to be. But perhaps that kept up your extraordinary courage and gave courage to others as well. Did you happen to notice a short paragraph that appeared on August 29 in the *American Daily Advertiser*, in the very same issue as your own article? Or were you too driven and too busy to read it? It went like this:

> As the late rains will produce a great increase of mosquitoes in the city, distressing to the sick, and troublesome to those who are well, I imagine it will be agreeable to the citizens to know that the increase of those poisonous insects may be much diminished by a

very simple and cheap mode, which accident discovered. Whoever will take the trouble to examine their rain-water tubs, will find millions of the mosquitoes fishing (?) about the water with great agility, in a state not quite prepared to emerge and fly off: Take up a wine glass full of water, and it will exhibit them very distinctly. Into this glass pour half a teaspoon full, or less, of any common oil, which will quickly diffuse over the surface, and by excluding the air, will destroy the whole brood. Some will survive two or three days but most of them sink to the bottom, or adhere to the oil on the surface within twenty-four hours. A gill of oil poured into a common rain-water cask, will be sufficient: large cisterns may require more; and where the water is drawn out by a pump or by a cock, the oil will remain undisturbed, and last for a considerable time. Hickory ashes have been tried without effect.

"How many lives would have been saved and how much misery averted if you, with all your intelligence and force and articulateness, had guessed the implications of this short paragraph!"

* * *

Two days before the contemporaneous appearance of this passage and his article in the *Daily Advertiser*, Dr. Rush had written to his wife with messages of love for each of the children, adding:

"For some days past, my mind has been so occupied with the immense objects now before me that I had almost forgotten them. Tell them all that the best proof they can give of their affection for their Papa is to pray for his health and life, and to be dutiful to their Mama and kind to each other."

Rush noticed that the symptoms of the disease are very different in different people. Sometimes it begins with a "chilly fit" and a high fever, but more often there is a gradual onset with headache, languor and a sick stomach. The first thing he observed upon entering a sick room was the countenance of the patient, which differed from that of one suffering from a common bilious fever as much as the face of a wild animal is unlike the face of a mild domestic one.

"The eyes were sad, watery, and so inflamed in some cases as to resemble two balls of fire. Sometimes they had a most brilliant or ferocious appearance. . . . The face was suffused with blood, or of a dusky colour, and the whole countenance was downcast and clouded."

After these initial symptoms there were often stupor, delirium, vomiting, a dry skin, cold hands and feet and a feeble slow pulse, sometimes as low as thirty strokes to the minute. Rush was particularly struck with the tendency of patients to self-deception, to deny the seriousness of their illness and to claim that they had nothing more than a common cold—even those who had nursed relations who had died of yellow fever.

By the third or fourth day of the disease, not only the eyes but also the skin became yellow. Few survived the fifth day; but more, Rush found, died on the second and third days. One of his patients stood up and shaved himself on the morning of the day he died. Death was usually preceded by bleeding from the nose, gums and bowels, and the vomiting of black matter. To his despair, Rush discovered that all the common remedies for malignant fevers failed him. Bark, wine and blisters made no impression on the disease, although he believed that some were saved by cold baths or by being wrapped in blankets steeped in warm vinegar. It was on August 29 that he first prescribed mercury, with some advantage, he thought.

On that day twenty-four persons succumbed to the disease in Philadelphia. People were beginning to think the plague had struck. Fear and terror, said Rush, sat on every countenance. A strange apathy pervaded all classes. The streets and roads leading out of the city were crowded with families fleeing for safety in every direction. Rush knew of only one preventive against the infection and that was to fly from it. Business began to languish. Water Street between Market and Race Streets became a desert. In nine days thirty-eight persons in eleven families died on Water Street alone. It was a common sight to see a corpse lying on the shafts of a chaise, without its top, being conducted through the streets by a Negro, with only a handful of mourners walking at a safe distance on the foot pavement. The sound of the wheels passing slowly over the pavement was the only sound to be heard on streets formerly rumbling and clattering with horse-drawn carriages, carts and drays. More than half the houses of the city were shut tight and about a third of the population had fled to the country.

Dr. Rush now seldom entered a house for the first time without meeting the parents or children of one of the sick, in tears. Many who had come to him to ask for advice concerning their relations wept aloud in his entry or parlor. But after a while, grief "descended below weeping" and people began to experience the loss of close relations or friends without shedding a tear. And yet, on September 1, Rush fears that "we have seen only the beginning of the awful visitation." He does not want to tire his wife with tales of woe, but he tells her he cannot help it. He assures her that he is more anxious to be delivered from his sins than to be preserved from the pestilential fever and begs her to help him to be more humble, more patient, more devout and more self-denying in everything.

His sister, Rebecca Wallace, had volunteered to keep house for him during his wife's absence. She and his mother did all they could to help him and protect him from infection. Rebecca placed a small mattress on some chairs, encouraging him to rest whenever he came into the house. Rush was exhausted, not alone from incessant labor, but from perplexity and bafflement. Consonant with his belief that good was commensurate with evil and that no disease existed for which Providence had not provided a remedy, he still hoped that this disease might be cured.

So he began to ransack his library and pore over every book that dealt with yellow fever, but to no avail. Finally he recalled a manuscript which Dr. Franklin had put into his hands shortly before he died. It had been written by a Dr. Mitchell, in 1741. Rush had read it before and had made extracts of it for his lectures. Now he read it for a second time. Suddenly, almost with the force of revelation, he felt the clouds of confusion lift. Whether the magic touch of Benjamin Franklin's influence lay behind this, who is to say?

What impressed him was the recommendation for vigorous purges to rid the viscera of their "feculent corruptible contents." He soon hit upon a powder. It consisted of ten grains of calomel and fifteen grains of jalap. This remedy he prescribed three times a day. Of the medication, Rush states, "It perfectly cured four out of the first five patients to whom I gave it, notwithstanding some of them were advanced several days in the disorder."

Apparently he discounted those who had recovered without such treatment. It is also possible that patients who could survive these heroic doses were so tough that they might have done so without them. But perhaps one should not judge Dr. Rush's methods from a distance of more than a century and a half. For example, he recounts the clinical history of one Richard Spain, a blockmaker in Third Street. After he had been pulseless and covered with a cold sweat for three days, this gentleman's neighbors were beginning to complain that no arrangements had been made for his burial. It was quite customary in these yellow fever cases to have a coffin in the house ready and waiting.

But in this instance it was not necessary. On Dr. Rush's direction, his patient took eighty grains of calomel and even more of jalap mixed with rhubarb, on three successive days. The Doctor's pupil, John Stall, mixed the medicine and gave it with his own hand three or four times a day. This resulted in a return of the pulse and a general warm moisture on the skin, replacing the cold sweat. In a few days Richard Spain was out of danger and soon restored to good health. Rush regarded him as "the first fruit of the efficacy of mercurial purges in yellow fever."

*　　*　　*

In the use of such gargantuan purges one can see the dead hand of Dr. Sydenham. His influence on Benjamin Rush's methods of treating yellow fever had been obvious at the outset, when in early August influenza was prevalent and had become, according to Rush, the "ruling epidemic." By his use of this phrase Rush acknowledged his adherence to the teachings of Dr. Sydenham, who had expounded his theory of epidemics a hundred years before. It was Sydenham whom Rush revered above all physicians and whom he studied to emulate. This great doctor had believed in a kind of hierarchical dominance among epidemics, the stronger one having the capacity to swallow up the weaker and impress its nature and character upon it. Two epidemics of unequal force could not long exist in the same place at the same time. Rush wrote: "Where the monarchy of a single disease was not immediately acknowledged, by a sudden retreat of all contemporary diseases, they were forced to do homage to it, by wearing its livery." To the 20th-century ear this pronouncement has little meaning and sounds much like sympathetic magic. But he was persuaded of the truth of this common law of epidemics. It undoubtedly led to great confusion.

Sydenham's doctrines about epidemics appear to have been based on his knowledge and experience of the recurrent plagues—the Black Death, which had ravaged Europe for more than 300 years after the middle of the 14th century and had therefore lasted into his lifetime. In the first two years, 1348–1350, a quarter of the people of Europe were killed by it, and two centuries passed before the lost population was regained. In England, bubonic plague reached its climax in 1665, when it killed nearly a tenth of the people of London. It is not surprising that Sydenham, who was then in the midst of his career, should have believed that only one epidemic could prevail at a time, because bubonic plague was so rapidly fatal that it seemed to dominate all other diseases.

From Sydenham, too, Rush derived his interest in climatology and his notions of debility, of proximate and predisposing causes, of putrefaction, and of vigorous bloodletting and purging. He joined his master, as well, in not trusting nature but in combatting her, and he applauded him "for having desposed the power of nature in medicine, and thereby put an end to the folly and mischief, which had arisen from a supine and blind attachment to her deadly operations." No wonder that both Sydenham and Rush earned obloquy and persecution from those who held views diametrically opposed to theirs.

Not that Rush thought Sydenham infallible, but in what were called putrid diseases he was satisfied that excessive stimuli produced inflammatory action in the system. In the case of malignant fevers, he adopted his master's further opinion that additional stimuli were imparted from the atmosphere in the form of morbific exhalations. Being no crude and ignorant empiric, but a scientifically-educated physician, Dr. Rush always proceeded according to principle; but far too often he appears to have been prescribing for his principles rather than for a sick man or woman. His devoted, almost obsessional, adherence to a formula, without which he would have felt lost, accounted for the frequent failures of his deductions in the face of what were often brilliant and correct observations on his part.

Although Rush was guided by the authority of Sydenham in the use of rigorous purges in his treatment of yellow fever, he had his own rationale for using them. He thought them detergent to the bile and mucus which lined the bowels, and he believed that they acted in a peculiar manner on the biliary ducts. The reason he repeated the doses so frequently while the fever continued was based partly on his notion that in all bilious fevers there is a reproduction of morbid bile as fast as it is discharged. To be sure, he did examine many organs after death, but to his surprise found little evidence of disturbances in the liver. Undoubtedly his methods were insufficiently refined to detect the necrosis of hepatic tissue, which is so characteristic of this disease, and which permits bile to pass from the biliary ducts directly into the blood stream.

This alone would account for many of the symptoms that puzzled Rush. Bile in the circulating blood is highly toxic and also has some very specific effects. It delays the coagulation of blood, leading to hemorrhages into the skin and viscera. It makes the capillary walls more permeable, so that the blood has a tendency to leak through them and accumulate in the stomach or intestines or lungs or kidneys. It depresses the action of the heart, leading to a phenomenon to which Rush frequently called attention— namely, a slow pulse in the presence of high fever, and, as everyone knows who has been jaundiced, it has a markedly depressing effect on the mood. These results were all too familiar to Rush, but he did not understand their cause. Accordingly he applied a remedy in which he had such unquestioning and unbounded faith that he could not help misinterpreting its effects, especially in a disease in which the outcome was so variable and unpredictable. Even in the same family, one member could have so light a case that it seemed only a negligible indisposition, and another could die within twenty-four hours.

The time-honored companion to purging was bloodletting. This, too, had the solemn sanction of Sydenham. Bleeding patients almost to death or at least to the point of fainting was no new medical maneuver. What induced Rush to resort to it were the following manifestations of the disease: the state of the pulse; the appearance of a moist, white tongue; frequent hemorrhages from every part of the body which, he found, gave perfect relief in some cases; and symptoms of congestion of the brain. He was reinforced in his belief by the appearance of the blood itself and by the highly inflammatory nature of the fever, which he attempted to counteract by depletion. Rush found that bloodletting raised the pulse rate when it was depressed, that it also reduced its force and frequency, checked vomiting, removed delirium, coma and obstinate wakefulness, and checked or prevented hemorrhages. It also imparted strength to the system, caused the redness of the eyes to disappear and eased pain.

This was particularly clear in the case of Dr. Redman's daughter. Her pains increased after three bleedings, but yielded to the fourth. He recalled Sydenham's remark that moderate bleeding did harm in the plague where copious bleeding was indicated. "Bloodletting," according to Rush, "when used *early* on the first day, frequently strangled the disease in its birth and generally rendered it more light, and convalescence more speedy and perfect."

It is, of course, self-evident that bleeding would raise the pulse rate and reduce its force, or even put an end to vomiting and to pain, if for no other reason than that of weakness and cerebral anemia. Many of his patients must already have been grossly anemic from nosebleeds or from internal hemorrhages and blood destruction. The oxygen-carrying capacity of their blood was certainly diminished, as was their blood pressure. Rush seems to have added insult to injury by reducing still further the blood supply to the brain, heart and other vital centers. Since he had no precise knowledge of the total volume of the circulating blood, his massive bleedings must have come close to exsanguinating some of his patients. Why they recovered so promptly—assuming that they did—is hard to explain.

Toward the end of the epidemic Rush drew from seventy to eighty ounces from a patient in five days, and in some cases much more. Mr. Gribble, a cedar-cooper on Front Street, lost 100 ounces in ten bleedings; Mr. George, a carter, was bled the same quantity in five days; and Mr. Peter Mierken, 114 ounces in five days. In the amount of blood to be withdrawn, Rush seems to have been governed by the state of the pulse and the temperature of the weather.

He was convinced that when he was called in to see a patient on the first day of illness and was immediately able to start his treatments, his patient was sure to recover. He does not seem to have counted on several important facts—namely, that his attendance caused the patient to take to his bed, to keep quiet and sometimes even to have the services of a nurse; that many patients recovered who did not have the benefit of being visited by him at all; and, furthermore, that Dr. Rush brought with him into the sickroom such courage, such confidence and such comfort that this alone must have had a healing effect.

Although he was exposed to constant anxiety, he kept calm. Dr. Hutchinson was dead; Dr. Kuhn was down with the disease; his great friend, Dr. Wistar, a little worse than the day before. Dr. John Morris expired just as Rush entered his room on the morning of September 8. His mother ran from her son's bed into the Doctor's arms and gave vent to such pathetic outpourings of grief that he was struck dumb and, finding himself "sinking into sympathy," broke from her arms and ran to other scenes of distress. He tells Julia that he is not only preserved in health "but in uncommon tranquility of mind." He has been depressed only twice "by a sudden paroxysm of sympathy with the distressed," and he has quite lost his fear of death from disease. In fact, he is possessed of perfect composure in the sickroom, where he stills his patients' fears by telling them that they have nothing but a yellow fever and that mercury and jalap are sure to cure them.

Between the 8th and 15th of September he visited and prescribed for between 100 and 120 patients a day; his pupils each visited between twenty and thirty more. For a while they refused no calls. The household then included his mother and sister, his Negro servant Marcus, a mulatto boy, and five pupils: Warner Washington and Edward Fisher of Virginia, John Alston of South Carolina, John Redman Coxe, the grandson of Dr. Redman, and John Stall of Philadelphia. With one heart, he says, they all devoted themselves to his service and to the cause of humanity. His house was filled with patients, chiefly poor ones, seeking advice. For many weeks he seldom ate a meal without prescribing for numbers of them as he sat at table. Soon Mr. Stall, Mr. Fisher and Mr. Coxe moved into the house to help round the clock.

*   *   *

Dr. Rush now changes his manner of living. He stops drinking wine and malt liquors, gives up eating meat, and instead eats sparingly of weak broth, potatoes, raisins, coffee, and bread and butter. This, he thinks, rids him of a troublesome headache which he feared meant that he was taking the fever. His body, he thinks, has become "highly impregnated with the contagion;" his eyes and even his face are yellow, and his pulse rapid. He suffers from profuse night sweats. It is improbable that any of these symptoms were evidence of his having contracted yellow fever. They sound much more like the beginnings of a pulmonary tuberculosis, which his frequent attacks of pleurisy and generally enfeebled health also suggest. His sleep begins to suffer. There is no rest or refreshment from it. People are constantly knocking at his door. In the evening he wishes it were morning and in the morning the prospect of what lies before him makes him wish for the end of the day. At one time he has more than thirty heads of families under his care, some of them with as many as ten dependent children, and all in imminent danger.

He would get up at six in the morning, drenched with perspiration, only to find a number of persons waiting for him. When he unlocked his front door, he would find notes begging his help. "Jacob Blackwell presents his respects to Doctr. Rush and informs him that he still has that fever hanging on him and begs the further attention of the Doctor. . . . Mrs. Clarkson [wife of the mayor] was seized this morning early with a chilliness & is now very unwell, I request you will call immediately & see her.". . . "Please to come & see my daughter," wrote William Innes. "She was taken this morning with a headache & sick stomach there is no person to bleed her. . . . Will the humane Dr. Rush condescend to step to the house of mourning—another of my family is ill & I have not a person to send out—my afflicted sister requiring two women to be constantly with her.":

No one called in vain. It was meat and drink to Rush to fulfill his duties. In spite of his illness, his sense of the success of his practice gave a tone to his mind and a "preternatural vigour" to his body. He needed both. He gives the following account of his activities on September 14, and the next days. After eight o'clock in the evening he visited the son of Mrs. Berriman, who had sent for him early in the morning. Dr. Rush found the young man very ill. He had already been bled in the morning on the Doctor's advice, but now the state of his pulse indicated a second bleeding. Since no bleeders were procurable so late, Rush bled the patient himself.

"From hanging over his breath and blood for ten minutes and afterwards riding home in the night air, debilitated as I was by the labours of the day, I found myself much indisposed the ensuing night. I rose notwithstanding at my usual hour. At 8 o'clock I lost ten ounces of blood, and immediately afterwards got into my chair, and visited between forty and fifty patients before dinner. At the house of one of them, I was forced to lie down a few minutes. In the course of this morning's labours, my mind was suddenly thrown off its pivots, by the last look, and the pathetic cries of a friend for *help*, who was dying under the care of a French physician. I came home about two o'clock, and was seized immediately afterwards with a chilly fit and a high fever. I took a dose of the mercurial medicine, and went to bed. In the evening I took a second purging powder, and lost ten ounces more of blood. The next morning I bathed my face, hands, and feet in cold water for some time. I drank plentifully during the day and night, of weak hyson tea, and of water, in which current jelly had been dissolved. At 8 o'clock I was so well as to admit persons who came for advice into my room . . . . The next day I came down stairs, and prescribed in my parlour for not less than an hundred people. On the 19th of the same month, I resumed my labours, but in great weakness. It was with difficulty that I ascended a pair of stairs, by the help of a banister. A slow fever, attended with irregular chills, and a troublesome cough, hung constantly upon me. . . . The contagion now began to affect me in small and infected rooms, in the most sensible manner."

Even his patients noticed how hot his hands were. On one of his visits he suddenly became dizzy and faint from the stench of the sickroom and he sank down on a bed. This was followed by a fever which kept him at home during the remaining part of the day. For five or six weeks, though far from well, he saw between fifty and 150 persons a day who came to him for advice. In the evening he answered letters from all over the Union and also continued his usual correspondence, including his touching letters to Julia. Now, for the first time, he had to refuse many patients every day and this caused him great distress. In one of his penetrating pieces of psychosomatic insight, he says, "Sympathy when it vents itself in acts of humanity, affords pleasure, and contributes to health, but the reflux of pity, like anger, gives pain, and disorders the body." In riding through the streets, he had to resist the entreaties of parents imploring a visit to their children or of children to their parents. He writes:

"I recollect, and even yet, I recollect with pain, that I tore myself at one time from five persons in Moravian-alley who attempted to stop me; by suddenly whipping my horse, and driving my chair as speedily as possible beyond the reach of their cries."

*   *   *

Now his distress reached its apogee. On September 11 his pupil, Warner Washington, fell victim to the disease. He had managed to conceal his danger from Dr. Rush until the day before he died. On September 23 a second pupil, his dear and amiable Johnny Stall, breathed his last in the back bedroom of Dr. Rush's house. He had been delirious from the start and had refused medication. His death seems to have touched Rush especially. He regarded him as a most accomplished youth, possessed not only of an uncommon genius for science, but talented also in music, painting and poetry. For years Rush carried with him a scrap of paper on which the young man had begun a note addressed to his father. A few months later Rush sent a silver cup to the young man's mother, inscribed as a mark of his "esteem for your late excellent son and my much beloved pupil."

"Scarcely had I recovered from the shock of the death of this amiable youth when I was called to weep for a third pupil, Mr. Alston, who died in my neighbourhood the next day." Alston had gone to take care of his fiancée, Miss Wilson, and caught the disease in her house. He would permit no one but Dr. Rush to bleed him, and Dr. Rush was not to be found. Next, Edward Fisher collapsed and was put to bed in the front room.

The house had turned into a hospital. Marcus, his Negro servant, who had been trained to mix powders, apply blisters and give enemas, as expertly as any apothecary, now came down with the disease and was put to bed in the laboratory. Only Coxe, Peter, the mulatto boy, and Mrs. Wallace, Dr. Rush's indomitable sister, were still up and about. At noon on the 26th of September, Coxe, his only remaining assistant, was seized with the fever and left to be with his grandfather, Dr. Redman, who himself was gravely ill and whom Rush had just attended. Two hours later his sister, overcome with fatigue and anxiety, had to take to her bed, as also did their mother, who was enfeebled and much indisposed.

At eight that evening, Rush tells us, a solemn stillness pervaded the streets. He had been putting up medicines to be distributed the next day among his patients and was seated in the back parlor, trying to chase away his melancholy thoughts by writing to his wife, when Marcus, just out of bed but weak from his bout of fever, crept to the door. Dr. Rush invited him in to sit by the fire, but his dull silence only added to the overwhelming sense of gloom.

Five days later, at two in the afternoon, his sister Rebecca died. Within an hour after she expired, Dr. Rush got into his carriage and spent the afternoon in visiting his patients. For years thereafter he worried about whether he had done the right thing by this apparently callous behavior. There seems little doubt of his devotion to her. She had been his nurse in sickness and had constantly helped him and advised him about where to spend his energies. She had refused an invitation to go to the country and was quite willing to risk her life—indeed, to sacrifice it—in order to save his. Her body was put in a plain coffin; there was no money for a mahogany one. Only Marcus and Peter and Billy Grey followed the hearse. Rush said that his heart descended into the grave with her. Some time later it was marked with a handsome tombstone bearing this inscription:

An Affectionate and Grateful Brother
Hath Caused this stone to be Erected
in Memory of
Rebecca Wallace
Who Died October 1, 1793. Aged 49 Years
While She Was Performing the Highest
Acts of Kindness to Him, And of
Humanity to the Distressed Citizens
of Philadelphia.

After this unhappy event, Rush's own health and strength declined. All motion became painful to him. He lost his appetite. His night sweats continued. His sleep was constantly disturbed by the most distressing and frightful dreams in which he rehearsed agonizing scenes from sickrooms and graveyards. He did his best to conceal his sorrows from his patients, but when alone he frequently wept over the loss not only of members of his family but also of many sincere and affectionate friends. He grieved as well for members of his own profession: Dr. Pennington, whose great and expanded mind was shattered by delirium; and Dr. John Morris, whose mother's grief had so upset him. He was literally surrounded by the infection. Four persons died in the house next door on the east, three a few doors beyond on the west, and five more on the opposite side of the street to the south. To the north, 150 feet from his house, the fever prevailed with great malignity in the family of Mr. James Gresson.

Many of the poor were bled by his pupils in his shop or in the yard, where, for lack of bowls, the blood was allowed to spill on the ground, only to putrify there and attract flies and mosquitoes. Streams of contagion, Rush believed, were constantly pouring into his house and being conveyed into his body by the air and in the food he swallowed. He gave up his ordinary precautions. He rested at his patients' bedsides and even drank milk or ate fruit in their sickrooms, so sure was he that he was already thoroughly saturated with the contagion. He felt as weak as an old man of eighty, hardly able to totter up a dozen stairs, and so reduced during the past two months that there was nothing left of him but his voice and his usual spirits. He had grown gaunt. His hands were blackened by mercury and his usual meticulous appearance was now shabby. There was a general breakdown of all services and supplies in the city. Cash was not to be had. The seat of government had moved to Germantown, where the President and his Cabinet met. Washington had been in Mount Vernon when the epidemic broke out and seldom returned to the city.

*   *   *

In spite of the relentless criticism of many of his colleagues, Rush stood unmoved by what he called their "dull and wicked confederacy." Of these, Dr. Kuhn was the captain, but Kuhn had attended only four patients when he was taken ill with a remittant fever, had fled from town and was now safe "in his lurking hole at Bethlehem." Perhaps what distressed Rush most was that his cordial friends, Dr. Wistar and Dr. Currie, stood up against him. They were joined by others. His former classmate and confidant, Ebenezer Hazard, described him as a perfect Sangrado, the bloodthirsty quack in *Gil Blas*, who "would order blood enough to be drawn to fill Mambrino's helmet, with as little ceremony as a mosquito would fill himself upon your leg." Next, Alexander Hamilton publicly lent the weight of his name in support of his own physician, Dr. Stevens, lately of the island of St. Croix, where he had had extensive experience in treating yellow fever. Dr. Stevens in turn addressed a most polite letter to the College of Physicians, outlining his plan of treatment, which was tonic and supportive and consisted of the administration of bark, Madeira wine, cold baths and good nursing care.

The difference in treatment was the logical upshot of the theoretical interpretation of what occurred in the disease. Stevens and others of his view aimed their treatment at the extreme debility of the animal functions and the great derangement of the nervous system which had to be counteracted by stimulating measures. Rush was persuaded that the debility resulted from an excess of stimulus of contagion upon the system, and thus only by depleting measures could these stimuli be abstracted.

History has favored the milder view. Where no specific remedy for a disease is known, supportive treatment has always been the better choice. But Dr. Rush was a stubborn and a stalwart man. He had resolved to stick to his principles, his practice and his patients to the last extremity. He was not alone in his stand; among others, Dr. Redman shared his views. On September 29 Rush wrote to his wife:

"Never was the healing art so truly delightful to me! and never had I more reason to be thankful than I now have for the honor God has done me in giving me health enough to renew my intercourse with my patients."

Now he began to keep his weather eye cocked. He knew that a heavy rain would weaken the contagion, but that nothing but a frost would finally and totally destroy it. Although the days started out cloudy and the barometer fell slightly, by October 5 the skies were fair again and no rain fell till the end of the month. Yet he could not be discouraged. He started to mend and "through divine goodness even to thrive on labor, care, persecution, and a milk and vegetable diet." In spite of all the purging and bleeding, all the bark and the wine, and all the acrimonious disputes of the doctors, the epidemic ran its course. According to Rush's figures, between the 1st of August and the 9th of November, 4,044 people had died. This was nearly 10 per cent of the citizens of Philadelphia. The peak of the death rate came on October 11, when the registry showed that 119 persons succumbed to the disease. On November 9, only six died. But by that time the cool weather and the autumn rains had arrived. A month before, Rush recorded:

"I visited a considerable number of patients, and as the day was warm, I lessened the quantity of my clothing. Towards evening I was seized with a pain in the back, which obliged me to go to bed at eight o'clock. About twelve I awoke with a chilly fit. A violent fever with acute pains in different parts of my body, followed it. At one o'clock I called for Mr. Fisher who slept in the next room. He came instantly, with my affectionate black man to my relief. I saw my danger painted in Mr. Fisher's countenance. He bled me plentifully and gave me a dose of the mercurial medicine. This was immediately rejected. He gave me a second dose, which likewise acted as an emetic, and discharged a large quantity of bile from my stomach. The remaining part of the night was passed under an apprehension that my labours were near an end. I could hardly expect to survive so violent an attack of the fever, broken down, as I was, by labour, sickness and grief.

"My wife and seven children, whom the great and distressing events that were passing in our city, had jostled out of my mind for six or seven weeks, now resumed their former place in my affections. My wife had stipulated, in consenting to remain in the country, to come to my assistance in case of my sickness; but I took measures, which, without alarming her, proved effectual in preventing it. My house was a Lazaretto, and the probability of my death made her life doubly necessary to my family.

"In the morning, the medicine operated kindly, and my fever abated. In the afternoon it returned, attended with a great inclination to sleep. Mr. Fisher bled me again which removed the sleepiness. The next day the fever left me, but in so weak a state, that I awoke two successive nights with a faintness which threatened the extinction of my life. It was removed each time by taking a little aliment. My convalescence was extremely slow. I returned in a very gradual manner to my former habits of diet. The smell of animal food, the first time I saw it at my table, forced me to leave the room. During the month of November, and all the winter months I was harassed with a cough, and a fever somewhat of the hectic kind. The early warmth of the spring, removed these complaints, and I now enjoy, through divine goodness, my usual state of health."

Rush never experienced any doubt that he and his pupils had saved hundreds of lives and that scores had been sacrificed to the mischief perpetrated by those doctors who disapproved of his methods. The fact that he had an attack of what he considered yellow fever and had submitted to his own treatment at the hands of his pupils was an added earnest of his belief in his method. Yet the fact that three of his five pupils and his own sister had died of yellow fever was ammunition for his enemies. Of course, he had his excuses and extenuations. He had been called in too late, or his patients had refused to be purged and bled sufficiently, or good nursing had become impossible to procure. On November 12 he wrote his wife:

"I want words to describe my emotions upon hearing that the dearest person to me upon the face of the earth, is at last within three miles of me after a long and most distressing separation. . . . If you come to town, you shall have the front room (now the purest in the house) to yourself. I will sleep in the room adjoining you with the door open between us. Kiss Ben. But—ah—who will kiss my dear Julia?"

12

A CONTROVERSIAL
FIGURE

❀ ALTHOUGH THE PEAK OF THE EPIDEMIC HAD PASSED,
Benjamin Rush continued to be attacked, criticized and excoriated
by his colleagues, by his enemies and by some of his former friends,
including Ebenezer Hazard. He believed that his colleague, Dr.
Kuhn, was in the van of those against him. However, a few of his
medical brethren shared his views and remained loyal to him. Rush
suffered severely from the opposition which his methods of practice
and his manner of defending them evoked. It was said of him that
his purges were meant for a horse, not for a man, and that he had
waded through the epidemic in a bath of his patients' blood. He
was even charged with murdering them by his excessive bloodlet-
tings.

Rush remained obdurate and immovable. Indeed, had he not
taught his methods to clergymen, to apothecaries and to Negroes
alike, as well as to the general lay public, instructing all of them to
take a mercurial purge and to send for a bleeder as soon as the first
symptoms of the disease appeared? Was this in itself not evidence,
he argued, for his good faith and his innocence of greed?

Rush attributed these acts of hostility to the sudden increase of
his practice and to public expressions of gratitude by the many persons whose lives he believed he had saved. Although he protested
seven years later in his autobiography that, in spite of the "most inveterate malice" to which he had been exposed, he had felt no

bitterness during this period of his life, his behavior belies his claim. He refused to consult with those of his colleagues whose views differed from his own, believing that the sick are made to suffer further when they are treated by physicians of opposite principles and practice. His former pupil, Charles Caldwell—the one with whom he had had so unpleasant a controversy—spoke of him as having become "much more than usually dogmatical in the assertion of his opinions, and more impetuous, irrespective, and overbearing in his manners." He was also accused of talking aloud to himself while walking on the street alone and of gesticulating as if he were conversing with someone. Such were the rumors about him, and they undoubtedly injured him greatly. If he was tense, overwrought, opinionated and irritable, he was also sick and worn out to the point of nearly complete exhaustion.

On November 5, 1793, Rush had sent a letter to Dr. John Redman, the President of the College of Physicians, tendering his resignation from fellowship in the College. Accompanying the letter was a copy of the works of Sydenham. In no way could he have better expressed his fundamental disagreement with his fellow members in the College. At the close of his account of the epidemic of 1793 he had written:

"My principal aim has been to revive, and apply to it, the principles, and practice of Dr. Sydenham, and however coldly those principles, and that practice may be received by some physicians of the present day, I am satisfied that experience in all ages, and in all countries, will vouch for their truth and utility."

One of Sydenham's chief contentions had been that epidemics occur only when a certain constitution of the atmosphere is present. It was this belief that had persuaded Rush that the yellow fever in Philadelphia had not been imported but was of local origin. His notions about bleeding also derived from Sydenham, but Sydenham and, later, Redman both gave up excessive bleeding. Not Rush, however. To him all diseases were due essentially to a single cause; namely, vascular tension, and for this there was one universal remedy—to decrease that tension by removing blood in great quantity. Bleeding, according to Dr. Rush, should be repeated while the symptoms which first indicated it continue, even if four-fifths of the blood contained in the body is withdrawn. He did not hesitate to remove a quart at a time every forty-eight or seventy-two hours. The remarkable recovery of a woman patient who had bled accidentally and profusely during the night from a vein that had been opened for bloodletting impressed him greatly, because it appeared to support his theoretical interpretation of fevers.

He taught, and this is recorded in his students' notes, that the body contained between twenty-five and twenty-eight pounds of blood. But he had no way of measuring blood volume such as we have. The fact is that the body of a man of average size contains about six quarts of blood and not twelve, as Rush believed. Because of this miscalculation he must, indeed, have nearly exsanguinated some of his patients. And yet such was his enthusiasm that he repeatedly claimed to have lost not more than one out of twenty patients, whereas at "Bush *Kill*," as he called the emergency hospital at Bush Hill, two-fifths of all the patients succumbed.

Besides the theoretical reasons, his indications for bloodletting were principally two—the state of the pulse and the appearance of the blood in the bleeding bowl. He listed ten variations from the full, frequent, tense pulse to an imperceptible one that made him decide to open a vein. As for the blood, the more *sizy* it was, the more clear the indications for bleeding became. By sizyness he was referring to the buffy coat of fibrin and trapped white corpuscles that forms on the surface of the shed blood in a container. This results from the sedimentation of the red blood corpuscles. We now know, and indeed Rush's own teacher, John Hunter, had taught in 1786, that in inflammatory states and in pregnancy the red cells sink more rapidly and are therefore not caught up in the clot, thus leaving a thick buffy coat behind them. Rush could have known this fact; but if he did, he paid no attention to it. He was partly right in regarding the thickness of the coat as evidence of an inflammatory process, but he was wrong in seeing it as an indication for bleeding, especially as the anemia, which he was inducing in his patients, increased the sedimentation rate and consequently the sizyness of the blood. Thus the more he bled, the greater were the indications to him for further bleeding.

The controversy over bloodletting was to rage for many years to come. It reached its peak in Edinburgh, where bleeding had been so much in vogue during Rush's student days. Many years later Dr. John Hughes Bennett, a graduate of the Edinburgh School and also a rebel like Rush but of a different turn of mind, would stand alone against the whole medical school and all the worthy descendants of Gregory and Cullen to point out the fallacy of bloodletting and the misconception of inflammation upon which it was based. He had been educated in Germany and France and was a pioneer in the use of the microscope in clinical pathology. Not until the middle of the 19th century was the useless spilling of blood finally discontinued as a routine medical procedure.

Rush's egregious and obsessional stubbornness and his singular incapacity for self-criticism must be looked upon as an automatic defensive maneuver in the face of the overwhelming anxiety and tragedy that surrounded him. He simply had to be right, especially since he felt appointed by God to save his afflicted city. He was the stuff that heroes and martyrs are made of. If he was condemned by some, he was as extravagantly praised and almost worshiped by the common people, to whom he appeared as the great and benevolent friend of mankind.

But he had not been alone in his heroism, nor in his devoted efforts to save his fellow citizens from doom. Mayor Mathew Clarkson, when his wife lay gravely ill with yellow fever and his young doctor son, a former student of Rush's, had died of the disease, had stood steadfast and alone at the head of the city government. President Washington and Governor Mifflin were gone. In the midst of almost total disintegration of the city, Clarkson had sent out a call for help. Nearly thirty volunteers had responded. With the Mayor they formed a committee to govern the city. They solicited funds in the form of bonds for $1,500 from the Bank of North America; they acquired a mansion, Bush Hill, and converted it into a hospital. It was at first a bedlam and a shambles, where the indigent and the moribund were brought to die or to share the beds of still warm corpses. Through the selfless and tireless efforts of two men it was gradually converted into a decent and efficient organization. Stephen Girard, sea captain and a prosperous French importer, and Peter Helm, a German cooper, together performed this quiet miracle.

Girard had managed to maneuver the American doctors out and to put in charge Dr. Jean Devèze, a French officer from the West Indies, who had had much experience with yellow fever at Cap François. Neither of these men looked on the disease as contagious, and they had no fears of infection; nor was Dr. Devèze a bloodletter. He used the French cure of stimulants and quinine, about which Rush was so skeptical. Rush claimed never to have lost a Negro patient from yellow fever and pointed, by contrast, to the high death rate among Negroes at Bush Hill, concluding that the difference was due to the methods of treatment. But he seems not to have taken into account the condition of the patients at the time of their admission to the hospital—that is to say, whether they were then already in the terminal stages of the disease.

The list of heroes could be lengthened to include some of the guardians of the poor, who searched out abandoned infants and orphans from deserted homes and brought them, and also paupers, to shelter either at Bush Hill or to the tent hospital established later. It would include as well the three Negroes, Billy Grey, Richard Allen, and Absalom Jones, on whose help Rush had so greatly depended. But at the head of the list was Benjamin Rush himself. He had not only shown superlative courage but had brought courage to others as well.

*   *   *

For the next decade and more, Rush was to be occupied with sporadic and endemic outbreaks of yellow fever. Almost each year from 1793 to 1805 his *Medical Inquiries and Observations* gives running accounts of the clinical and pathological manifestations of the disease with all its protean changes. Since he recognized how unwelcome bloodletting had become and how reluctant many patients were to submit to it, he began to propose other depleting remedies, such as sweating and salivation by mercury inunction. But he never abandoned bleeding and purging as the two sovereign remedies. He was confident of a patient's recovery when he was called in on the first day of illness and was allowed to apply his remedies at once. Indeed, he offered a kind of crude statistical evidence for his belief, but, of course, it was without adequate controls.

Concerning one aspect of this dread disease, however, he did change his mind. He finally became convinced that it was not contagious, but was transmitted through a particular quality of the atmosphere. In this opinion he was supported and helped not only by Noah Webster, who had published in 1799 *A Brief History of Epidemic and Pestilential Diseases,* but also by his erstwhile pupil

Charles Caldwell, with whom after the initial contretemps Rush became reconciled. Rush freely acknowledges his indebtedness to both men.

In discussing the cause and the means of transmission of yellow fever, Rush exhibited an analytical astuteness that he seldom displayed when it came to treatment, where he was more the advocate and propagandist than the critical observer. He might have been comforted, and perhaps dismayed, as well, to learn that after more than a century and a half we still do not know how to cure this disease even though we do know how to prevent it. One of his colleagues wrote him in 1799 from Charleston, quoting a local physician:

"I wish no person would send for me, for I know nothing of this disease, and am as ignorant as a child unborn—for let me do as I will, puke, purge or bleed, still they die."

And Rush himself wrote a little later:

"There is a grade of benevolence in our profession much higher than that which arises from the cure of diseases. It consists in exterminating their causes."

Dr. Rush was not one who could accept criticism or tolerate opposition without redoubling his efforts to prove himself right. As many innovators have been since, he was up against a kind of chamber of commerce mentality in the community. Each time yellow fever showed its frightening face, the first need was either to deny its existence or to call it by some other name. On Christmas Eve 1794, Elizabeth Drinker made the following entry in her diary:

"I have been led to think, I may say to conclude, on reading Doc^r Rush's acct. of the Yellow fever, that my daugh^r Nancy had it towards the end of October last, at Clearfield—and do suppose that Doc^r Kuhn, who attended her, knowing that we would steadily attend her, be it what it would, kindly endeavoured to conceal it from us—he say'd it was the Jaundice and some thing of the fall fever—it is possible it may be so,—but as it has pleas'd kind providence to restore her, I intend at a sutable oppertunity to tell the Doctor my opinion of the matter, and I have no doubt of his candour on the occasion,—I suspected it while nursing her by many of the symptoms, and finding many others in D^r R^s book, seems a confirmation."

Then a few months later she added:

"I ask'd Doc^r K——— the other day, if it was not the Yallow fever that Nancy had last fall, he answer'd in the negative. Notwithstanding all my conjectures."

This was to be a commonly repeated experience. Each time a denial, each time an assertion that it was imported or had been caught from someone else by direct contact. To believe that it was in some way indigenous would have been to cast aspersions on the fair city of Philadelphia, the flower of the United States, or on New York, or Providence, or Baltimore, or Boston, or on the aristocratic Commonwealth of Virginia. But it occurred also in Chester, Wilmington, New London, Connecticut, and Windsor, Vermont. In all of these places yellow fever kept erupting from time to time. Surely there could be nothing balefully unsalubrious about the atmosphere in such widely scattered places.

Rush's arguments were in the main tough and logical. He could see no virtue in quarantine laws nor in shunning afflicted citizens, which only frightened them and distressed their relatives. Here are some of his incidental observations: Of the year 1797, as bad a year as 1793, although more people had fled from town, he wrote "that moschetoes were more numerous during the prevalence of the fever than in 1793." He thought the disease more malignant than the fevers of 1793 and 1794. On the 21st of July (1798) the ship *Deborah* arrived from the West Indies and discharged her cargo in the city. She was moored at Kensington, where the foul air from her hold produced several cases of yellow fever. In August the disease appeared in nearly every part of the city. Any change in the weather short of frost, Rush believed, caused the disease to spread. He states specifically that the origin of the fever was from the exhalations of gutters, docks, cellars, common sewers, ponds of stagnating water and from the foul air of the ships such as the *Deborah*.

Rush observed that yellow fever did not spread in the country when carried there from cities. Nor did it spread in yellow fever hospitals when they were beyond the impure air in which it was generated; nor again in the cities from any specific matter emitted from the bodies of sick people. He cites the experiment of Dr. Ffirth, who inoculated himself more than twenty times in different parts of his body with the black matter discharged from the stomachs of yellow fever patients, and also with their blood, serum and saliva, without coming down with the disease. This intrepid man had even swallowed their vomitus with no ill effects.

Again and again, Rush comes back "to certain noxious qualities in the atmosphere, as the exclusive causes of the prevalence, not only of that fever, but (with a few exceptions) of all other epidemic diseases. It is true, we are as yet ignorant of the precise nature of those qualities in the air which produce epidemics." He was narrowing his focus to dirty streets and gutters, to stagnant water, poor drainage and the exhalations of putrifying animal and vegetable matter. He therefore favored the proper ventilation of sickrooms, the drainage or covering of marshy grounds and the cleaning up of streets, gardens, yards, privies and cellars. He pointed to the extraordinary degree of cleanliness of those cities in Holland and Great Britain which had rid themselves of the plague.

Although Rush first believed that yellow fever was contagious in the sense that smallpox is, passing from person to person by direct contact, he later quite changed his mind and thought it arose locally from miasmata produced by decaying vegetable matter. He therefore vigorously upheld local sanitation as against quarantine, which his opponents favored. Of course, time has shown that both sanitation and quarantine are essential to prevention.

Dr. Rush never differentiated clearly between bubonic plague and yellow fever, although their clinical history and the means of their transmission are quite different—the one by the rat flea, the other by the mosquito—as was to be proved much later. Nor had he a clear notion of specific causes. In fact, he lent an ear, although perhaps a skeptical one, to various superstitions and old wives' tales. For example, certain trees give out a bad odor before yellow fever breaks out, cattle sicken and cats when rubbed do not emit sparks of electricity or when thrown from a window do not land on all four feet. Thus did the dead hand of medievalism press upon Dr. Rush in spite of his clear-eyed and realistic appraisal of the circumstances that gave rise to this disease.

*   *   *

After 1797 Benjamin Rush's practice began steadily to decline. No new families, except foreigners, came to him for treatment and many of his old patients deserted him. Nothing, he thought, could

resist the tide of public clamor that had been raised against his practice. "My name," he wrote later, "was mentioned with horror in
some companies, and to some of the weakest and most insignificant
of my brethren false tales of me became a recommendation to popular favor." During the winter of 1798 Rush helped form the
Academy of Medicine, whose principal purpose was to prove the
domestic origin of yellow fever. This was in opposition to the College of Physicians, from which he had resigned. The real case
against him was based partly on his opinions about the origin of
yellow fever and partly on his methods of treatment and on his insistent claims for them. He was supported in his views by such a
distinguished physician as Dr. Philip Syng Physick, and by others.
Even his adversary, Kuhn, in the extremity of the epidemic of
1797, finally resorted to bloodletting, as did other members of the
College. Rush, however, began to feel deserted and ringed about
by his enemies. He was too sensitive and too idealistic to tolerate the
foray against him. But if his judgment and his tact were wanting,
no one could possibly have questioned his motives nor his devotion
to what he felt to be the public good.

Two years before this his mother had died in her seventy-eighth
year. He had been inordinately attached to her, and although now
deeply bereft he was comforted by his religion. With her dying
breath she had uttered the words, "Sweet Jesus." Rush never
doubted that she would be reunited with his father, by whose side
she was buried in Christ Church graveyard. Not long thereafter his
only remaining sister, Rachel Montgomery, died in Harrisburg.
She, too, was full of faith and hope of happiness beyond the grave.

Except for his stalwart Julia, always the sensible helpmeet, who
did her best to calm him through his turbulence and grief, Rush
felt abandoned and alone. She seems never to have hesitated to
speak her mind when she found him in the wrong. During the epidemic of 1797 she entreated him not to expose himself again but to
leave town, and in this she was joined by the tears of their thirteen-
year-old daughter Mary. But Rush, of course, was adamant in his
determination to remain at his post, despite the fact that his beloved
city had become alien to him. He said of himself that he was
scarcely tolerated there. An excerpt from a letter from Samuel
Hodgdon, a former quartermaster of the Army, written August
17, 1797 to Timothy Pickering, then Secretary of State, shows

how he was regarded by one of his fellow Philadelphians:

"Rush behaves like a Man escaped from Bedlam, he has told two Gentlemen of my acquaintance within two days past, to *fly*, for Contagion was every where, and that respiration could not be performed without the utmost hazard. One of the persons laughed at him, the other whose nerves were not so strong was very much affected. If I should hear such language from him I shall advise him to have his head shaved and take his seat in the Hospital. I am not disposed to be severe upon him, but such speeches coming from *him* will do our City more injury than a thousand such Men and such talents as he has credit for could ever with the best disposition do it good . . . . Good God can the people be any longer deceived by a Mountebank and resign all their comforts into the bloody hand of experiments and inconsistency."

In the autumn of 1797, Rush wrote to Dr. John Rodgers in New York, "Ever since the year 1793 I have lived in Philadelphia as in a foreign city." Rodgers was professor of midwifery at Columbia and would later become a trustee of the College of Physicians and Surgeons in New York. He was about ten years younger than Rush and had had a similar medical education, first at the College of New Jersey, then at the University of Pennsylvania and at Edinburgh. The two men had been founding members of the College of Physicians. Rush wrote to him as to an old and trusted friend. In his letter he first broached the subject of his leaving Philadelphia and settling in New York. A condition of his moving would be the certainty of getting a professor's chair at Columbia, so that he could continue to disseminate his medical principles. He wanted a consultation practice only. The income of a professorship, with that of his estate in Pennsylvania, plus a garden and pasture lot, would suffice to maintain his family. This suggestion that he move to New York and join the medical faculty at Columbia was met enthusiastically by both Rodgers and his colleagues. They unanimously resolved to recommend him for the Chair of the Practice of Medicine. But the plan came to nothing. It was blocked by Alexander Hamilton. Three days later Rush expressed his most grateful and affectionate acknowledgment to Rodgers and to the medical faculty. Though still determined to retire from the present scene of strife, which had become so disagreeable both to his family and to himself, he now asked Rodgers to go no further in the matter. He added: "It is peculiarly gratifying to me to learn that the opposition to my appointment has come from that gentleman."

Hamilton was quite aware of Rush's Antifederalist views and of the fact that he was a staunch and loyal friend of Jefferson's, who had vigorously opposed Hamilton's funding system, as had Rush. More important than this, Alexander Hamilton had come down with yellow fever in the early autumn of 1793, when panic was abroad and the condition of the city desperate. A few days later his wife was stricken. Both were treated by Hamilton's boyhood friend from the West Indies, Dr. Edward Stevens, whose methods, unlike Rush's, were moderate and conservative. Dr. Stevens saw the couple through to a happy recovery. It was natural for Hamilton to extol him in all the newspapers, as well as in a letter addressed to the College of Physicians. By implication this was a slap at Rush, who, of course, took it so, although he expressed a high opinion of Dr. Stevens' candor and liberality, even if they differed in practice. Hamilton had great public prestige; his joining the swelling ranks of Rush's opponents was an added source of injury to Dr. Rush's professional reputation. Thomas Jefferson, like Franklin a man of scientific genius, had little patience with medical theorists and system builders. But being both Rush's patient and friend, he never opposed him publicly.

Fortunately, Rush had made some shrewd investments in real estate in central and northern Pennsylvania, and Mrs. Rush had inherited valuable land near Princeton from her father, Richard Stockton, but the Doctor's income from practice had nearly vanished. At this time the Rushes had eight living children, of whom John, the eldest, was twenty, and the youngest, Samuel, but two months old. There were plenty of mouths to feed.

His wife's uncle, Elias Boudinot, a lawyer, and one-time president of Congress, applied on Rush's behalf to John Adams to have him appointed Treasurer of the Mint in place of Dr. Nicholas Way, who had died in office. Even Abigail Adams tried to influence her husband against this appointment, as did many others. Because of his sympathy with the French Revolution, people called Rush a "French Democrat." This has been likened to calling a "New Dealer" a "Red." John Adams stood firmly against all remonstrances and appointed Rush. He is quoted as saying, "I know Dr. Rush's principles perfectly. He is no more a French Dem-

ocrat than I am." When Rush called on Mr. Adams to thank him
for his great kindness, the President took him by the hand and said,
according to Rush, "You have not more pleasure in receiving the
office I have given you, than I had in conferring it upon an old
Whig." Adams had written:

"When the office of Treasurer of the Mint was vacant, I had, as
nearly as I recollect about 40 applications for it. I never had
more difficulty in examining and comparing testimonies, qualifications, merits &c., in order to determine conscientiously in my own
Mind, whom to nominate. After the most serious deliberation, and
weighing every Mans pretensions I concluded to give the office to
Dr. Rush who had not applied for it." :

He called Rush's nomination one of the actions of his life which
he recollected with the most entire satisfaction, even though it had
made him about thirty-nine enemies. Although the post carried a
salary of only $1,200 a year, it served as an anchor to windward in
the storm that Rush was trying to ride out.

During this troubled period he was again preoccupied with yellow fever. The number of deaths in the epidemic of 1798
amounted, according to him, to between three and four thousand,
although there were far fewer cases than in 1793 because the city
was deserted by nearly all its inhabitants. Julia and the younger
children had removed to Princeton; Rush, to "Sydenham," the
country seat he had acquired two and a half miles from the city,
where he had about twelve acres under cultivation. His first mention of it is in a letter to his wife, dated August 26, 1798:

"I write to you for the first time from our little *hut* on Timber-
lane. I lodged here last night and was well accommodated. The noise
of rural insects, the sight of domestic animals coming to the well to
drink before they retired to rest, the purity and coolness of the air,
a pleasant and frugal supper of fruit and milk, and the greatest
kindness and attention from Betsey, Charlotte, Billy, and both our
sons, created for a few hours a flow of peaceful and happy feelings
such as I have seldom experienced since I left the country school in
which I received the first elements of my education. I forgot for a
while the disputes and convulsions which now agitate our country
and the globe. . . . I forgot the persecutions of my enemies and
felt as if I could welcome the most inveterate of them to partake
of the simple fare of our little cottage. One thing I could not forget

—the sufferings of the sick, the afflicted, and the dying in the city of Philadelphia. My heart was torn with anguish in looking towards it. The deaths yesterday were 40."

Three days later he again writes her from "Sydenham Hut." He tells her not to be uneasy about her "best friend." "I have escaped a Lion and a Bear in 1793 and 1797. Why should I fear to meet our present Goliath? . . . Public confidence is again placed in me, and my opinions and advice have at last some weight. Under these circumstances I cannot think of retiring altogether. My business is confined chiefly to my old patients, to strangers, and the poor. I refuse applications daily to wealthy and respectable people. I go to town about 9 o'clock in the morning and return to our hut always before sunset. I am seldom fatigued and have as yet felt (one day excepted) none of the aches and pains of 1797."

In order to surprise and please his wife, Rush had not up to this point told her of the improvements he had made on their little farm. He now tells her he has a neat brick kitchen, 16' x 12', with a convenient garret room over it, between the old brick house and the well. He has also added a story and a half to the house.

Julia is to divide these new additions as she wishes. She can have either a small room and a pleasant cool entry, or one large room. When finished, he promises her that the building will be convenient, cool, tight, and large enough to accommodate all of the family who prefer to leave the city in the warm weather. He hopes that the garden, under her eye, will be greatly productive. He tells her that Richard, their second son, then eighteen, has enlarged the strawberry bed to nearly half an acre.

*　　*　　*

In spite of the bucolic calm, an ill wind was soon to blow from an unexpected quarter. William Cobbett, a young Englishman, had reached Philadelphia in 1794, where he soon became a political pamphleteer, whose bitterly trenchant and sarcastic pen served as a powerful weapon for the Federalists. It was used without mercy on Republican-Democrats and Francophiles alike. Rush soon became one of his prize victims. The fact is that Cobbett hated America. He had come here with his wife, having fled first from England and then from France. Hoping to make his home and fortune here, he found the landscape hard and inhospitable, the climate unbearable in its extremes and the people lazy and dishonest. Other Englishmen have shared Cobbett's opinion that life in this country is good only for making money.

When Cobbett arrived in Philadelphia from Wilmington, where he had been teaching English to French refugees from the West Indies, anti-British feelings were running high. The seizure of our vessels to prevent shipments of supplies to France had led to a popular outcry and, in spite of President Washington's proclamation of neutrality, to demands for war on England. Cobbett was a passionate monarchist, whose nostalgia and chauvinism led him to glorify everything English. He had, moreover, suffered a grave personal misfortune shortly after he reached Philadelphia. His wife not only gave birth to a stillborn baby, but their only child died as well. Embittered, he lashed out against this country and all those who were hostile to his own.

Early in life he had come under the influence of the writings of Jonathan Swift. He proved himself an apt pupil. He first wrote anonymously, but later adopted the pseudonym "Peter Porcupine." His blacklist included many of the courageous, liberal Anglo-American patriots who still dwell in our Valhalla—Joseph Priestley, "Citizen Madison," as he called him, Lafayette, Noah Webster, Benjamin Franklin or "Old Lightning Rod," Thomas Jefferson and, of course, Tom Paine, in Cobbett's eyes the worst traitor of them all. He soon added Benjamin Rush's name to the others and for him he drew his sharpest double-edged sword. He slashed him first for his democratic principles, then for his medical practices.

On December 17, 1796, Dr. Rush delivered a eulogy in memory of his friend David Rittenhouse, the distinguished astronomer, mathematician and patriot, who had succeeded Benjamin Franklin as president of the American Philosophical Society. The members of the Society met at the First Presbyterian Church on High Street. The Church was crowded with the élite, including George Washington, Thomas Jefferson, members of the Senate and the House of Representatives, Judges of the Courts of the United States and Pennsylvania, the Corporation and Clergy of the City, the College of Physicians, the Faculty of the University, and many influential citizens. This was the kind of audience before which Rush naturally wanted to shine. In approximately one hour of florid oratory he praised his subject for his virtue, his wisdom, his piety and his genius. He made only passing references to Rittenhouse's republicanism and his attachment to an elective and representative form of government. Though to our ear the address has the ring of oratorical sentimentality, this was the genre style of the day. No one could have doubted Rush's fervid sincerity.

"Be just, and loose the bands of the African slave. Be wise, and render war odious to our country. Be free, by assuming a national character and name, and be greatly happy, by erecting a barrier against the corruptions in morals, government, and religion, which now pervade all the nations of Europe."

Cobbett was quick to detect the political propaganda in Rush's address and thereupon he let loose the first of his poisoned barbs. Hyperbolic bombast and a glaring departure from truth, he called it. Rittenhouse had never done good to anyone. "The remorseless Dr. Rush shall bleed me till I am white as this paper before I'll allow that this was doing good to mankind."

A few months later Rush wrote:

"My remedies for yellow fever would have met no opposition this year had I not signed the Declaration of Independence and latterly declared myself a Republican in the *Eulogium* upon Mr. Rittenhouse.

The fact is, strident and devastating opposition came not only from Cobbett, but also from John Fenno, the editor of the *Gazette of the United States*, whose tirades against Rush for his fanaticism and his "lunatic system of medicine" finally drove the Doctor to sue him for libel. But his lawyers advised him to drop this suit, fearing that Fenno would never be convicted by a jury of his fellow countrymen.

Others joined the hue and cry. An article in the *Gazette* for October 6, 1797, erroneously supposed to have been written by Dr. Andrew Ross, so enraged young John Rush, who was a medical apprentice to his father, that it ended in the exchange of heated words and finally the caning of Dr. Ross.

Cobbett was the principal assailant. He was a more vicious adversary, more slanderous, more cunning, more ruthless than the others, a master of ridicule and of the poisonous art of character assassination. He had written in *Porcupine's Gazette*, "I affirm this John Rush to be an *impertinent puppy*, a *waylaying coward*, a *liar*, and a *rascal*." Outraged by this attack on his son, Benjamin

Rush decided to sue for libel on his own right. This time no one tried to dissuade him. As Fenno had been, Cobbett was also furious at what they considered an assault on the sacrosanct freedom of the press. He declared openly that he would persecute Rush while living, and his memory after he had died. Of the Rittenhouse eulogy, he said, "The doctor had better have confined himself to medicine, and let politics alone . . . . Damn him," he added, "I will attack him for it." And attack he did. When the papers announced that Rush was to be offered a professorship of the practice of physic in Columbia College and said of him that he was a man born to be useful to society, Cobbett's comment in the *Gazette* was, "And so is a mosquito, a horse-leach, a ferret, a pole-cat, a weazel: for these are all bleeders, and understand their business full as well as Dr. Rush does his." To Rush's claim that mercury is "the *Samson* of medicine," Cobbett replied, "In his hands and in those of his partizans it may indeed be justly compared to *Samson;* for, I verily believe they have slain more Americans with it, than ever Samson slew of the Philistines. The Israelite slew his thousands, but the Rushites have slain their tens of thousands."

Each number of *Porcupine's Gazette* brought new insults and fresh provocations. Rush was called a "potent quack," a "barefaced puff," who, like Sangrado, would bleed his patients to within an inch of the grave.

Cobbett wrote:

> The times are ominous indeed,
> When quack to quack cries, *purge* and *bleed.*

*   *   *

Then came the trial. On Friday, December 13, 1799, Rush made his early morning rounds as usual at the Pennsylvania Hospital and then drove to the State House—the familiar scene of his former political ventures and where he had delivered his maiden speech. Here the court was sitting. The Doctor was late. Julia was already seated and beside her their daughter Mary, and Richard, who was already a practicing lawyer. The courtroom was crowded, not only because the case had attracted wide and excited interest for political reasons and because Dr. Rush was so celebrated a man with an international reputation, but also because Congress was in session and President Adams was in town. This alone brought great numbers of people to the square outside the red-brick building.

For Benjamin Rush much was at stake—perhaps final ruin, as against a release from gross and scurrilous abuse. So much for the issue of libel. But even more was at stake than the feelings and reputation of a high-minded if sometimes misguided man. On one side was the right of a physician to practice his own system of medicine without interference from the outside or hindrance to new and hitherto untried methods; and on the other side was the freedom of the press, held so sacred in this country. It was between these issues that the battle was joined.

The Chief Justice of the State, Edward Shippen, presided, assisted by two associate justices. He was a cousin of Dr. William Shippen's, Rush's antagonist during the Revolutionary War. The Judge was a Federalist, the father-in-law of Benedict Arnold and a man noted for his kindness, his generosity and the dignity of his manners. The jury was drawn from Rush's fellow townsmen— artisans, tradesmen and shopkeepers. Rush was represented by four attorneys, the defendant by three. His chief counsel was Joseph Hopkinson, a young man not yet thirty, who had been admitted to the bar at twenty-one, and this was his first important case.

Hopkinson opened by declaring that Dr. Rush was "as well known for his peaceful habits and amiable manners, as William Cobbett is for his . . . malignant disposition and his inveterate hate." He spoke of the "barbarous and unprovoked injuries" Cobbett had inflicted on the Doctor, how he had made Rush the "sport and play-thing of malicious ridicule and vulgar wit," and of Cobbett's "dark and virulent spirit," of his "insufferable arrogance," of his "ridiculous vanity" and of the names on his blacklist of all the honorable men whom he had persecuted. His attack was as deadly and violent, Hopkinson argued, as "malice could invent or abandoned depravity execute." Then the young advocate warmed to his plea and let himself go.

"When tempests agitate the ocean to its foundation, and rock it in convulsions, numerous noxious animals are thrown up, which would otherwise never have seen the light; so in a troubled state of things, wretches are cast up from the very dregs and slime of the community, who, in more happy times, would have lived and rotted in obscurity."

Cobbett did not hear these words. He had left town before the trial and had gone to New York.

The first day of the trial ended with public feeling much inclined toward Rush's side of the controversy, despite the fact that the volatile people of Philadelphia had drifted with the tides of events. Since John Jay's successful negotiation with England, which had averted war, pro-British sentiments had been growing, as had hostile feelings toward France and Jefferson. This was a complete reversal. In the minds of the populace, Cobbett was Britain and Rush was France. Yet Cobbett had gone too far. He had angered President Adams by attacking him for making peace with France, and for deserting the rigid Federalist party line. For five years the brazen Cobbett had been screaming for war with France. Now the President threatened to invoke the Alien and Sedition Acts and deport him. Perhaps this accounted for the sudden flight from Philadelphia to New York.

The next morning Mr. Moses Levy took up the case for the plaintiff. It was like Rush to pick a Jew for his counsel—the first one to be admitted to the Philadelphia bar, and at the age of twenty-three. With his dark complexion, his aquiline features and his black gown, he cut an impressive figure and this lent weight to his calm, penetrating, logical argument. He emphasized that this was an action for libel, not slander, that what is committed to paper—what is printed—has a lasting impression and is capable of much and universal mischief. "The law," he declared, "is pointedly against the defendant, he having written what would have been a libel even if spoken. I shall take it for granted then, that this newspaper attacking of Dr. Rush, as 'quack,' 'potent quack,' 'grand empiric,' 'who has slain his tens of thousands,' is a gross and infamous libel. . . ."

Moses Levy warmed to his argument.

"The opinions of Dr. Rush were circulated from an idea that they were just; he submitted them to public search and inquiry. . . . We do not contend that Dr. Rush has established the true mode of practice; he thinks so, and has given to the world his reasons for thinking so. But the case does not rest upon that point; it is all one to you whether his practice is right or wrong. Did Cobbett say that he knew a better mode? No. He endeavoured to rise a public laugh upon Dr. Rush, and put him forth in a most degrading point of view, at a moment . . . when the state of the city was enough to appal the stoutest heart; when the confidence of men in general was placed on the advice of this man;—at that moment his reputation is pulled down; his mode of treatment, almost the only one then practised, is destroyed, and no effort is made to put another in its place! Dr. Rush does not pretend to say he is right; he thinks so: But the superior genius of Cobbett *does* presume to declare that he is wrong. . . ."

Levy closed his argument with telling words:

"It is high time to rescue the American character from the indifference which has too long prevailed amongst us . . . it is time to punish crime so daring. This man has declared, that he would 'persecute the defendent while living, and his memory after his death.' How can you check this vindictive spirit, but by timely and exemplary punishment? Let him be taught that he has wantonly attacked, and that with cool deliberate malice, an unoffending individual, and though he has removed himself out of the jurisdiction of this court, yet that he is a marked man, and that a respectable jury of Philadelphia have studied only principles of truth and justice with impartiality. Let others be taught by his punishment to avoid his offense."

These sober and judicious words seemed to turn the tide of the case. The defense attorneys, led by Mr. Tilghman, sought to extenuate the offense by asserting that there had been no attempt to render Dr. Rush himself odious or to injure him in his profession. The attack had been leveled at his use of mercurial purges and at the excessive bloodletting, they held, and they argued valiantly for the freedom of the press.

In Judge Shippen's charge to the jury, libel is defined as "malicious defamation, expressed either in printing, or writing, or by signs or pictures tending to blacken either the memory of one who is dead, or the reputation of one who is alive, or to expose him to public hatred, contempt or ridicule." He called the publications of Cobbett clearly libelous. He spoke of the liberty of the press as "a valuable right in every free country, . . . never to be unduly restrained." But the law, he said, considered public attacks on private character as "a very atrocious offense" which threaten the public peace. He adjured them to put political and partisan considerations completely out of their minds in reaching their decision. It was their responsibility, he said, to fix the amount of the damages.

When the jury filed out, Dr. and Mrs. Rush and Mary left the courthouse, but Richard remained. Later that night he came home to tell his parents that after two hours of deliberation a verdict in favor of his father had been returned, and that William Cobbett was to pay damages of $5,000 plus the cost of the suit, which amounted to $3,000 more.

The trial was over and a certain peace descended on the community. Feelings against Dr. Rush became less hostile for a while, until another turn of events stirred them up again. On the second day of the trial George Washington had lain dying, but not until six days later did the *General Advertiser* of Philadelphia carry this modest and inconspicuous notice:

> Died at Mt. Vernon on Saturday evening,
> December 14th (1799), at 11 o'clock of an illness of 24 hours
> George Washington
> Commander-in-Chief of the American Armies

Death was attributed to croup or inflammatory quincy—what we should probably call a septic sore throat. Rush wrote in his diary:

"This day died, universally lamented, General Washington. His disease was the Cynanche Trachialis. It proved fatal in 14 hours. He was patient and resigned in his illness. He said his will was made, his private affairs settled, and his public business but two days behind. He wished his physicians to enable him to die easy. Congress instituted public honors to his memory. The whole United States mourned for him as for a father."

Washington had been bled copiously, nine pints in twenty-four hours, but of his three physicians, one alone, Dr. Elisha Dick, a former pupil of Rush, had opposed bloodletting. Even so, the great man's death was attributed to Rush's system of medicine. Cobbett lost no time in blaming him and devoted the last issue of *Porcupine's Gazette* to driving this point home.

Although financially ruined, Cobbett soon resurrected himself. Safely removed from the jurisdiction of the Pennsylvania courts, and with the beneficent sanction of Alexander Hamilton, Cobbett again raised his strident voice against Rush. From February to June 1800 he brought out a periodical called *The Rush-Light*, which he devoted entirely to abuse of Benjamin Rush. His previous diatribes paled before these. "Can the RUSH grow up without mire?" he queried. Quoting the Book of Job, he stated that the rush withers before any other herb. But beyond his personal animus against Rush, and aside from the legal malice involved, the doubts that Cobbett cast on Rush's claims for his methods were, as matters of fact, justifiable. Indeed, in the long run, they probably helped discredit a system of medicine that time has not sustained. Cobbett claimed to have established mathematically that Rush had killed more patients than he had cured.

Although *The Rush-Light* achieved considerable popularity in Philadelphia and helped recoup its editor's fortunes, in time his vein of anger exhausted itself. In June 1800 he sailed from New York for England on the packet *Arabella*. He never paid the $8,000; he paid half the sum and Benjamin Rush gave the money to charity.

13

THE DISEASES OF THE MIND I

✿ THE DEPARTURE OF COBBETT FOR ENGLAND MARKS a turning point in the life of Benjamin Rush. Shortly thereafter, in the summer of 1800, he started writing his *Travels Through Life,* a document addressed to his children in order, as he said, to afford them entertainment and instruction. But it clearly served another purpose: to put himself in a good light in their eyes, and to help him recover from the many injuries he felt he had suffered, the worst at the hands of Cobbett. Now came a change of mood in Rush and also a change in his chief concerns. No longer the gallant optimist, he became more introverted and more withdrawn and given to self-justification. For solace he turned to religion.

Yet, some of his best work was before him. Rush was now in his middle fifties, an age which in some vigorous men often marks new beginnings or at least a consolidation and redirection of past interests. As he wrote his friend Jefferson: "My persecutions have arrested or delayed the usual languor of 55 in my mind. I read, write, and think with the same vigor and pleasure that I did fifteen years ago." Then he reflects that slander can be a much more powerful stimulus to our mental faculties than fame.

His mind seems to have been turning away from politics and toward religion. He was fond of inserting aphorisms in his correspondence. "We should found our laws wholly upon the mild religion and just precepts of Jesus Christ. . . . All true wisdom begins in true religion." But he could not quite share the expectations of the pious people who thought we were on the eve of the millennium. He was convinced that a great deal of preparatory work had to be done before that blessed state of grace could be achieved. Civilization, human knowledge and liberty must first pervade the globe. These, Rush thought, were the heralds of true religion, and he was ready to do his part in paving the way for its advent.

His deep concern with the suffering caused by diseases of the mind was a part of this grand design—part of his effort to create a more perfect world—less fraught with evil, misery and human waste. This attitude was all of a piece with his passionate dedication to democracy, and with his hatred of brutality and tyranny. Indeed, Rush's contribution to what would later be called psychiatry must be understood in the spirit of the Declaration of Independence—and of the Enlightenment heralded by Locke and Hume and their disciples in France. In his youth he had met Hume and Diderot face to face, and he had steeped himself in the writings of Locke and Rousseau. It was natural for him to be lifted up on the wave of humanitarianism, individualism and nationalism that had swept and was still sweeping 18th-century Europe and the young American states. If he differed with the French Encyclopaedists, it was in the depth of his religious feelings and convictions.

It has been well said that whenever the spirit of humanism arises a new contribution to psychiatry follows. In fact, the whole development of psychiatry has been marked by man's struggles to rise above the prejudices of his age. Benjamin Rush played a major part in such a struggle. One need think only of his battle for the abolition of slavery, of his tireless campaign against the use of strong drink and against capital punishment, of his efforts to improve the condition of jails and the treatment of prisoners, of his leadership in the emancipation of women, his insistence on the just and decent treatment of minority groups and his plans for free and liberalized public schools and colleges throughout the new nation. This was the background, the culture medium, in which his interest in the mentally deranged had been planted and grew.

During the last decade of the 18th century, even while burdened with the care of patients suffering from yellow fever, Rush had been engaged in investigating the "causes, seats, and remedies of madness and other diseases of the mind." He writes to Jefferson, "Before I commit the results of my inquiries and observations to the press, I wish to read everything that has been published upon those subjects." There is reason to believe that he did so, both because of his familiar studious habits and because he refers to many by name in his famous textbook which would be published ten years later, a year before his death. In this same letter to Jefferson, he begs the loan of a history of the Bastille, by Henri Le Tude, who had been committed, under the pretense of madness, to the Bicêtre in Paris. The Bicêtre housed within its walls a prison for criminals, a hospital for patients with venereal diseases, a house of correction for children, a poorhouse for indigents and beggars, and an asylum for lunatics. Le Tude's book, Rush had been told, contained many curious facts about madness.

Rush had already introduced certain reforms in the care of patients confined in the asylums for mad people at the Pennsylvania Hospital. On his urging, the managers had provided two warm and two cold bathrooms on the lowest floor of the Hospital and a pump to supply them with water. For those deranged people capable of working, he suggested spinning, sewing and churning, for women; and, for men, grinding Indian corn in a hand mill to provide food for the horses or cows of the Hospital; also cutting straw, weaving, digging in the garden and sawing or planing boards. These were among the first provisions for what would later be called occupational therapy. This is now so much taken for granted that it is hard to realize how extraordinarily bold Rush's proposals appeared to his contemporaries. They represented a giant stride forward, a radical change from the brutalizing, punitive behavior that had prevailed, to an imaginative, human and humane attitude, characteristic of the physician rather than of the jailer.

Pioneer though he was, Rush's efforts were not unique. They were part of a wide movement for reform, arising almost simultaneously, though independently: in England, by the work of the Quaker, William Tuke, who had founded the York Retreat in 1796 for the cure of the insane; in Germany, by Reil and Müller; in Italy, by Chiarugi; and in France, by Jean Colombier, Joseph Daquin, and the greatest of them all, Philippe Pinel.

These men were exemplars of the so-called moral treatment of insanity. This was based on the assumption and observation that mental derangement or lunacy could sometimes result from stress, from disappointment, from shock or grief, or from what today would be called emotional causes. Moral treatment consisted of keeping patients clean, of making them comfortable, of trying to build up their self-respect, of meeting them with friendliness and encouragement and of explaining their difficulties to them. This was a relatively new departure. It depended, first of all, on a rejection of notions of possession, demonology and witchcraft that had dominated the Middle Ages and had lasted until much later. Even well into the 18th century witchcraft trials continued to recur— trials in which both accused and accusers showed unquestionable evidence of mental derangement.

Madmen were regarded as brutes or wild beasts and treated as common criminals. They were thrown into dank and filthy dungeons, where they lay on vermin-infested straw, sometimes remaining imprisoned for a lifetime. Not a ray of light or of human kindness reached them. They were the butt and sport of brutal keepers or of prurient visitors who paid a fee for a sight of them. In Colonial America incarceration in jails was the common practice, as it had been in England and on the Continent, with frequent resort to the pillory or the whipping post. For the relatively well-to-do, care was entrusted to their families, who provided crude medical treatment consisting of semi-magical medieval medicinal plants, as well as copious bloodletting. Violent persons were locked up and chained by their families in strong rooms, cellars, or outhouses. Sometimes communities contributed to the cost of building such blockhouses, which were often not much larger than a dog kennel.

In Massachusetts, at Braintree, the birthplace and home of John Adams, it was voted "That Samuel Speere should build a little house 7 foote long & 5 foote wide and set it by his house to secure his Sister good wife Witty being distracted & provide for her." This was in 1689. A century and a half later, in 1844, in another New England town, Little Compton, Rhode Island, one Abram Simmons, an insane pauper, was entombed in a stone vault about seven feet square, with a heavily-bolted iron door. Here, secured by a chain to a rock overhead, he lived, winter and summer.

Conditions such as these formed the setting in which Benjamin Rush functioned and provided the backdrop against which he wrote his celebrated *Medical Inquiries and Observations upon the Diseases of the Mind*. In the next generation many people would become aware of them because of the work of one of the most remarkable of America's 19th-century female reformers.

Dorothea Lynde Dix—a frail, retired school teacher from the state of Maine, where she was born in 1802—first observed the sufferings of "lunatics," as they were then called, in a jail in East Cambridge, Massachusetts. This was in 1841. From that date she dedicated her life and her energy toward improving the condition of the mentally ill. Reared in the Unitarian tradition of social idealism, and once a governess in the household of William Ellery Channing, from whom she drew her inspiration, Miss Dix became, with the possible exception of some of the abolitionists, the greatest social reformer in American history. She had a particular genius for touching the pocketbooks of rich Victorian gentlemen and of moving legislatures to found new and better institutions. Throughout the country, asylums appeared in her wake. Nothing could stop her; no corruption or self-complacency could discourage her, no personal risk or danger deter her. She made her presence felt and her voice heard. She appeared before the Congress of the United States and Parliament in London. Sir George Gray, the Home Secretary, in approving one of the bills for which she was responsible, regretted only that the reform had been achieved by "a foreigner, and that foreigner a woman, and that woman a dissenter!"

In the *Providence Journal* for April 10, 1844, Miss Dix published an article called "Astonishing Tenacity of Life." It is not written over her signature, but over that of Thomas G. Hazard. It is known, however, from a public document of her own, that she provided the writer with the facts on which his article was based. They concerned her first visit to Little Compton, where she had discovered Abram Simmons, confined in complete darkness, in that unheated cell seven feet square and six and one-half feet high, built entirely of stone. This dungeon stood in the courtyard of the poorhouse. Simmons had been imprisoned there for over three years. One of his legs was fastened by an ox-chain, shackled to an iron staple in the rock overhead. The article stated:

"There he stood, near the door, motionless and silent; his tangled hair fell about his shoulders; his bare feet pressed the filthy wet stone floor; he was emaciated to a shadow and more resembled a disinterred corpse than any living creature. Never have I looked upon an object so pitiable, so woe-struck, so imaging despair. Notwithstanding the assertions of the Mistress that he would kill me I took his hands and endeavored to warm them by gentle friction. I spoke to him of release, of liberty, of care and kindness. A tear stole over the hollow cheek, but no words answered my importunities; no other movement indicated consciousness or perception of sensibility."

All this happened right here in New England, just a little over one hundred years ago, and about two miles from where this book was written.

When relatively harmless, these poor distracted individuals would be farmed out, often to ignorant people of ill will, or they were treated as paupers at a time when pauperism itself was looked upon as a crime. Or again, they would be warned out of town or be spirited away under cover of night to wander aimlessly, hopelessly and in tatters from village to village.

Public almshouses did not come into existence until the end of the 18th century, when the growth and concentration of the population made them necessary. Closely allied to them were houses of correction and workhouses, which combined the functions of a penal institution and a poorhouse. Confinement and incarceration gradually replaced corporal punishment. All manner of derelicts, eccentrics and criminals were thus thrown together.

When the first house of correction was built in Connecticut in 1727, it provided for the confinement of

> . . . all rogues, vagabonds and idle persons going about in town or country begging, or persons . . . feigning themselves to have knowledge in physiognomy, palmistry, or pretending that they can tell fortunes, or discover where lost or stolen goods may be found [this was undoubtedly aimed at gypsies], common pipers, fidlers, runaways . . . common drunkards, common night-walkers, pilferers, wanton and lascivious persons . . . common railers or brawlers . . . as also *persons under distraction* and unfit to go at large whose friends do not care for their safe confinement.

Upon entering such a house of correction each person was automatically whipped on the bare back not more than ten times unless otherwise ordered.

*   *   *

The foregoing in general describes the lot of the insane during Rush's childhood and youth. In Pennsylvania before 1732, concern for the poor and care for the sick, the abandoned and the deranged had rested mainly with the Quakers. But with the rapid growth of the city of Philadelphia the effects of poverty became more acute and soon all sects were combining to share the burden. In 1732 an almshouse was built and for a time this was the only refuge for the demented.

On January 23, 1751, while Benjamin Rush was still a child, a petition written in Benjamin Franklin's hand had been presented to the Provincial Assembly, proposing the establishment of a hospital. Within four months the assembly acted favorably and voted a grant of £2,000 for the initial expenses, provided that an equal amount be raised by private subscription. Although Franklin gives full credit to his particular friend, Dr. Thomas Bond, for the idea of building a hospital in Philadelphia, Bond assured him that he could get nowhere with the project without Franklin's sponsorship and support. The opening words of Franklin's petition deserve quotation:

> That with the Numbers of People, the number of Persons distempered in Mind and deprived of their rational Faculties, hath greatly increased in this Province. That some of them going at large are a Terror to their Neighbours, who are daily apprehensive of the Violence they may commit; . . . That few or none of them are so sensible of their Condition, as to submit voluntarily to the treatment that their respective Cases requires, and therefore continue in the same deplorable state during their Lives; whereas it has been found, by experience of many Years, that above two Thirds of the Mad People received into Bethlehem Hospital [Bedlam in London], and there treated properly, have been cured.

Although the accuracy of this last statement may be open to question, Franklin, with his usual sagacity, recognized mental illness not only as a demographic problem, statistically related to the size of the population, but also as a medical one, deserving proper treatment rather than incarceration and punishment. Not less important was the idea that a general hospital could undertake the care of "poor distempered Persons, who languish long in Pain and Misery, under various Disorders of Body and Mind . . . ."

The Pennsylvania Hospital thus became not only the first hospi-

tal to be established in the Colonies, but also the first to accept patients both mentally as well as physically ill. In this it has served as
a guide for later developments in the United States. Since there
were no insane asylums in the Colonies, a general hospital was the
only possible humane refuge for the demented. The first asylum in
this country exclusively for mentally deranged persons was established in 1773 in Williamsburg, Virginia.

It was in the Pennsylvania Hospital between Spruce and Pine
Streets that Benjamin Rush had received in the days of his apprenticeship his first instruction in medicine, and here also it was that he
later had his first experiences with the insane. But it was not until
the year 1783 that he became a regular member of its staff, and this
was the beginning of a thirty-year period of service.

In this new Hospital mad people were consigned to the cellar,
where they received whatever medical treatment seemed necessary.
Their scalps were shaved and blistered; they were bled almost to
the point of insensibility and purged until there was nothing left in
their intestines but mucus. They were watched over by cell-
keepers equipped with whips, who more closely resembled prison
guards than trained nurses or orderlies. Discipline was rigidly enforced and any infraction of rules was severely punished. Patients
were chained by their waists or ankles to iron rings in the floors or
walls of their cells; or they were restrained in handcuffs or ankle-
irons or confined in a "madd-shirt"—a closefitting, sleeveless can-
vas garment which completely deprived them of free motion.

In spite of the persistence and survival of these unenlightened
and savage practices, including the shocking one of exhibiting insane patients to the curious in return for a fee, the fact that they
were now housed in a hospital designed for their treatment rather
than in a penal institution was a great step forward. This was the
first time in American history that a public institution received
mentally ill patients explicitly for medical treatment rather than for
punishment. The admission procedures were dangerously simple.
To have a patient committed required only the application of a relative or friend (or sometimes an enemy) to one of the managers of
the Hospital, signed by one of the physicians. If the patient remon-
strated or resisted, he was simply put in chains.

In 1796, because of insufficient space, a new wing was added to
the western part of the Hospital. Over this wing Dr. Rush pre-

sided. By now he had had the exclusive care of these patients in the primitive setting of the Hospital cellar for nine years. How excruciating such surroundings must have been to a man of his sensibilities can easily be imagined. In a previous communication to the managers of the Hospital he had complained of the cells where these patients were confined. They were cold and damp in winter, he wrote, hot in summer, lacking in ventilation, stuffy and malodorous; and then he continued:

"These facts being clearly established, I conceive that the appropriating of the cells any longer for the reception of mad people will be dishonorable both to the science and humanity of the city of Philadelphia."

These reforms in the care of the mentally sick that Rush introduced had come on the heels of the American Revolution. The French Revolution was the harbinger of similar changes. The new note was best sounded by Joseph Daquin, a contemporary of Philippe Pinel and in some respects his precursor. He wrote:

"The course of treatment of insanity should be highly analogous to the methods used in the study of natural history, and that only in hospitals could one observe the various guises in which the malady appears, describe its history, regulate the therapeutic methods which cannot be always the same in all varieties of mental derangements, rid one's self of all the prejudices one has about the various types of insanity, and apply moral treatment in all cases."

This extraordinary statement might have been taken as a preface to much of the work of reform that sprang from the convulsive social forces that shook the world at the end of the 18th century. The salient characteristic of reform was the spread of humanism. In the case of the insane, kindness and compassion were substituted for cruelty, and careful clinical observation and study began to replace the routine reliance on archaic procedures. There was both the conviction and the hope that the tragic problems of insanity would yield, not to torture and exorcism, but to the methods of science. This belief was implicit in the optimism of the period and it was shared by all the great reformers of the time. Each had witnessed the existing horrors and barbarities: Tuke at the lunatic asylum in York and at Bedlam in London; Colombier and Daquin at the Hôtel Dieu, said to have been one of the most backward hospitals in all Europe; Pinel at the Bicêtre, described by him as a "vast pandemonium;" and Rush at the Pennsylvania Hospital. With vehemence, courage and determination each of these heroic men started the slow process of change.

A typical lunatic asylum of the 18th century is described by Dr. John Conolly, the famous English champion of non-restraint. He wrote:

"These were but prisons of the worst description. Small openings in walls, unglazed, or whether glazed or not, guarded with strong iron bars; narrow corridors, dark cells, desolate courts, where no tree, nor shrub, nor flower, nor blade of grass grew; solitariness, or companionship so indiscriminate as to be worse than solitude; terrible attendants armed with whips . . . free to impose manacles, and chains, and stripes, at their own brutal will; uncleanliness, semi-starvation, the garotte, and unpunished murders: these were the characteristics of such buildings throughout Europe."

The reader will be reminded of the famous picture of Bedlam painted by Hogarth in 1730. Here the experienced eye can detect all manner of patients jumbled together in one apartment: the hysterical, the feeble-minded, agitated patients with manic excitement, posturing catatonics, melancholics, and many who are obviously delusional and hallucinating—to portray them in the terms of the 20th century.

Private consulations were not much different. In 1740 Dr. James Monro, physician to Bethlehem Hospital, was consulted by a poor woman about her son Peter. Dr. Monro said to the mother:

"Choose your apothecary, and I will prescribe." The next day they "blooded him largely, confined him to a dark room, and put a strong blister on each of his arms, with another over all his head. But still he was as 'mad' as before, praying or singing, or giving thanks continually; of which having laboured to cure him for six weeks in vain, though he was now so weak he could not stand alone, his mother dismissed the doctor and apothecary, and let him be 'beside himself' in peace."

The rich and the great fared no better. This same Dr. Monro lured Alexander Cruden, the famous author of the Biblical Concordance, to Mrs. Wright's private madhouse in Bethnal Green. There his patient was given a physic, handcuffed and chained to the bedpost. However, each morning before Dr. Monro's visit the keeper unchained him. Poor Cruden suffered from repeated attacks of insanity which would later be called megalomanic paranoid delusions.

Dr. Monro was one of a large coterie of famous physicians, including such well-known men as Heberden and Willis, who watched over King George III in his recurrent attacks of madness. The King was kept in strict seclusion away from his family and ministers. He was given laudanum and bark (quinine) and calomel. His head was shaved and blistered. He was threatened with a straight waistcoat and was strapped to a chair, which he called his "coronation chair." The royal person was held down by four strong attendants, who stuffed a handkerchief in his mouth when he became too obscene. He had five episodes of a manic-depressive psychosis, beginning in 1765 at the age of twenty-seven, and ending in 1810 in a final attack from which he never recovered.

Rush read the work of Sir Alexander Crichton, physician to the Westminster Hospital and an expert in mental illness, on the madness of the King. Although he did not find that Crichton's works led to anything new or useful in practice, today they seem remarkable in view of the fact that they were published in 1798. For example, he said that murder was not uncommonly committed from despair and hid the wish for suicide. He believed that the actions and mental processes of the insane were not haphazard and random, but that they had their motives which could be understood. He anticipated Freud by more than a century by demanding that the physician must understand himself before he can hope to understand his patients. He even used the word *analysis* as the genuine "touchstone of truth." Of the physician, he said:

"He should be able to go back to childhood, and see how the mind is modelled by instruction. He who cannot do this will never proceed farther in knowledge than what he has acquired by books or by tuition; and how very limited this knowledge is, in regard to the pathology of the human mind, need not be mentioned.

"When the work of analysis is completed, the most useful and difficult part remains; that of applying the result, or general principle, to explain and arrange the individual facts. It is this, indeed, which distinguishes the man of science from the mere scholar. It is, of all mental employments, the most difficult, the most liable to error, and yet the most valuable when well accomplished. . . ."

Although the credit for reform is usually given to Pinel in

France, who has since been called the Father of Psychiatry, just as Rush is called the Father of American Psychiatry for his enlightened and liberalizing work, the honors should be more widespread. The work of these two men was obviously part of a ground swell which carried many on its crest. No reform movement comes in full-blown. It is usually gradual in onset, and far from being finally and permanently established all at once, it ebbs and flows for a long time. When a new level of excellence is achieved, it must be constantly defended. Undoubtedly Rush was influenced by the writings of his famous French colleague, whom he quotes several times, but to what extent he felt indebted to him is not entirely clear. Although the two men saw eye-to-eye as to questions of humanitarianism and soon discovered that kindness, decency and relative freedom reduced the frenzy of their charges, there remained certain important differences between them.

Of Rush and Pinel it may be said that each man brought to his art his own temperament and the summation of his life's experience, which was, of course, in part the product of his culture. Pinel was born in Provincial France, the same year that Rush was born in Byberry, Pennsylvania. In his childhood he lost his mother, just as Rush had lost his father. After his mother's death Pinel withdrew from an active life and then devoted himself to the study of philosophy and mathematics. He, too, came under the influence of Locke and Rousseau. From mathematics he turned to physiology, but not until he was twenty-eight did he take a degree in medicine. At this age Rush was already well launched on his variegated career, combining practice, teaching and politics. Pinel came to Paris from Montpellier in 1778, at a time when Rush had already had his profoundly moving and disillusioning military experiences. He became a member of the Society of the Encyclopaedists and then contributed various articles on hygiene in the *Gazette de Santé*, which he directed.

His great shyness at first caused him to fail his examinations for his doctorate. This had its advantages because, being unable to practice, he saw only a few patients, but he observed them very carefully. One of his friends now had an attack of mania. Pinel viewed him daily and made very full notes on his progress, reading meanwhile widely on the subject of mental illness. He then joined the staff of a *petite maison*, a small hospital that received mentally disturbed private patients, and here his interest and expertness and reputation grew. In 1793, just when Rush was beginning to emerge from the horrors of the first wave of yellow fever, Pinel was appointed to the staff of the Bicêtre and the next year he became Professor of Internal Pathology and Director of the Salpêtrière.

It is of interest that Pinel translated the works of Cullen into French and was much influenced, as we know Rush to have been, by Cullen's interest in the classification of diseases and by his physiological theories. But on the whole Pinel was skeptical of the prevailing medical methods in the treatment of the insane. He criticized blistering and bloodletting and the drugs that most of his contemporaries used so freely and indiscriminately. He himself was sparing in the use of them, relying principally upon moral treatment. Rush, whose background was medical and who, in his most impressionable years, had sat at Cullen's feet, never freed himself from his master's teachings, although he tried to do so by modifying them somewhat.

It could be said of these two men, both propelled on the wave of humanism, and both essentially kind, that Pinel was introverted and Rush was the opposite. To this extent their psychotherapy was bound to differ. In political affairs Pinel might have been called conservative and Rush radical, but in psychiatric matters it was Rush who was relatively conservative, and Pinel the radical. Pinel's greatest contribution was his insistence upon careful observation, his painstaking systematic description of his cases, uncontaminated by the prevailing metaphysical speculations or physiological fictions and freed from the anecdotal style of the day. Rush, for his part, was more a child of his time and was swayed in his thinking by these very fictions.

14

THE DISEASES OF THE MIND II

❀ AN AMERICAN PSYCHIATRIST IN THE MID-20TH century, reading Benjamin Rush's *Medical Inquiries and Observations upon the Diseases of the Mind,* feels as if he were crouching on a sunny riverbank somewhere in the wilderness, panning for gold. Amid great mounds of gravel he will be rewarded by an occasional glittering nugget of the truth. At least it will so appear to him, but unfortunately in our test of what the truth is, there is no *aqua regia* which will dissolve it out. Rather, the truth is a recognizable and comfortable feeling of kinship with beliefs and theories that have been tested and accepted and are held today, coupled with full awareness that these are changing and will continue to change. Whatever does not fit into this mold is discarded as dross or looked upon indulgently and curiously with an antiquarian eye.

Just as with Rush's political and social philosophy, so with his medical and psychiatric beliefs, he can be understood only in the context of his culture. In this setting he was a bold pioneer, conspicuous for his fruitful literary allusions, for his intuitive prescience, for his ingenious and comprehensive grasp of a chaotic subject, in many respects far ahead of his times. But judging his contribution from our vantage point, and it is impossible not to judge him so, he was often embarrassingly naïve and anecdotal, with an uncritical propensity for anological thinking and for attributing

false causes and drawing dubious inferences, and with an obsessional need for fostering and defending a unitary theory of disease,
mental as well as physical. This was the natural upshot of the confused classification of the day, based as it was on symptoms rather
than an understanding of causes. Sydenham had tried to bring some
order to this confusion, but the texts of Rush's day listed all possible combinations of symptoms, each as a separate disease entity.
Fevers, for example, were classified as *remittents, intermittents,
continuing, putrid,* and the like.

In his characteristically imperious way, Rush now declared that
there was in truth only one disease and since there was but one disease there was, logically enough, but one remedy. In this sweeping
generalization he included diseases of the mind with diseases of the
body. There was some advantage in this point of view, because it
focused his attention on what are today called psychosomatic
phenomena—that is, on body-mind relationships.

According to Rush, underlying all disease was a predisposing
debility or, in modern terminology, a lowered resistance. Operating on this debility was a stimulus or an exciting cause and these
together produced excessive action or convulsive excitement in the
walls of the blood vessels. Madness, according to Rush, resulted
from the morbid irregular action of the vessels in that part of the
brain which is the seat of the mind. Thus it was nothing more than
a chronic non-specific form of fever, to be treated by preventing
or reducing the exciting cause and lowering the resulting tension.
To achieve this, bleeding and purging, as in yellow fever, were his
stand-bys. Now it is possible to translate into modern equivalents
some of Rush's physiological hypotheses, for which, to be sure, he
could adduce no direct or experimental evidence. Instead of convulsive excitement in the walls of the blood vessels, a modern psychiatrist would substitute electrical impulses in the brain and rever-
berating circuits. But even these, plus the refined techniques of
modern brain physiology, have as yet contributed little to our understanding of insanity except perhaps in epilepsy, in the presence
of gross pathological cerebral lesions.

Dr. Rush had little interest in pathological anatomy. He seemed
hardly aware of the work of Bichat and the French school and
their efforts at the localization of lesions. Indeed, on the whole he
was indifferent to the laboratory approach to medical problems, so

much was he absorbed in his practice and dedicated to helping his patients and his students. He brought to psychiatry the urgent need, which he shared with Franklin and Jefferson and Rittenhouse, to make the world a better place for man to live in, and this he thought he could do best by attending to the thing in hand, in spite of his obvious penchant for theoretical speculations.

But one should not belittle his substantive accomplishments. Nor should one dismiss his errors with an air of superiority. A hundred and fifty years from now our present convictions and theories in medicine may be looked upon with equal disregard by our descendants, if, indeed, they do not return to his views. In an historical survey, the errors of a great man do not count. What counts are his moral ideal and the push he gives to man's fate. On this score one can only admire Rush, in spite of the unevenness of his thinking. The fact is, he was so persuasive, so passionate, convinced and articulate, that he swept objections before him. And soon he had a devoted band of student-followers who continued to practice his mistakes. This is the fate of most great men—to put a drag anchor on their generation at the very time they are launching it on hitherto uncharted seas. Rush was not unaware of this danger. In a lecture on Hippocrates delivered six years before his work on diseases of the mind was published, he said:

"While we thus felicitate ourselves upon the present highly cultivated and improved state of medicine, let us check a disposition to pride, by looking forward to a time when there will probably be the same difference between our degrees of knowledge, and those that are to exist hereafter, that now exists between us and Hippocrates. Should discoveries in our science be multiplied but for a century to come, in the same ratio they have been for the last thirty years, this difference will probably take place. Then will the opinions and modes of practice of modern physicians, furnish subjects for animadversion, such as you have heard this day upon those of Hippocrates.

"Perhaps from the chair which I now occupy, your successors in this seminary may hear expressions of surprise and contempt at our ignorance of the most simple modes of curing diseases which now elude our skill, or of our tedious, painful, and offensive, remedies for such as are under the power of medicine. Should the humble labours of your teacher, who now addresses you, attract his notice,

I hope he will do him the justice to admit, before he consigns his name and opinions to oblivion, that he experienced the same pleasure in renouncing an old error that he did in teaching a new truth; and that the health and lives of his patients, and the improvement of his pupils were always dearer to him than interest or fame."

In a century and a half Rush's name and opinions have not been consigned to oblivion. From the nature of this peroration, and because of his unequalled personal charm, one can understand what a hold he had on the young minds of his students, of whom he had taught as many as 3,000. Whether he really experienced as much pleasure in renouncing an old error as he did in teaching a new truth may well be questioned. Who, indeed, does? But it must be admitted that he did change his mind about the means of transmission of yellow fever and that he admitted his mistake in believing it to be a contagious disease.

As for his animadversions on the teachings of Hippocrates, whose aphorisms Rush had translated into English before he was twenty years of age, these should be explored further. They spell out much about Rush's medical philosophy. Beginning with Hippocrates' ignorance of anatomy, physiology and pathology, Rush goes on to charge him with believing in the healing powers of nature and regarding a physician as the servant of nature. Of this attitude, so congenial to a 20th-century physician, Rush had this to say:

"The result of his confidence in these powers appears in the histories of many of his cases, most of which terminated in death. . . . It is impossible to calculate the mischief which Hippocrates has done by first marking nature with his name, and afterwards letting her loose upon sick people. Millions have perished by her hands in all ages and countries."

Hippocrates and Rush should have been of one mind. Both were activated by what Edith Hamilton has called "the greatest spirit that moves in humanity, the spirit that makes men free." But Hippocrates lived in the golden age of an ancient civilization which had achieved a kind of human wisdom perhaps never equalled, whereas Rush had followed on the heels of pioneers whose energies were consumed in conquering a wilderness, in subduing nature and bending her to man's will. For Rush and for many of his contemporaries the demand for such action was loud and imperative.

Americans have not yet come to realize the dangers inherent in this belief. In the day of the pioneer, nature was more often than not man's enemy. He had to set her aright. It is no wonder that people today are confused in their semantics; that they can no longer distinguish between what is radical and what is conservative and so continue to spoil our landscape, waste our resources and poison our environment.

But medicine has returned to the Hippocratic view. It believes in the healing power of nature, in *working with nature and never against her.* This is implicit in the moral treatment in psychiatry, which Rush supported with one hand, while with the other he continued to use remedies which today, to use his own words, would be considered "tedious, painful, and offensive." But in this respect we cannot call the kettle black. Who knows what a future generation of doctors will say of electric shock treatment and lobotomy?

His other stricture against Hippocrates, whom he venerated and whose fame, he said, rose "like a stupendous and solitary mountain," had to do with his classification of diseases. According to Rush, Hippocrates enumerated 239 general and local diseases, and described several more to which he gave no names. "In designating symptoms, like plants and animals, by specific characters," Rush wrote, "and afterwards prescribing specific remedies for them, he has rendered medicine complex, useless, or fatal, in many instances." History had repeated this error from Hippocrates to Cullen, and Rush set about to correct it. He began by reclassifying mental diseases into certain well-defined categories. To Rush's famous French colleague Pinel, who was distinguished rather for his succinct case presentations, such systematic classification was of less interest; but for Rush, to whom quasi-philosophical speculations came naturally, it was meat and drink.

*   *   *

In the preface to his *Diseases of the Mind,* Rush tells his readers that he has been obliged to employ a new nomenclature because new opinions are proposed and new symptoms are described. This is as necessary as is an increase in the number of words and their combinations to meet the growing wants and objects of civilized society. Many of Rush's terms have not stuck or there has been a shift in their meaning, so that a kind of glossary is needed to understand them. For example, the word *melancholia* (from black bile), he replaced by a much more appropriate term—*tristimania*—which, however, has never been officially accepted in psychiatry. The characteristic symptom of this form of derangement, which he also designates as *hypochondriasis*, is *distress*, of which the causes are both numerous and of a personal nature. Here are some of Rush's examples:

The patient "erroneously believes himself to be afflicted with various diseases, particularly with consumption, cancer, stone, and above all with impotence and the venereal disease. Sometimes he supposes himself to be poisoned, or that his constitution had been ruined by mercury, or that the seeds of the hydrophobia are floating in his system. . . . He believes that he has a living animal in his body. A sea-captain, formerly of this city, believed for many years that he had a wolf in his liver. . . . There is now a madman in the Pennsylvania Hospital who believes that he was once a calf, and who mentions the name of the butcher that killed him, and the stall in the Philadelphia market in which his flesh was sold. . . . One of the princes of Bourbon believed he was transformed into a plant and stood in his garden, where he insisted upon being watered in common with all the plants around him." Or again the patient may think he is transformed into glass, or that if he discharges the contents of his bladder, he will drown the world, or indeed that he is dead.

"It is worthy of notice," writes Rush, "in all these cases of erroneous judgment, the patients reason correctly, that is, draw just inferences from their errors." All their erroneous opinions about themselves are of a degrading nature. Rush states that these patients, afflicted with hypochondriasis or tristimania, are often peevish, irascible, quarrelsome, very sensitive to noise, restless and unstable. They are given to paroxysms and remissions and can be favorably influenced "by company, wine, exercise, and, above all, the weather."

There is nothing here that will astonish a present-day psychiatrist. For Rush's word *tristimania* he would substitute involutional psychosis or agitated depression with somatic delusions; and for *amenomania*—another one of Rush's terms—paranoia, signifying a thought disorder in which the individual projects his own inner turmoil onto the outer world or, in the case of hypochondriasis,

onto his own body. The relationship of these two states, hypochondriasis and paranoia, can be verified daily by any psychiatrist.
Even the relationship of hypochondriasis to hysteria, which Rush
recognized, is still often apparent. But what is different in our
thinking is that we have progressed a little further toward finding
the underlying causes of some of these disturbances and sometimes
we can treat them, whereas Rush, who was even more ignorant
than we are, could deal only with the symptoms—that is, the
derangement which he conceived of in terms of the excessive and
morbid action of the vessels of the brain.

A case in point would be general paresis, or syphilis of the central nervous system. Rush did in fact recognize *tabes dorsalis* or
locomotor ataxia, but in his day the cause of it was still an unsolved
mystery. Nor could he possibly have guessed that the excitement,
the mood changes, the memory defects, the euphoria, the inappropriate behavior and the degradation of character so commonly observed in sufferers from general paresis were caused by changes in
the brain due to a microscopic protozoan parasite, the *Treponema
pallidum*, the existence of which was not discovered for another
eighty years. And it would take another eight years before this
same organism was actually found in the brains removed at autopsies from the unfortunate patients. Then several more decades
would elapse before the discovery of penicillin and its use as a preventive of this dread and once common disease—now so rare that
most present-day medical students have never seen a case.

On the basis of its symptoms, and perhaps because of changes in
the pulse, Rush included this disease under the rubric of General
Intellectual Derangement or General Madness and, according to its
severity, or chronicity, classified it under *mania, manicula,* or
manalgia—words no longer in use. For the last two we might substitute "hypomania" and "catatonia." He would have treated them
with depleting measures because of the assumed arterial excitement.
Although such treatment would have been inappropriate, Rush's
implication of the blood supply to the brain was nearer the truth
than he could have known. In general paresis the degeneration of
brain substance results from pathological changes in the arterial
system. When Rush speaks of "those cases in which persons of exemplary piety and purity of character, utter profane, or impious,
or indelicate language, or behave in other respects contrary to their

moral habits," he was probably referring to general paresis, then a common disease, because this behavior is characteristic of it. But such behavior can also be encountered in a great variety of other psychotic states, some of known origin, others still unknown.

In addition to the various other kinds of treatment that Rush recommends, he makes the following comment:

"An epidemic fever, many years ago, pervaded the cells of our hospital, which restored the greater part of the maniacs to their reason. These accidental cures struck the late Dr. Bond so forcibly, that he attempted to exercise a fever in several of his patients . . . by sending them to the swamps of Gloucester County. . . in the State of New Jersey, With what success I have never heard."

The dear old Jersey mosquito! A modern physician, if he is not too young, will recall that the Viennese neurologist, Wagner von Jauregg, noticed that patients suffering from syphilis of the brain improved when they had fever from some other infection. In 1917 he deliberately gave them malaria. Later, fever was induced by various kinds of electrically generated heat waves.

Rush comments on the immense changes in the human mind that are induced by a little alteration in the circulation of the blood in the brain. "What great effects are produced in this instance by little causes! How slender the tenure by which we hold our intellectual and moral existence! and how humiliating our situation from its loss!" He frequently turns to the poets to exemplify his points—"many things arrest their attention, which escape the notice of physicians." He is fond of quoting *King Lear* or the poet Cowper, and many of the great names of English and classical literature and quotations from the Scriptures punctuate his writing.

With regard to the obscene and profane talk of deranged patients who believe themselves to be the Messiah, Rush says:

"There was a time when persons thus deranged were subjected to fines, imprisonment, the extirpation of their tongues, and even to death from fire and the halter. To the influence of the science of medicine we are indebted, for teaching that these opinions are generally as devoid of impiety as an epileptic fit . . . ."

Rush believed that derangement could derive from a sense of guilt, either real or imaginary. But no two divines are ever agreed in what constitutes the unpardonable sin, and many wise and good men believe it is not possible to commit it. Even murder and theft

Rush accounts for, not as vices, but as symptoms of the disease he calls *moral derangement*, hoping thus to rescue persons affected with it "from the arm of the law, and to render them subjects of the kind and lenient hand of medicine." Lying and drinking, he thinks, are still other symptoms of this disease.

Here he is clearly speaking of what would later be called pathological lying, for he says:

"Persons thus diseased can not speak the truth upon any subject nor tell the same story twice in the same way, nor describe any thing as it has happened to other people. Their falsehoods are seldom calculated to injure any body but themselves, being for the most part of a hyperbolic or boasting nature, but now and then they are of a mischievous nature, and injurious to the characters and property of others."

He infers that it is a corporeal disease because it sometimes appears in mad people who are remarkable for veracity in the healthy states of their minds.

"Lying, as a vice, is said to be incurable," says Rush. "The same thing may be said of it as a disease, when it appears in adult life. It is generally the result of a defective education." As for the habitual use of strong drink, Rush recognizes the limitations of the religious and moral approach when not combined with remedies of a physical nature. He urges "the establishment of a hospital in every city and town in the United States, for the exclusive reception of hard drinkers." Of them he says:

"They are as much objects of public humanity and charity, as mad people. They are indeed more hurtful to society, than most of the deranged patients of a common hospital would be, if they were set at liberty. Who can calculate the extensive influence of a drunken husband or wife upon the property and morals of their families. . . ."

After more than a century and a half we can only echo and applaud these sentiments. Rush regards the drunkard as more dangerous to society than the thief and recommends that before confining him to a hospital or "Sober House" he be examined by a commission consisting of a physician and two or three magistrates appointed by the Court. Society has not, as yet, followed his advice nor met this still imperative need.

Another of his suggestions has been lost sight of. In writing of the care of patients who exhibited taciturnity, downcast looks, a total neglect of dress and person, long nails and beard, dishevelled or matted hair, indifference to heat and cold, or what we would probably call a patient in a severely retarded depression or in a schizophrenic catatonic state, Rush laments the want of the right kind of attendant.

What is needed, he says, is "some person of prudence and intelligence," who should live constantly with the mad people and "have the exclusive direction of their minds." He should converse with them, read to them from entertaining books, and let them read to him, dine with them and protect them from the rudeness and insults of their keepers, walk out with them and ride with them, partake in their amusements and "measure out their punishments." (sic!) "Such a person would do more good to mad people in one month, than the visits, or the accidental company, of the patient's friends would do in a year." Rush was proposing a kind of resourceful psychiatric social worker or psychiatric nurse, or perhaps a lay visitor. But no such person appeared on the medical scene for many years to come. Rush paid strict attention to cleanliness in the person and apartments of mad people, believing this to be indispensable not only to their comfort but to their cure. The ragged dress, the dirty skin, the long nails and beard and the uncombed hair of the madman cause him to lose the consciousness of his personal identity—these are his words.

Many of his comments are singularly apposite and familiar: "A conscience, burdened with guilt, whether real or imaginary, is a frequent cause of madness. The latter produces it much oftener than the former." Worldly success can be followed by a severe depression. This, every present-day psychiatrist can attest. Thus, "Sir Philip Mordaunt shot himself immediately after succeeding to a great estate . . . and while he appeared to be in possession of everything that could constitute the plenitude of human happiness." Or again, "The eldest son of a Scotch nobleman, of high rank and large fortune, destroyed himself in the same way, a few weeks after the consummation of all his wordly prospects and enjoyments by his marriage to a most accomplished and amiable young lady."·

Depression of the mind, according to Rush, "may be induced by causes that are forgotten; or by the presence of objects which revive the sensation of distress with which it was at one time associated, but without reviving the cause of it in the memory." To counteract the morbid effects of envy, malice and hatred, Rush followed a suggestion that had been given him by a madman in the Pennsylvania Hospital. This patient had the habit of writing down everything that passed in his mind, and particularly malice and revenge. "In recording the latter," this man said, "I feel my mind emptied of something disagreeable to it, just as a vomit empties the stomach of bile. When I look at what I have written a day or two afterwards, I feel ashamed and disgusted with it, and wish to throw it into the fire." Rush was convinced from this and similar cases of the salutary effects of this remedy. The present generation of psychiatrists would recognize this method as representing free association, or perhaps what they call "abreaction" or "catharsis."

Although given to a variety of bodily treatments, some of which seem inappropriate and archaic today, Rush found, in keeping with his extraordinary psychological insight, that intellectual derangement is more common from mental than corporeal causes. He quotes the figures cited by Pinel in the Bicêtre Hospital in Paris. Of 113 patients confined in this hospital, 34 were there because of domestic misfortunes, 24 from disappointments in love, 30 from the distressing events of the French Revolution, and 25 from fanaticism. Rush's own figures correspond roughly to these. In his group of patients, 34 became ill from mental causes and 16 from corporeal. Among the latter he lists sunstroke, intemperance, parturition and onanism, and certain toxic substances such as opium, hemlock, nightshade and aconite. As for the influence of the moon in inducing or increasing madness, Rush believed that the moon, when full, increased the rarity of the air and the quantity of light, and that these act upon sick people in various diseases, and, among others, in madness. Such action, he thought, required a predisposition. He agreed with his English colleagues that a predisposition to madness was connected with dark-colored hair. He could find no correlation with the size and shape of the skull. He was quite aware of the familial incidence of some forms of derangement, citing the example, among others, of identical twin brothers, both captains in the Army, who committed suicide by cutting their throats with their razors. They lived 200 miles apart, one in Vermont and the other in Deerfield, Massachusetts; both were happily married but subject to fits of melancholy.

As for the incidence of madness, Rush found a greater disposition to it between the ages of twenty and fifty than at any other time in life. His own figures agreed with both Pinel's and with Mr. Haslam's at Bethlehem. Women are more susceptible than men, and single persons more than married ones. "Celibacy," he says, "is a pleasant breakfast, a tolerable dinner, but a very bad supper." The rich are more predisposed than the poor—a statement which we cannot support today. He quotes Dryden in saying that great wit and madness are nearly allied. He agrees with Pinel that poets, painters, sculptors and musicians are most subject to madness, but he never knew "a chymist, a naturalist, a mathematician, or a natural philosopher" to be afflicted. This he attributed to the fact that the artist exercises his imagination, the scientist his understanding. Modern psychiatric experience could support neither the observation, nor its explanation.

Rush believed that suicide was more common in men than in women, and more in Protestants than in Catholics because the latter relieve their minds from the pressure of guilt, by means of confession and absolution. In a government in which all the power of a country is representative and elective, general suffrage and free presses served, he thought, like chimneys in a house, to conduct from the individual and public mind all the discontent, vexation and resentment which had been generated in the passions, by real or supposed evils, and thus prevented the understanding from being injured by them. Were he living today perhaps he would recommend that we clean our flues. Perhaps he would find many of our citizens still afflicted with what he called "tory-rot"—a name for the timidity of those Americans who played no active part in the Revolution. Rush was fully aware of the rôle of the major emotions in causing not only bodily but mental disturbances and he even recognized that arousing a moderate degree of anger in depressed persons would counteract their depression.

*   *   *

In the light of these almost prophetic insights it is the more remarkable to consider some of his therapeutic procedures. To understand these there must be kept in mind the fact that fever was Rush's presiding conceptual model—fever which implied the excitability of the blood vessels. He must have assumed some kind of balance, hydrostatic or otherwise, between the brain and more distant parts of the body. Hence his use of blisters and purges to set up a competing inflammatory reaction elsewhere—in the mouth through mercury, or in the stomach, the bowels, or, for example, on the shaved cranium. This was but a part of the mystical pathophysiology of the day.

This led to other absurdities. A patient was forced to assume an erect posture for many hours at a time, or he was placed in a gyrator which, by centrifugal action, was supposed to influence the cerebral circulation by carrying blood away from the brain. When he was too unruly he was encased in a contraption called, euphemistically enough and again prophetically, a "tranquilizer." Rush abandoned this because the restrained and immobilized patient was still able to damage himself. Reward and punishment were implicit in his treatment. A not too subtle method of control was that of pouring cold water inside a patient's sleeve.

Control was the essence of Rush's therapeutic activity. Through his eye, his voice, his countenance he aimed to secure the obedience of his deranged patient. But he cautioned that a physician's conduct "should be uniformly dignified. . . . He should never descend to levity." He must be just and have a strict regard to truth. Above all, if he wished to acquire the obedience and affections of his deranged patients, this he could do only by acts of kindness.

The 18th-century physician was an authoritarian figure and Rush, because of his extraordinary personal magnetism and intelligence and his reputation as America's greatest doctor, was the very embodiment of authority. He did not hesitate to exploit this by the use of moral and emotional persuasion. He tried to meet irrationality with cogent reasoning, but he was not above the use of the "pious hoax." If his patient thought he had a snake in his stomach, Rush would not hesitate to have one placed in what he calls his close-stool. To a hypochondriacal patient who feared that he had a venereal disease, Rush recommended marriage and at the same time offered him a bond for a large sum of money if any bad consequences should follow taking this advice.

No modern psychiatrist, worthy of the name, would so behave. Yet, at the same time, Rush was capable of proposing a definition of *phobia* at which no one could cavil today. Phobia he called a fear of an imaginary evil or an undue fear of a real one. He even permitted himself in this connection a few of his rare pleasantries, poking fun at those who spun out a multiplicity of diseases.

"Rum-phobia is a very rare distemper. I have known but five instances of it in the course of my life. . . . Doctor-phobia is complicated with other diseases. It arises often from the dread of taking physic, or of submitting to the remedies of blistering and bleeding. It might be supposed to be caused by the terror of a long bill, but this excites terror in few minds, for who ever thinks of paying a doctor's bill while he can use his money to advantage in another way?"

*   *   *

Rush finished writing his *Diseases of the Mind* at the end of February 1812, and in late October he was correcting the last of the proof sheets. During the next quarter-century this work, bearing the ponderous title *Medical Inquiries and Observations upon the Diseases of the Mind,* went through five editions, as well as numerous translations into foreign languages. For many years it remained the only textbook on mental diseases in America. It was widely quoted by foreign authors, particularly by Esquirol, who was Pinel's successor and the leading European alienist of the first half of the 19th century. Rush began his book in this fashion:

"In entering upon the subject of the following Inquiries and Observations, I feel as if I were about to tread upon consecrated ground. I am aware of its difficulty and importance, and thus humbly implore that BEING, whose government extends to the thoughts of all his creatures, so to direct mine, in this arduous undertaking, that nothing hurtful to my fellow citizens may fall from my pen, and that this work may be the means of lessening a portion of some of the greatest evils of human life."

An earlier longhand manuscript of lectures on the mind had opened thus:

"The knowledge of the human mind is the most *important* branch of all the sciences. . . . The history of the faculties and operations of the human mind is the most *certain* of all kinds of knowledge. It consists of facts only. It relates to feelings and actions which take place within ourselves, and in which it is not possible for us to be deceived."

Little did Rush realize how terribly easy it is for us to deceive ourselves, especially in the realm of the emotions. The distant echo of Descartes' *cogito ergo sum* can be heard in this and also in Rush's psychophysical dualism. Descartes lived in the century before Rush; he does not mention his name in his autobiography or published letters. But knowing his wide reading and his familiarity with the great, both living and dead, it is scarcely possible that he was not influenced by the French philosopher, as he was by Locke. Descartes believed that the emotions are based on physiological —or what Rush would have called "corporeal"—processes, and that to control them one would have to control the underlying bodily reactions.

Benjamin Rush's views were entirely consonant with this. In like manner he believed that "All the operations on the mind are the effects of motions previously excited in the brain," and that "every idea and thought appears to depend upon a motion peculiar to itself." He believed that the mind was located in an unspecified area of the brain and that it could migrate from an injured to a healthy part. He objects to "madness" being "placed exclusively in the mind . . . because the mind is incapable of any operations independently of impressions communicated to it through the medium of the body."

And yet Rush escapes the charge of materialism by regarding the mind as a reality distinct from the body, although stimulated and influenced by it. Whatever his metaphysical beliefs, it is quite clear that he thought mental illness could begin with emotional disturbances due to fear or anger, for example, or to intellectual causes. But in both instances the effects were the same—excessive action in the blood vessels of the brain. Perhaps, as Descartes had done, he reconciled his dualism by the conviction that God's intervention served to connect the two worlds. This would have been as consistent with his religious views as his dualism was consistent with the fundamental ambivalence of his personality.

Just because of his dualism, he avoided the exclusively physical approach to mental illness and exhibited a great concern with his patients' total personality. This was evident in his treatment, which, apart from the physical measures already mentioned, included almost everything still in use in a modern mental hospital. The list would include exercise, hydrotherapy, occupational ther-

apy, productive work, music, reading, travel and even malarial
therapy. But more important than these was his emphasis on the
decent environment of his patients and on the attitude and character of the personnel who had the "mad" men and women in their
charge.

He brought to his work a natural dignity, an earnestness, and an
optimism that probably transcended in effectiveness all his therapeutic measures. He was an artist endowed with unusual intuitive
gifts for empathy and understanding, who met his patients, perhaps
as an authoritarian figure, but also with kindness and with the intellectual curiosity so characteristic of him. Nothing escaped his
interest—what they ate, the clothes they wore, the climate in
which they lived and worked, their hopes and their fears.

If he was confused and stubborn in his theories and in his insistence on a unitary interpretation of all disease, at least he escaped
the error of his immediate followers in overemphasizing a phreno-
logical interpretation of mental phenomena. He brought to his
work a psychological orientation, even an interest in dreams, which
has presided over much of modern psychiatry ever since. It is so
often true of dominating figures that their gifts seem to be par-
celled out among their offspring. Some will inherit some of them
and others others. Present-day psychiatrists, descended from this
progenitor, are as divided as Rush was in himself—some emphasiz-
ing the psychological, others the anatomical-physiological point of
view.

In terms of method and critique, Rush was certainly no great
scientist. Some of his therapeutic devices not only seem unusual,
but are based on a rationale little short of fantastic. For example, he
maintained that:

"Mercury acts . . . by abstracting morbid excitement from the
brain to the mouth, by removing visceral obstructions, and by
changing the cause of our patient's complaints and fixing them
wholly upon his sore mouth. The salivation will do still more service if it excite some degree of resentment against the patient's
physician or friends. . . . [Mercury] stimulates every part of the
body, renders the vessels pervious to their natural juices, conveys
morbid action out of the body by the mouth, and thus restores the
mind to its native seat in the brain."

Mercury was an old remedy introduced into medicine by Paracelsus, who lived two and a half centuries before Rush. It had been used since the 15th century for the treatment of syphilis, but Rush could not possibly have known that some of his mad patients suffered from syphilis of the brain. If mercury actually helped them, it was not for the reasons that Rush advanced, but perhaps because it worked as an anti-syphilitic. However, Rush's notion of exciting some degree of resentment against the physician is perhaps more sensible than it sounds. As is now known, this might easily lighten a patient's burden of depression or awaken him from a state of apathy. Rush had, to be sure, other ways of doing this by practicing a kind of ingenious intimidation—ducking his patients in water or threatening them with burial if they imagined that they were dead. Fortunately in science the evil that men do and their fallacies are buried with their bones, and the good lives after them because it withstands the test of time.

*   *   *

Perhaps Benjamin Rush's most important contribution to psychiatry was his discussion of what, in a lecture on medical jurisprudence, delivered to his students in 1810, he called "moral derangement." Here he touches on many questions that still plague our criminal courts, such as, what constitutes knowledge of right and wrong, what is the nature of responsibility, and of irresistible impulses. His illustrative cases have a familiar contemporary ring:

"A respectable schoolmaster of the name of Reuse in Hamburgh, in the year 1804, murdered his wife and five children in the course of a single night, and afterwards attempted to destroy his own life. This man bore a good character, lived happily with his family, and retired to rest apparently in harmony with them all. He had just before been unsuccessful in a trifling lawsuit, which he feared would involve his family in distress. He expiated his disease, says Rush, for it cannot be called murder, upon the rack.

"In the year 1804, a certain David Williams at Milton in the State of New York, became weary of life and contemplated destroying himself by suicide; but changed his purpose, and with uncommon circumstances of cruelty, killed a little boy of the name of Ira Lane, who had never offended him, and whom probably he had never seen before.

"A certain Catharine Zigler murdered her child. She instantly confessed her crime, was tried, and acquitted, probably from a suspicion that she was somewhat deranged. She became pregnant soon afterwards, on purpose, as she said, that she might have another object upon which she might gratify her propensity to murder. She was delivered of a child, which she immediately destroyed. For this act she was dragged to a court of law, where she was condemned, and finally suffered the punishment of death."

These cases, and many others like them, Rush regarded as instances of moral derangement. In his energetic and articulate way he defended them against what he considered the cruel retribution of the law. By "moral derangement" he meant "that state of mind in which the passions act involuntarily through the instrumentality of the will, without any disease in the understanding." This is what the French were later to call *manie avec conscience* and the English psychiatrist Prichard named "moral insanity" in 1835. In all of this Rush took the lead, arguing vehemently that such people were suffering from a disease and should not be guilty in the eyes of the law. Nor was he primarily concerned with whether they were able to distinguish right from wrong, on which Macnaughton's rule would later be based in England. Rush was again far in advance of his time in recognizing irresistible impulse as a sound legal plea.

The unevenness of Rush's views and his own ambivalence have elicited equally ambivalent responses from his critics. Some extol him as a great pioneer; others find him confused and his work all but worthless. Certainly, from a strictly modern point of view his clinical data were sketchy and amateurish; he had no statistical proof for most of his statements, nor any way of testing his theory of arterial excitement. He was often guilty of analogical and circular thinking and of *post hoc* arguments. But he said this:

"The first thing to be done by a physician . . . is to treat the disease in a serious manner. To consider it in any other light, is to renounce all observation in medicine. However erroneous a patient's opinion of his case may be, his disease is a *real* one. It will be necessary, therefore, for a physician to listen with attention to his tedious and uninteresting details of its symptoms and causes. . . . He [the doctor] should hear with silence their rude or witty answers to his questions and upon no account ever laugh at them or with them. . . ."

And this:

"In reviewing the slender and [in]adequate means that have been employed for ameliorating the condition of mad people, we are led further to lament the slower progress of humanity in its effort to relieve them, than any other class of the afflicted children of men. For many centuries they have been treated like criminals, or shunned like beasts of prey; or, if visited, it has only been for the purpose of inhuman curiosity and amusement. Even the ties of consanguinity have been dissolved by the walls of a mad house, and sons and brothers have sometimes languished or sauntered away their lives within them without once hearing the accents of a kindred voice.

"Happily these times of cruelty to this class of our fellow creatures, and insensibility to their sufferings, are now passing away. In Great Britain a humane revolution, dictated by modern improvements in the science of the mind, as well as of medicine, has taken place in the receptacles of mad people, more especially in those that are of a private nature. A similar change has taken place in the Pennsylvania Hospital, under the direction of its present managers, in the condition of the deranged subjects of their care. The clanking of chains, and the noise of the whip, are no longer heard in their cells. They now taste of the blessings of air, and light and motion, in pleasant and shaded walks in summer, and in spacious entries, warmed by stoves, in winter, in both of which the sexes are separated and alike protected from the eye of the visitors of the Hospital. In consequence of these advantages, they have recovered the human figure, and with it, their long forgotten relationship to their friends and the public.

"Much, however, remains yet to be done for their comfort and relief. To animate us in filling up the measure of kindness which has been solicited for them, let us recollect the greatness of its object. It is not to feed or clothe the body, nor yet to cure one of its common disease; it is to restore the disjointed or debilitated faculties of the mind of a fellow creature to their natural order and offices, and to revive in him the knowledge of himself, his family and his God."

Of the treatment of the criminally insane, he wrote:

"We bestow much study and great labor in restoring the wandering reason of our fellow creatures; but we neglect their

erring hearts. We erect splendid and commodious buildings to
confine persons, when intellectual derangement has rendered them
dangerous to society, and we employ our skill and humanity to relieve them; but with an unmerciful impatience, we consign persons,
whom moral derangement has rendered mischievous, to the exterminating ax and halter." [1]

Benjamin Rush recognized deviant behavior as illness rather than
deliberate wickedness and thus helped lay the groundwork for the
modern conception of personality disorder. Although his psychological insights were often astute, the therapeutic measures he employed by no means kept pace with them, because he was bound
by the mechanistic attitudes that prevailed in his time and that he
had brought with him from Edinburgh. Nevertheless, as the
harbinger of American psychiatry he needs no further apology.

15

WHAT MANNER
OF MAN?

❀ THE PUBLICATION IN 1812 OF HIS MEDICAL IN-
quiries and Observations upon the Diseases of the Mind was the
crowning achievement of Benjamin Rush's professional life. When
sending a copy to his friend, John Adams, he wrote:

"The subjects of them [mental diseases] have hitherto been en-
veloped in mystery. I have endeavored to bring them down to the
level of all the other diseases of the human body, and to show that
the mind and body are moved by the same causes and subject to
the same laws. For this attempt to simplify the *medicina mentis* I
expect no quarter from my learned brethren. But time I hope will
do my opinions justice. I believe them to be true and calculated to
lessen some of the greatest evils of human life. If they are not, I
shall console myself with having aimed well and erred honestly."

Since this time many psychiatrists have made similar attempts—
that is, to reduce the laws of mental life to the same principles as
govern the actions of the body. This laudable ambition is difficult
to achieve, because in the case of the mind the number of variables
is so great that a quantitative experimental approach has thus far
hardly proved feasible.

Rush assured Adams that his work had been well received by the
gentlemen of the bar, but not a single physician, with one exception, had taken the slightest notice of it. He now lived at peace
among his medical brethren, although he claimed to have no

friends among them. "Leave off writing books, Doctor," Judge Peters had said to him, "and they will cease to be your enemies."

In the course of his preparation of this book, Rush had undergone a poignant personal experience. In his *Commonplace Book*, on December 11, 1802, he made this note:

"This day my son John resumed the study of medicine. So anxious was he to return to my house and business that he said 'he would supply the place of one of my men servants and even clean my stable rather than continue to follow a sea life.' "

John had been a lieutenant in the Navy. He took his medical degree in 1804 and his graduating thesis was: "An inaugural essay on the causes of sudden death and the means of preventing it." The dissertation was dedicated to his father, and in the context of the young man's life this title was perhaps a prophetic one.

Then, instead of accepting an appointment at the Philadelphia General Hospital, the young doctor set off for South Carolina, where he re-entered the Navy as a sailing master. From 1805 to 1808 he was in command of various gunboats in Boston and New Orleans. On October 1, 1807, he fought a duel with Lieutenant Benjamin Taylor, in command of Gunboat No. 15 at the New Orleans Station. Taylor was killed. He had been one of John's closest friends. John was arrested, but a few weeks later he was returned to duty. Within a year he was again in trouble because of a quarrel and gunplay on his vessel. He was then ordered to Washington. The next news of him came in a letter from Captain David Porter, bringing to his father the unhappy message that John was insane and had attempted suicide. While at first there was hope of his recovery, he was brought home in February 1810 in a state of deep melancholy. His father described him thus:

"Neither the embraces nor tears of his parents, brothers, or sister could prevail upon him to speak to them. His grief and uncombed hair and long beard added to the distress produced by the disease of his mind," a disease with which Dr. Rush was all too familiar. John was hospitalized on his father's ward in the Pennsylvania Hospital.

In time, Rush recovered from the anguish and distress of his son's illness, which cast a pall over the whole family, but for some time he was quite unfitted for study or professional work. On January 2, 1811 he wrote Jefferson:

"My son is better. He has become attentive to his dress, now and then opens a book, converses with a few people, but still discovers, with a good deal of melancholy, alienation of mind upon several subjects, particularly those which associate with the cause of his derangement. He is now in a cell in the Pennsylvania Hospital, where there is too much reason to believe he will end his days."

This prognosis was an accurate one. With the exception of one short remission, John Rush remained there for twenty-seven years, until 1837. His constant walking to and fro had worn deep grooves in the planks of the ward flooring. These were known as "Rush's walk." It was like his father to face up to this agony with quiet courage, and to let it goad him on in his major life work.

If Benjamin Rush was in fact the first American psychiatrist, this was not because of any special training. Such training was not available in Colonial America nor in the early years of the United States. What knowledge he had, he had gained, as psychiatrists still do, from the observation of his patients, from reading and from an extraordinarily wide acquaintance with his fellow men. He had come to know all kinds: philosophers and statesmen and scholars; laborers and artisans; Negroes and Indians; slaves and freedmen; Jews and Germans and ignorant drunken Irish immigrants; Tories and Whigs; Baptists, Episcopalians, Lutherans, Methodists, Presbyterians and Quakers; Southern aristocrats, New Englanders and farmers; prospectors and woodsmen. His relationships with all of them were by no means superficial. Because of his intelligence, his inordinate curiosity and his capacity for feeling his way into other people's lives, he possessed ideal gifts for understanding. Perhaps his arrogance, his lack of humor and his need to moralize may be looked upon as liabilities, but in those days a doctor of medicine was still a man of singular learning, a model of deportment and, above all, an authoritarian father-figure. Rush's personality lent itself to this stereotype, but it was softened by great kindness and by a real concern for suffering and oppressed people, and as well by the sentimental streak in his nature.

* * *

In his later years Benjamin Rush's reputation and fame spread beyond the parochial confines of his native state and even across the Atlantic. He had become famous not only for his work on yellow fever and for his studies on *Diseases of the Mind*, but also for bringing out an American edition of the works of Sydenham and for many important medical observations. In 1805 he had received a gold medal from the King of Prussia for his great services during the yellow fever epidemic of 1793. In 1807 the Queen of Etruria awarded him another gold medal; and four years later, on the eve of Napoleon's defeat, the Czar of Russia sent him a diamond ring. In addition to these honors, the King of Spain ordered the account of yellow fever to be translated into Spanish, and sent his minister, Don Carlos Martinez, to express the royal thanks; and Rush was also given diplomas from several literary and philosophical societies in different parts of Europe. He never mentioned these various tributes to more than two or three persons outside his own family, but they were clearly a source of great gratification to him. John Adams had written him: "Every Sprigg of Laurell you receive at home or from abroad gives me pleasure because I believe it well merited."

Although he was now more successful in his profession than he had ever been before, more sought after and both respected and honored, he claimed, nevertheless, to have felt more a stranger in Philadelphia than he would have in London or in Constantinople. To a younger colleague who had enquired "how you keep your body in health, and intellects in a state of such regular excitement, as to write with such correctness at all times," Rush replied with these words:

"I am now in my sixty-eighth year, and through divine goodness possess the same facility in doing business and the same pleasure in study that I did when I was a young man. I generally sleep about seven hours in the four-and-twenty, and spend from three to seven hours at my desk every day, according to the greater or less hurry of my business. I continue to prefer tea and coffee with their usual accompaniments to all other kinds of aliment. At dinner, but at no other time, I eat sparingly of animal food, with the common vegetables of our country, and generally drink one glass or a glass and a half of old Madeira wine after them. I never drink ardent spirits in any way nor at any time. I see well with spectacles and my hearing is unimpaired. I appreciate the continuance and perfection of these two senses at 100,000 dollars a year. Blessed be God for them; without them life would be a living death."

From necessity, he said he had conformed to the Spanish proverb of "being *old* when I was young, that I might be *young* when I was old." Dr. Rush was now Dean of the Medical School, having replaced Shippen.

He was the last survivor of the pre-Revolutionary professors. Morgan, Kuhn and Shippen were dead. Shippen, like Morgan, ended his life in solitary bitterness. Six of his eight children had died, his only son in early manhood, and in addition his daughter's life was wrecked through an unhappy marriage. At least he had the satisfaction of knowing that he was the first to remove the prejudices against male accoucheurs. In his last illness he sent for Rush and, though unable to speak, conveyed to him through his look the feeling that their old enmity was a thing of the past. Rush had written Adams on July 13, 1808: "The papers will inform you of the death of my brother professor and old enemy, Dr. Shippen. He sent for me in his last illness and discovered after he was unable to speak that he carried no hostility out of the world against me." Rush delivered a brief eulogy about Shippen to his students.

As Dean, Rush often spent as many as four hours a day examining candidates for degrees—a task which he called a "dull, mechanical, and fatiguing business." Political life had lost its allure for him, at least so he claimed. He stated repeatedly that he loathed political controversy above all things and seldom read anything in the newspapers but informative articles. "The few sands that remain in my glass," he wrote to Jefferson, "urge me constantly to quicken my labors." He had projected a great work on hygiene but this never came to fruition.

Judging from his lectures to his students, now numbering 300, during the years of the preparation of his life work on mental diseases, Rush seems to have kept up his other interests. Their subject matter ranges widely. There are homilies on the vices and virtues of physicians, on the proper education to qualify a young man for the study of medicine, on the pains and pleasures of a medical life. There are practical discussions on the construction and management of hospitals, with the most meticulous and thoughtful recommendations; on the means of getting business and of acquiring knowledge; and there are critical historical essays on two of his heroes, Hippocrates and Sydenham. The lectures were introductory in nature and designed to arrest and capture the young minds of his students and to offer them a model of professional sagacity which they might emulate.

"Observation without principles is nothing but empiricism. . . . The mind of a man pervades everything he does and says. . . . it is never too late to learn that which is necessary to be known. Dr. Franklin learned to write a fair and legible hand after he was 30. . . . In the present state of morals, and government, the stock of private sympathy can never be commensurate to the mass of sickness and distress which occur in our world."

Among the unjust causes for the loss of a doctor's business, Rush mentions writing poetry upon subjects unconnected with medicine.

"Mankind are in general ignorant of the relation of our science to all subjects, and that the mind acquires a versatility and facility in its operations upon medicine, by being occasionally exercised by other studies. They consider medicine as a trade; and that physician to be the most dextrous workman who knows least of other things. . . . a physician who knows nothing but the sciences which are supposed to belong exclusively to his profession, is a nonentity. . . . there should be no day nor night to a student; and above all, to a student of medicine. He should always, like a plant, be in an absorbing state."

One of the lectures in this series deals with the advantages to a physician of studying the diseases of domestic animals. In it, Dr. Rush makes a strong plea to establish a veterinary institution in this country and a Chair of Veterinary Medicine at the University of Pennsylvania. Here he showed his customary imaginative foresight. In another lecture he urged the keeping of records throughout the country of the ages and diseases of persons who die and of the months in which their deaths occur. Such information, he thought, would be of incalculable advantage to medical science.

Rush was again in advance of his time in believing that pain was not decreed by Heaven to be a necessary accompaniment of childbearing. It had been regarded by some divines as an unchangeable punishment for the original disobedience of women, and by some physicians as essential to enable the uterus to relieve itself of its burden. But in one instance Rush had observed delivery to take place during an epileptic seizure and in another during a fit of drunkenness, without any awareness or recollection of pain. In

1802 he expressed the hope that a medicine would be discovered that would produce insensibility to pain without impairing the muscular contractions of the uterus. Opium was then the drug of choice for destroying useless pain and shortening the progress of labor, but it was far from adequate. Rush's hope foreshadowed by nearly half a century the discovery and use of general anaesthetics in obstetrics.

In lecturing on the pleasures of the senses Rush remarked:

"Pleasure is not only one of the ingredients of health; but its deficiency and its excess are frequent causes of disease. . . . Man is said to be a compound of soul and body. . . . However proper this language may be in religion, it is not so in medicine. He is, in the eye of a physician, a single and indivisible being, for so intimately united are his soul and body, that one cannot be moved, without the other. The actions of the former upon the latter are numerous and important. They influence many functions of the body in health. They are the causes of many diseases; and if properly directed, they may easily be made to afford many useful remedies."

These notions, now so familiar in psychosomatic medicine, actually go back to Plato. But they had long been forgotten, as they were forgotten again after Rush. And not until Freud introduced the concept of repressed emotional conflicts and Cannon demonstrated the rôle of the major emotions in bodily processes were they revived and systematically studied.

In a lecture on the faculties of the human mind, or on what we should call clinical psychology and its usefulness to a physician, Rush spoke of cures performed by faith. He tells how labor pains are shortened by assuring the patient that each pain is the last one. "Hope may be considered as the diet of the mind in sickness." He believed it could support and even prolong life. To render his prescriptions successful, a physician "should pry into the state of his patient's mind, and so regulate his conduct and conversation, as to aid the operation of his physical remedies." Rush spoke of "dissolving unpleasant and creating agreeable associations of ideas," sometimes by the use of a key word or phrase. Here he was anticipating by many decades the work of the French school at Nancy.

*   *   *

Rush told his students that even their dreams "should not be permitted to sport themselves idly" in their brains, because if they
acquired habits of observation, useful inferences could be deduced
from them. He was obviously interested in his own dreams, and he
seems to have had no hesitancy in recounting them to John Adams,
who held a special place in his trust and affection. In 1805 he described to Adams a dream that he had had about fifteen years
earlier. This was about the time that Adams became Vice-President
of the United States and that Rush, after having devoted sixteen
years to his country, could see nothing ahead but labor and self-
denial in his profession. However, he protested that he had then
envied no man and blamed no man. In this setting the dream tells a
different story.

Rush dreamed that a great number of people were assembled
near Christ Church. They are gazing at a man seated on the ball
just below the vane of the steeple. On asking what was going on,
Rush is told that this man has discovered a method of regulating
the weather. Interestingly enough, this was the year that Franklin
had died. The man could produce rain and sunshine and cause the
wind to blow from any quarter. He has a trident in his hand which
he would wave in the air, commanding the wind to blow from the
northwest instead of the northeast. But this time the weather vane
refuses to move. The man then calls for rain, but none falls. Then
becoming agitated and dejected, he complains bitterly of the
refractory elements. At this point Rush says to a friend, "The man
is certainly mad." Then a figure dressed like a flying Mercury
descends rapidly from the steeple, holding a streamer bearing the
inscription *De te fabula narratur* ("About you a story is being
told"). And Rush then says: "The impression of these words was
so forcible upon my mind that I instantly awoke, and from that
time I determined never again to attempt to influence the opinions
and passions of my fellow citizens upon political subjects."

In another dimension the figure of Mercury is an archetype
sent to earth from on high (the church steeple) to bring Rush a message, and the gist of the message was for Rush to stop deceiving
himself and to become aware of his limitations.

Knowing what we do about Rush, this dream is not too difficult
to interpret. He had, indeed, retired from political life because he was
not tough enough for it and had been hurt by it. He is both the

dreamer and the man on the steeple—that is, in the highest position, playing the part of God who commands the elements; but the elements do not obey him. He recognizes his impotence, but he is consoled by the prophetic device on the streamer and then he awakens with the resolution never again to play the political game.

The dream tries to resolve this conflict between his burning political ambitions and his realization that this career is now closed to him. What is more natural than his wanting to tell this dream to John Adams, whom he describes as his "first preceptor in the science of government" and who has taught him "to despise public opinion when set in competition with the dictates of my judgment and conscience." Yet Adams had been pricking his friend's conscience. He had just written him that it is the duty of every man who loves his country to step forth in the defense of its institutions.

In the next dream reported to Adams, Rush is no longer God, sitting on top of Christ Church, nor Jupiter Pluvius. Rather, as Adams had recently been, he is himself the President of the United States. Dr. Rush had just lost a patient from "the fatal effects of intemperance in the use of ardent spirits." While ruminating about this case and the incalculable evils spreading through the country from the use of strong drink, he falls asleep. He dreams that he has been elected President. At first he objects to accepting so high and honorable a station. But then he recollects that it will give him the opportunity to put a final stop to the abuse of ardent spirits in his country, and with this thought in mind he accepts the office and enters upon its duties with enthusiasm and zeal.

Up to this point the two dreams are similar. Rush is exalted to a position of power—his wish—where he can work magic. He tells his secretaries, who bring him many letters to sign, that he will do no more work until he gets Congress to pass a law prohibiting the importation, distilling and consumption of hard liquor in the United States. Such a law is passed. It recommends molasses and water and small beer in place of ardent spirits. Wise and humane and patriotic as the law is, it nevertheless meets with great opposition.

Here, as in the first dream, the ugly face of reality obtrudes itself on the dreamer's wish. Petitions come from all quarters urging Congress to repeal the law. Then one day, while Rush is sitting alone in his council chamber, a venerable but plain-looking man is introduced to Rush by a servant. This old man comes to protest about the law, pointing out its injustice and all the damage that will follow its enforcement. Rush hears him out but protests that his visitor does not know the people of the United States as well as he, adding that they will always "submit to the empire of Reason." But the old man contradicts him, saying that there is an empire of another kind, more powerful than Reason, namely, the empire of Habit. To this, people yield a willing and involuntary submission.

"You might as well," he says, "arrest the orbs of heaven in their course as *suddenly* change the habits of a whole people. . . . Indeed, Mr. President," he continues, ". . . you are no more of a philosopher than you are a politician, or you never would have blundered upon your spirit law. Let me advise you to retire from your present station and go back to your professor's chair and amuse your boys with your idle and impracticable speculations, or go among your patients and dose them with calomel and jalap. . . ." Rush is outraged. He shouts, "Stop, stop, sir. . . . What do you mean by thus insulting the first magistrate of your country?" At this point he calls for his servant, John, and tells him to "turn this man out of doors." Then the noise and vexation awakens him and he feels the relief that the whole scene has been "nothing but a dream."

Again Rush is confronted with his impotence, this time in the face of his determination to put a stop to the evils of drink. He is forced to realize that a professor's chair is not a seat of power. The dream again intimates a feeling of rivalry, if not jealousy, with Adams, whom he loves and admires, and yet who, unlike Rush, had won the political laurels that Rush undoubtedly, but unconsciously, coveted. It is perhaps no accident that the servant in the dream is called John. These feelings may have been responsible for his vehemence in wanting his sons to shun politics.

There is another element in the dreams that should not be overlooked. Rush is beginning to be aware of his age and perhaps of his waning powers. He is now sixty-two. As is usual in dreams, the old man very probably represents both the dreamer and, in this instance, Adams as well. The two dreams contain intimations of mortality; but to Rush, who lacked the necessary insight and understanding to interpret them, they appeared only bizarre, although somehow threatening.

There is yet another of Rush's dreams on record in his voluminous correspondence with John Adams that has a singular prophetic aspect. In it, Rush's son Richard, while reading a history of the United States, calls to his father's attention the following passage:

"1809. Among the most extraordinary events of this year was the renewal of friendship and intercourse between Mr. John Adams and Mr. Jefferson, the two ex-Presidents of the United States."

When Adams hears of this from Rush, he writes:

"A Dream again! I wish you would dream all day and all Night, for one of your Dreams puts me in spirits for a Month. I have no other objection to your Dream, but that it is not History. It may be Prophecy."

Two years pass. In 1811 Rush is in receipt of a letter from Adams upon the then all-engrossing topic of banks, in which the letter comments as follows:

"The Banking Infatuation pervades all America. Our whole system of Banks is a violation of every honest Principle of Banks. There is no honest Bank but a Bank of Deposit. A Bank that issues Paper at Interest is a Pickpocket or a Robber. But the Delusion will have its Course. You may as well reason with a Hurricane. An Aristocracy is growing out of them, that will be as fatal as The Feudal Barons if unchecked in Time."

Thereupon Rush transmits this paragraph in a letter to Jefferson, with this remark:

"When I consider your early attachment to Mr. Adams, and his to you; when I consider how much the liberties and independence of the United States owe to the concert of your principles and labors; and when I reflect upon the sameness of your opinions at present upon most of the subjects of government and all the subjects of legislation, I have ardently wished a friendly and epistolary intercourse might be revived between you before you take a final leave of the common object of your affections. Such an intercourse will be honorable to your talents and patriotism and highly useful to the course of republicanism not only in the United States but all over the world. Posterity will revere the friendship of two ex-Presidents that were once opposed to each other. Human nature will be a gainer by it."

That Rush's rôle as mediator should have been presaged by a dream was a not uncommon experience for him, and the dream itself can be put down as a simple childlike wish-fulfillment dream, prophetic in its implications.

The olive branch which Rush had proffered was accepted by both men. Few acts of his life gave him more pleasure than this rekindling of the friendship between Adams and Jefferson, which led to the long and well-known exchange of letters between Quincy and Monticello. He called Adams and Jefferson "The North and the South Poles of the American Revolution." Both men died in 1826 and on the same day, the 4th of July!

*   *   *

In early July 1812 Rush was called to see a patient who lived about nine miles from town. Since it was a holiday, he took along with him to do the driving, instead of his Negro servant, his youngest son, William, then a boy of eleven. After visiting his patient, Rush realized that they were within three or four miles of the farm on which he had been born and where his ancestors for several generations had lived and died. This farm was in a settlement known as Byberry, about twelve miles up the Delaware River from Philadelphia. He decided to visit it, and as they approached the place Rush was amazed to find himself peculiarly agitated. Except for the approach to the house, everything seemed just as he had left it sixty years earlier, when, at the age of six, he had lost his father, and his mother had moved away. He took his young son upstairs to see the room in which he had made his "first *unwelcome* noise in the world." Then he asked to see the cedar tree his father had planted, only to learn that it had been cut down to make pillars for a piazza on the front of the house. Rush stepped up to one of the pillars and embraced it. He saw again the orchard of old straggling apple trees, and for each apple he felt "something like the affection of a brother."

The house—a long, low two-story structure, with a central dormer—showed signs of age and decay. On one of the stones near the front door he could make out his father's or grandfather's initials—J.R. On their way home, Dr. Rush and the small boy went to see the family graveyard in which four successive generations of Rushes were buried, all descended from that Captain John who had commanded a troop of horse under Cromwell, and whose sword and watch Rush had inherited. Here too was buried his grandfather, James, the gunsmith for whom Benjamin's third son, the physician, had been named.

While standing near his grandfather's grave, Rush's thoughts became confused. He saw his forebears risen from their graves and surrounding him, dressed in their homespun and working clothes. They said, "What means that *gentleman* by thus intruding upon us?" And then, in his imagination, Rush soliloquized and spoke to them thus:

"Dear and venerable friends! Be not offended at me. I inherit your blood, and I bear the name of most of you. I come to claim affinity with you and do homage to your Christian and rural virtues. It is true my dress indicates that I move in a different sphere from that in which you passed through life, but I have acquired and received nothing from the world which I prize so highly as the religious principles I inherited from you, and I possess nothing that I value so much as the innocence and purity of your characters."

A century and a half later the author took occasion to repeat this pilgrimage of Dr. Rush's. After miles of urban sprawl, one approaches Byberry, where there are trees, green grass and some space between the houses. Then up a short country lane, where the old house comes into view, recognizable at once by its stone exterior and the square columns that support the roof over the porch. But it is all in great disrepair, lacking paint, impoverished and shabby. Worse than this, the garden is now blighted by the derelict bodies of abandoned cars. The house itself is of good proportions, which still lend it dignity. From the upstairs room in which Rush was born, one looks in vain for the apple orchard or the bucolic scenes of his childhood which he had treasured in his memory up to the time of his death.

At supper on the night of his visit to his birthplace Rush had regaled his family with the story of the day's excursion and with the cherries which William had gathered from a tree supposedly planted by his grandfather.

Such a day was a rare one for Dr. Rush. He had always found it difficult to relax; his principal form of recreation had been more work, for which he had an inexhaustible capacity.

One of Rush's students, Dr. Samuel Jackson, has left a description of him as he appeared at about this time of his life. He was above middle height, very erect and rather slender, small-boned, and finely formed. His face was thin, his nose aquiline, and his eyes were beautifully set, large, blue, mild and benevolent. His forehead was broad and high and his head, which was long, was nearly bald from the crown forward; his hair clubbed behind and powdered. Although his complexion was healthy, he could not be called handsome, for his cheeks were fallen in and many of his front teeth were missing, and his face was wrinkled with care and age.

This description corresponds closely with the posthumous portrait by Thomas Sully. In conversation, Rush's expression was highly animated, his face often showing intense thought, preoccupation and firmness of purpose. He hardly ever laughed, but his infrequent smile was peculiarly gracious. His bearing was rather military; he walked with a firm, elastic step, arms folded on his chest; and he carried a stick. To everyone who bowed to him, poor or rich, he took off his hat, greeting them in his mild but strong voice with, "I hope you are very well, sir."

His clothes were plain and usually of drab color, and the vehicle in which he rode was also plain. It had two wheels and was drawn by one horse. Marcus, his Negro servant, who had been with him for more than thirty years, always rode with him in his open carriage.

Dr. Jackson goes on to describe his teacher, whom he venerated but did not idolize, as very simple and artless in bearing, "without a semblance of affectation, remarkable for kindness, cordiality, and even condescension."

Another student, Dr. Caldwell, with whom Rush had had the unpleasant contretemps, described him as "among the most polished of that polished age." Pre-eminent in conversation, he never interrupted or tried to monopolize the talk. His predominant feelings at the end of his life were said to have been piety and benevolence and on first appearance he was so imposing as to subdue every mind and win every heart.

Jackson writes of his teacher: "Of the six professors of our time, he was the only one who was never seen angry,—over his face there never came the shadow of a cloud." If he was subject to irritation, "he had acquired a perfect dominion over it in public."

From time to time he had to take to his bed from exhaustion, and because of a chronic cough. Even so, as late as March 1813, he said that although now and then he was aware of his age his cough did not impair his strength nor lessen his capacity for work. But, as March wore on, the cough grew more troublesome and exhausting. On Wednesday, April 14, Dr. Rush visited his patients as usual. At dinner he had a sudden chill and felt miserable. This sent him to bed at nine o'clock, but he first drank some brandy and soaked his feet in hot water. During the night he grew worse. He developed a fever and had severe pains in his side, which caused difficulty in breathing. One can guess that he had pneumonia, probably of tuberculous origin. Toward morning a bleeder was sent for, who drew ten ounces of blood. This relieved him so that he was able to fall asleep. But the next morning he was nearly exhausted, his pulse gradually becoming weaker. Dr. Dorsey, who was in attendance, thought his patient had typhus, but Rush himself believed that his pulmonary tuberculosis had reached an acute state. Dr. Physick was called in. Rush was again bled, but this time only three ounces by cupping. On Sunday morning his spirits were better and he was able to talk freely, but by four in the afternoon his temperature began to mount and by nine o'clock his condition was critical. On Monday afternoon, April 19, at about five o'clock, Benjamin Rush joined his ancestors.

He was laid to rest in a grave near his father's and his mother's and that of Benjamin Franklin. His body lies beside that of his wife, who survived him by a third of a century. They are buried beneath an oak in Christ Church Burial Ground, at Arch and 5th Streets in Philadelphia. Around the Rush tomb are the headstones of several of their children, many of the names almost effaced by time. His son John's headstone is fractured, as his life was fractured —the part bearing his name lying carelessly on the ground. On Benjamin Rush's tomb are inscribed these words from Matthew:

> Well done good and faithful servant
> Enter thou into the joy of the Lord.

Thomas Jefferson wrote these words to John Adams:
"Another of our friends of seventy-six is gone, my dear Sir, another of the co-signers of the Independence of our country. And a better man than Rush could not have left us, more benevolent,

more learned, of finer genius, or more honest." ⋮

But Jefferson's devotion to his friend did not blind him to his palpable shortcomings. A year after Rush's death Jefferson wrote in a letter to Dr. Thomas Cooper: "For classical learning I have ever been a zealous advocate; and in this, as in his theory of bleeding and mercury, I was ever opposed to my friend Rush, whom I greatly loved; but who has done much harm, in the sincerest persuasion that he was preserving life and happiness to all around him." Jefferson was too gentle and too loyal to offend the man for whom his friendship and respect, to use his own words, would always remain unaltered and unalterable.

And John Adams' words were these:

"As a man of Science, Letters, Taste, Sense, Phylosophy, Patriotism, Religion, Morality, Merit, Usefulness, taken alltogether Rush has not left his equal in America, nor that I know in the World. In him is taken away, and in a manner most Sudden and totally unexpected a main Prop of my Life." ⋅

On the one hundred and fifty-second anniversary of his death, the American Psychiatric Association, whose official seal bears Rush's portrait, caused a bronze plaque to be placed at the grave. It bears this legend:

Benjamin Rush
1746–1813
Father of American Psychiatry
Signer of the Declaration of Independence
Heroic Physician, Teacher, Humanitarian
Physician General of the Continental Army
Physician to the Pennsylvania Hospital
Professor of Physic, University of Pennsylvania

*   *   *

What manner of man was this Benjamin Rush? He had, to be sure, his own answer to this question.

The good opinion of good friends is a balm to any man, and especially to one who so often contrived to be hurt as Benjamin Rush did. If he was irritated and distressed by what he considered the follies of his fellows, he tried to explain them away by saying that most men were "*madmen at large.*" They differed in their degrees of insanity, but the maddest of all were those who by writing and reasoning attempted to cure them. He was fond of quoting Nathaniel Lee, the 17th-century playwright, who spent five years in a cell at Bedlam. When asked what had brought him there, he declared, "The world is mad, but the world believed the same thing of me and I was outvoted." Rush felt that he had lost his "character for sanity" by being outvoted by his medical brethren in 1793, when he had first introduced the use of mercury and bleeding for the cure of yellow fever. He felt, moreover, that this would never have happened had he not been an ardent Whig. He had countered the charges against him by saying:

"There is not a single instance of a discovery or improvement in any art or science made by a Tory that I know of in any part of the United States. Their prejudices are as cartilaginous or bony upon all subjects as they are upon subject of government."

But even enemies have their place in the economy of nature. A man's evil passions help to keep him alive as much as his good ones, and "individual enemies help to make men wise, prudent, and successful in life." At least, so Rush thought.

Julia Rush had understood him better. She was, as he had often said, the faithful companion of his pains and pleasures. She had once said that there was no character in history more like him than Martin Luther—ardent in all his pursuits, fearless of the consequences of attacking old prejudices and often hasty in his manner of speaking of his enemies. Rush had readily admitted having yielded now and then to the natural irritability of his temper when unjustly treated, but on the whole his view of himself had been that of a kind and forgiving man who harbored no grudges. He had listed all his offenses, beginning with subscribing his name to the Declaration of Independence and ending with his insistence on the domestic origin of yellow fever. And of his own reputation he had said:

"My opinions upon many subjects and my innovations in the practice of medicine have so much divided my fellow citizens upon the subject of my talents and character, that it will be impossible for many years to decide the controversy respecting either of them. Those who come after me (if my works should survive my interment) will be the best judges whether I have added by them to the knowledge and happiness or to the errors and miseries of my fellow citizens."

Although Benjamin Rush had readily admitted to possessing all the defects of Luther's nature, there was yet another character in history who, in his judgment, was closer to his own. This was the prophet Jeremiah, and, by way of illustration, he had quoted this:

"Woe is me, my mother, that thou hast borne me a man of *strife* and a man of contention to the whole earth. I have neither lent on usury nor have men lent to me on usury, yet every one of them doth curse me."

Jeremiah and Luther and Rush did, indeed, have traits in common: fierce singleness of purpose, an equally fierce conviction that they were right, and the belief that they were called upon by God to set the crooked straight. Tender and sensitive by nature, each of them lacked sufficient humor to temper the hostility which their relentless diatribes evoked from others. For each of them the ultimate gospel was his sense of inner integrity. But neither Luther nor Rush was a prophet of doom, and in this they differed from the author of the austere and dolorous complaints of the Old Testament.

With advancing years, Rush had given up some of his self-righteous aggressiveness. He had grown more mellow and tolerant and had even admitted that he was kindly treated by his fellow citizens and that at last he lived peaceably with all men. But he had declared he *still* felt like a stranger in his native state. His patients were his only acquaintances, his books his only companions, and the members of his family nearly his only friends. Small wonder that he then turned with so much warmth, affection and loyalty to the friends of those memorable years 1774, 1775 and 1776, and especially to Thomas Jefferson and John Adams. With each, Rush carried on a spirited and pithy correspondence, ending only with his death.

With John Adams particularly, Rush had been in constant correspondence, their letters increasing in frequency, in warmth, affection and mutuality of interest, after a lapse of some twelve years, when Adams had written him in 1805: "It seemeth unto me, that you and I ought not to die without saying Goodby or bidding each other Adieu."

This had been the starting point. Rush was able to unbend with Adams, to write from "a heart that loves you," to tell him that he still lived in his affections and that few persons occurred oftener to his thoughts than his venerable and dear friend. In fact, he said that he owed more to Adams' friendship than he had ever owed any other human being except his excellent mother and his beloved and faithful wife.

Julia Rush had twitted them for carrying on like a couple of school girls about their sweethearts, but Rush had insisted that he would not be outdone by the number or promptness of Adams' letters. His own were often tardy because of the press of his business. But what he had valued above all were his older friend's honesty, integrity, firmness, courage and vigor, and the brilliance of his imagination. He described his style as bold, original, electrifying, full of nerve without a redundant word. He called it "the artillery of language."

And Adams had been outspoken with Rush. He had reprimanded him for having burnt all his notes on the Revolutionary War, except for his characterization of the men who had signed the Declaration of Independence. Adams had written Rush in August 1805: "The burning of your Documents was, let me tell you, a very rash action and by no means justifiable upon good Principles." Of himself, Rush had written but three words, "He aimed well." Rush surely had had Adams in mind when he said that integrity takes "a stronger hold of the human heart than any other virtue." The world, he thought, stands in more need of justice than of charity; indeed, it is the want of justice that renders charity everywhere so necessary.

At the time of these exchanges of sentiments, Adams was in his seventy-seventh year, while Rush was approximately ten years his junior. But he had felt himself aging physically, if not yet intellectually. The infirmities of old age, he had observed, did not unfit a man so much for study as they did for company or business. He had agreed with Adams that there is a coincidence of decay in the mental faculties and the bodily organs, although the former are often less perceptible than the latter. Adams, as was once said of Dr. Johnson, was like tin—bright to the last. "Some men's minds wear well, but yours don't appear to wear at all," Rush had written his friend, to which Adams replied that he always felt at least forty years younger when writing to Rush. The old gentleman had recently attended a meeting in Boston and thereafter had ridden twelve miles on a winter's night back to Quincy. A New

Englander, he had said, is a "meeting-going animal." Rush always admired the plainness, simplicity and intelligence in the New England character.

One detects in Rush in these latter days a certain worldly wisdom or perhaps disillusionment, if not bitterness. The sanguine optimism of his early manhood had paled. He quoted Louis XIV as saying, ". . . we were only fit to live in the world when we were called to leave it." And he himself thought that men seldom do right until they have reached the extremity of error. The same skeptical spirit seems to have invaded his erstwhile patriotic idealism. He often wished for the time he had wasted in the days of his political activities. "I feel pain," he wrote Adams, "when I am reminded of my exertions in the cause of what we called liberty, and sometimes wish I could erase my name from the Declaration of Independence." But Adams, who had suffered as much as Rush at the hands of political enemies, did not feel sorry for himself. Instead, he administered a quick and unanswerable rebuke to such pusillanimous thoughts. He was made of tougher stuff than Benjamin Rush.

*　　*　　*

The biographer's job, like the diamond cutter's, is to display the facets of a personality so as to bring out its inner light.

Rush's light burned in him fiercely and made him the champion of justice and the enemy of cruelty, ignorance and bigotry. In many respects he was far ahead of his time; in others he lagged behind. He was a modern in spite of his 18th-century dogmatism and sentimentality, and in spite of a critical lack of insight into himself. As were many of his contemporaries, he was moved by a sublime optimism untroubled by intimations of ultimate failure. The Kingdom of Heaven would surely be at hand, if only one worked hard enough. And Benjamin Rush was never idle.

He lived in an heroic time and he took on heroic stature when he brought his unusual gifts to bear on the thorny and complicated aspects of mental illness. Throughout his life Rush was moved by piety and a trust in the ultimate wisdom and goodness of the Creator.

The portraits of him, both paintings and etchings, are so varied that it is difficult to choose among them. Some are clearly sentimentalized into a picture of the good gray Doctor; others make him look so sick and ravaged that one cannot imagine him so. The one chosen for the frontispiece of this book has been taken from an etching by Savage made in 1800, when Rush was fifty-five years old, perhaps at the height of his powers, having survived the perilous and melancholy years of the yellow fever epidemics. This portrait brings out his manliness and vigor, his stubbornness and pride, his self-assurance touched by sensitiveness and vanity. It seems to reflect him most fully. In looking at this likeness of Rush, one can well imagine his having written to Noah Webster at about the same time: "*Expect* to be persecuted for doing good, and *learn* to rejoice in persecution."

Benjamin Rush's flaws are manifest and we can learn from his mistakes as well as from his accomplishments. Mark Van Doren wrote, "Man has become most noble, most transparent, through his errors." Rush's errors were costly both to himself and to his patients, but he had a human heart, not one of stone. And he had courage, the captain of all virtues. After courage comes compassion.

BIBLIOGRAPHY
OF FREQUENTLY CITED REFERENCES

	Abbreviations
A Report of an Action for a Libel "brought by Benjamin Rush, against William Cobbett, in the Supreme Court of Pennsylvania, December term, 1799, for certain defamatory publications in a news-paper, entitled *Porcupine's Gazette*, of which the said William Cobbett was editor," Philadelphia, 1800	Action
The Autobiography of Benjamin Rush: His "Travels through Life," Together with His Commonplace Book for 1789–1813, ed. George W. Corner, Princeton, The American Philosophical Society and the Princeton University Press, 1948. "*Travels through Life*" (pp. 23–169) was largely written retrospectively in the year 1800, whereas the *Commonplace Book* (pp. 173–360) is in the form of a contemporaneous diary written between 1789 and 1813.	Autobiog.
John Morgan, Continental Doctor, Whitfield J. Bell, Jr., Philadelphia, University of Pennsylvania Press, 1965	W. J. B.
"Benjamin Rush's Journal of a Trip to Carlisle in 1784," L. H. Butterfield, *The Pennsylvania Magazine of History and Biography* (October 1950)	L. H. B.
Medical Inquiries and Observations upon the Diseases of the Mind (5th ed.), Benjamin Rush, Philadelphia, 1835	Dis. of Mind (B.R.)
Not So Long Ago, A Chronicle of Medicine and Doctors in Colonial Philadelphia, Cecil K. Drinker, New York, Oxford University Press, 1937	C. K. D.
Essays, Literary, Moral & Philosophical, Benjamin Rush, Philadelphia, 1798	Essays (B.R.)
"Extracts from the Journal of Miss Sarah Eve," *The Pennyslvania Magazine of History and Biography*, V (1881)	Eve
Doctors on Horseback, James T. Flexner, New York, 1937	Flex.
French Journal, manuscript journal kept by Benjamin Rush relating his "Account of Journey to Paris," J. Pierpont Morgan Library	Fr. Jr. (B.R.)
Benjamin Rush, Physician and Citizen, 1746–1813, Nathan G. Goodman, Philadelphia, University of Pennsylvania Press, 1934	Goodm.
Sixteen Introductory Lectures, to courses of lectures upon the Institutes and Practice of Medicine, delivered in the University of Pennsylvania, Benjamin Rush, Philadelphia, 1811	Lectures (B.R.)

Abbreviations

Letters of Benjamin Rush, L. H. Butterfield (ed.), Vol.   L. I (B.R.)
I and II, Princeton, The American Philosophical So-   L. II (B.R.)
ciety and the Princeton University Press, 1951

Medical Inquiries and Observations (2nd ed.), Benjamin   Med. Inq. &
Rush, Vol. I, Philadelphia, 1794   Obs. I (B.R.)

Medical Inquiries and Observations (2nd ed.), Benjamin   Med. Inq. &
Rush, Vol. II, Philadelphia, 1805   Obs. II (B.R.)

Medical Inquiries and Observations (2nd ed.), Benjamin   Med. Inq. &
Rush, Vol. III, Philadelphia, 1805   Obs. III (B.R.)

Old Family Letters, copied from the Originals for Al-   O. F. L.
exander Biddle, Series A, Philadelphia, 1892

Scottish Journal, manuscript record of Benjamin Rush's   Scot. Jr. (B.R.)
visit to Edinburgh, 1766–1768, in possession of the Indi-
ana University Libraries, Bloomington, Indiana

The Development of Modern Medicine: An Interpreta-   R. H. S. 1
tion of the Social and Scientific Factors Involved, Richard H. Shryock, New York, 1947

Benjamin Rush from the Perspective of the Twentieth   R. H. S. 2
Century, Richard H. Shryock, Benjamin Müsser Lecture, No. III, College of Physicians, Philadelphia (November 1946)

Syllabus of a Course of Lectures on Chemistry, A Fac-   Syllabus (B.R.)
simile Reprint of the 1770 Edition, Benjamin Rush
(With an Introduction by L. H. Butterfield), Philadelphia, Friends of the University of Pennsylvania Library, 1954

Verdict for the Doctor—The Case of Benjamin Rush,   Verdict
Winthrop and Frances Neilson, New York, 1958

An Account of the Bilious remitting Yellow Fever as   Yellow Fev.
it appeared in the City of Philadelphia in the year 1793
(2nd ed.), Benjamin Rush, Philadelphia, 1794

A History of Medical Psychology, Gregory Zilboorg,   Zilb.
New York, 1941

ADDITIONAL SOURCES

"Benjamin Rush and the Theory and Practice of Republican Education,
1783 to 1813" (typescript of dissertation), James Bonar, The Johns Hopkins
University, December 1962

The Counter-Revolution in Pennsylvania, 1776–1790, Robert L. Brunhouse,
Philadelphia, 1942

"Further Letters of Benjamin Rush," L. H. Butterfield, *The Pennsylvania
Magazine of History and Biography*, LXXVIII (Jan. 1954)

"Dr. Rush to Governor Henry on the Declaration of Independence and the Virginia Constitution," L. H. Butterfield, *Proceedings*, The American Philosophical Society, Vol. 95, No. 3 (June 1951)

"Benjamin Rush: A Physician as Seen in His Letters," L. H. Butterfield, *Bulletin of the History of Medicine*, XX (July 1946)

"Benjamin Rush as a Promoter of Useful Knowledge," L. H. Butterfield, *Proceedings*, The American Philosophical Society, Vol. 92, No. 1 (1948)

"Moral Persuasion as Therapy," Eric T. Carlson and Meribeth M. Simpson, *Current Psychiatric Therapies*, IV (1964)

Battles of the American Revolution, 1775–1781, Henry B. Carrington, New York, 1876

Medicine in England during the Reign of George III, Arnold Chaplin, Fitzpatrick Lectures, Royal College of Physicians, London, 1919

A Brief Narrative of the Ravages of British and Hessians at Princeton in 1776–1777, Varnum L. Collins, Princeton, 1906

Two Centuries of Medicine, A History of The School of Medicine, University of Pennsylvania, George W. Corner, Philadelphia, 1965

Concepts of Insanity in the United States, 1789–1865, Norman Dain, New Brunswick, New Jersey, 1964

George Washington Himself, A Common Sense Biography, John C. Fitzpatrick, Indianapolis, 1933

"Dr. Rush and General Washington," Paul Leicester Ford, *Atlantic Monthly*, Vol. 75, 1895

London Life in the XVIIIth Century, M. Dorothy George, New York, 1925

Benjamin Rush and His Services to American Education, Harry G. Good, Berne, Indiana, 1918

A History of Medicine, Douglas Guthrie, London, 1945

"The Influence of the Leyden School upon Scottish Medicine," Douglas Guthrie, *Medical History*, III (April 1959)

The Medical School of Edinburgh, Douglas Guthrie, Edinburgh, 1959

"The Three Alexander Monros and the Foundation of the Edinburgh Medical School," Douglas Guthrie, *Journal of the Royal College of Surgeons of Edinburgh*, II (Sept. 1956)

Currents and Counter-Currents in Medical Science, Oliver Wendell Holmes, Boston, 1860

The Life and Morals of Jesus of Nazareth, Thomas Jefferson, Washington, D.C., 1904

"Benjamin Rush and American Psychiatry," Charles K. Mills, *Medico-Legal Journal*, New York, 1886

Commemorative address: centennial anniversary of the institution of the College of Physicians of Philadelphia, S. Weir Mitchell, *Transactions*, College of Physicians, 1887

The Character of Rush, an Introductory to the Course on the Theory and Practice of Medicine in the Philadelphia College of Medicine, Thomas D. Mitchell, Philadelphia, 1848

The Turning Point of the Revolution, or Burgoyne in America, Hoffman Nickerson, Boston, 1928

An American Boswell, C. E. Osgood, Princeton University Library, Chronicle V, 1943–44

Medical Inquiries and Observations upon the Diseases of the Mind, by Benjamin Rush, M.D. Issued under the auspices of the New York Academy of Medicine (The History of Medicine Series, 3, No. 15). With an introduction by Dr. S. Bernard Wortis (New York, 1962)

Medicine and Society in America, 1660–1860, Richard H. Shryock, New York, 1960

The Psychiatry of Benjamin Rush, Richard H. Shryock, Philadelphia, The American Psychiatric Asociation, May 1944

The Medals of Benjamin Rush, Obstetrician, Horatio R. Storer, Newport, Rhode Island, American Medical Association, June 1889

The Entire Works of Dr. Thomas Sydenham, London, 1753

Modern Sanitary Conditions, George E. Waring, Jr., American Medical Association, June 1889

"Clinical Transformations in Psychiatry and Psychoanalysis," Gregory Zilboorg, *Journal of the American Medical Association,* Vol. 171 (Oct. 1959)

NOTES

The motto is taken from a speech by Oliver Wendell Holmes Jr. on Memorial Day in 1913, when he was Justice of the Supreme Judicial Court of Massachusetts. It can be found in *The Occasional Speeches of Justice Oliver Wendell Holmes,* ed. Mark de W. Howe, Harvard University Press, 1962, pp. 6–7.

CHAPTER 1

Page	Line	
17	17	Scot. Jr. (B.R.)
18	5	*Ibid.*
18	14	Autobiog., p. 40
18	17	Scot. Jr. (B.R.)
18	13	*Ibid.*
19	3	Autobiog., p. 41
19	15	*Ibid.,* p. 24
21	6	Goodm., p. 4
22	6	Autobiog., pp. 29–30
22	14	*Ibid.,* p. 31
22	19	*Ibid.,* p. 32
22	21	*Ibid.*
23	12	*Ibid.,* p. 36
24	5	*Ibid.,* p. 37
24	12	*Ibid.,* p. 38

Page	Line	
24	12	*Ibid.,* p. 37
25	5	*Ibid.,* p. 38
26	13	*Adventures in Medical Education,* G. C. Robinson (Cambridge, Massachussetts, 1957)
28	1	"John Redman," in *Annals of Medical History,* William S. Middleton, VIII (Autumn 1926), p. 219
28	7	*Ibid.,* p. 220
29	9	*Ibid.,* p. 217
30	5	L. I (B.R.), p. 13
30	1	*Ibid.,* p. 14
31	9	*Ibid.,* p. 23

CHAPTER 2

Page	Line	
34	3	Quoted in *M. D.,* III, 10 (New York, October 1959), p. 164
36	3	Scot. Jr. (B.R.)
36	14	*Ibid.*
37	2	Quoted in *The Medical Side of Benjamin Franklin,* William Pepper (Philadelphia, 1911), pp. 72–73
38	14	R. H. S. 1
38	12	*Ibid.*
38	4	*Ibid.,* p. 16
39	7	Quoted by R. H. S. 1, p. 26; first lines of the *Practice of Physic,* I (Edinburgh, 1796)
39	3	L. I (B.R.), p. 41
40	1	*Ibid.,* p. 62
41	2	*Ibid.,* p. 39
42	4	W. J. B., p. 57

Page	Line	
42	5	Autobiog., p. 45
42	10	L. I (B.R.), p. 40
42	17	Autobiog., p. 47
43	18	*Ibid.,* p. 46
43	9	*Ibid.*
44	13	L. I (B.R.), p. 40
45	6	*John Witherspoon Comes to America,* L. H. Butterfield (Princeton, 1953), p. 21
45	10	L. I (B.R.), p. 38
46	15	*Ibid.,* p. 60
46	14	*Ibid.,* p. 53
46	3	*Ibid.,* p. 40
47	3	Autobiog., p. 51
47	11	Scot. Jr. (B.R.)
47	20	*Ibid.*
47	6	*Ibid.*
48	3	L. I (B.R.), p. 65

CHAPTER 3

Page	Line	
50	9	Autobiog., p. 54
50	13	*Ibid.,* p. 56

Page	Line	
51	5	L. II (B.R.), pp. 632–633
51	6	L. I (B.R.), p. 68

Line numbers in roman type are counted from the top of the page; those in *italic* are counted from the bottom.

Page Line
53   6   Quoted in *A Memoir of William and John Hunter*, George C. Peachey (Plymouth, 1924), p. 114
54   9   Quoted in *The Great Doctors: A Biographical History of Medicine*, H. E. Sigerist (New York, 1933), p. 221
55 19   Quoted by R. H. S. 1, p. 20; letter from Cotton Mather to John Woodward, September 28, 1724
58 14   "Observations on Jail and Hospital Fever," J. Hunter, in *Medical Transactions of the College of Physicians* (Philadelphia, 1779)
59   4   Fr. Jr. (B.R.)
59 12   *Ibid.*
60   2   *Ibid.*
60 17   *Ibid.*

Page Line
61   4   Quoted in William Pepper, *op. cit.*, p. 49; letter from Benjamin Franklin to Barbeu Dubourg, London, July 28, 1768
62   7   Fr. Jr. (B.R.)
62 12   Autobiog., pp. 67–68
62   5   Fr. Jr. (B.R.)
63   6   *Ibid.*
63 16   *Ibid.*
66   2   Quoted in *Franz Anton Mesmer, A History of Mesmerism*, Margaret Goldsmith (New York, Doubleday, 1934), pp. 154–155
66 16   Autobiog., p. 70
66   7   Fr. Jr. (B.R.)
67 16   *Ibid.*
68 18   Autobiog., p. 69
68 10   *Ibid.*, p. 75

CHAPTER 4

Page Line
70 13   Autobiog., p. 78
70   2   L. I (B.R.), p. 43
71   2   Autobiog., p. 78
72 15   *Annals of Philadelphia and Pennsylvania*, John F. Watson, Vol. 1 (Philadelphia, 1857), p. 394
72   7   C. K. D., p. 29
73 16   *Rebels and Gentlemen: Philadelphia in the Age of Franklin*, Carl and Jessica Bridenbaugh (New York, Oxford University Press, 1962), p. 264
75 14   Quoted in W. J. B., p. 111
75 15   *Discourse upon the institution of medical schools in America*, facsimile of original edition (Philadelphia, 1765, Baltimore, Johns Hopkins Press, 1937)
75   4   W. J. B., p. 52
76   6   Bridenbaugh, *op. cit.*, p. 285
76 20   Autobiog., p. 79
78   6   L. I (B.R.), p. 49
79 12   Quoted in *The Story of Chemistry*, Georg Lockemann (New York, Philosophical Library, 1959), p. 74

Page Line
82 18   Goodm., p. 27
83   9   *Ibid.*, from the *Pennsylvania Packet*, April 22, 1776, p. 28
85   2   Syllabus (B.R.), p. 5, p. 7, p. 10
85 11   Herbert S. Klickstein, "A Short History of the Professorship of Chemistry of the University of Pennsylvania School of Medicine, 1766–1847," *Bulletin of the History of Medicine*, XXVII (1953), p. 53
88   9   *Lectures on the Practice of Physic*, Benjamin Rush, I, No. 31, II, No. 1, 1796 (Manuscript, Library of the University of Pennsylvania). Quoted by R. H. S. 1, p. 3
90   7   R. H. S. 1, p. 70
90 19   *Observations on the Duties and Offices of a Physician and the Methods of Prosecuting Enquiries in Philosophy* (London, 1770), pp. 110–112. Quoted by R. H. S. 1, pp. 70–71
90 14   L. I (B.R.), p. 51
91   5   Autobiog., p. 85

CHAPTER 5

Page	Line	
92	17	*Adams Family Correspondence*, ed. L. H. Butterfield (Cambridge, Mass., The Belknap Press of Harvard University Press, 1963), Vol. 2, p. 109
92	3	Eve, p. 193
93	15	*Ibid.*
93	19	*Ibid.*, p. 26
93	12	*Ibid.*, p. 191
93	4	*Ibid.*, f.n. 1
94	9	*Ibid.*, p. 199
96	1	L. I (B.R.), p. 81
96	11	*Ibid.*, p. 76
96	6	Med. Inq. & Obs. I (B.R.), p. 9
97	6	*Ibid.*, p. 56
97	14	*Ibid.*, p. 57
97	15	Autobiog., p. 223
98	4	L. I (B.R.), p. 430
98	18	*Ibid.*, p. 431
99	6	*The Oxford History of the American People*, Samuel Eliot Morison (New York, Oxford University Press, 1965), p. 207
99	9	Autobiog., p. 112
100	4	L. I (B.R.), p. 84
100	14	Autobiog., p. 114
101	6	*Ibid.*
101	18	L. II (B.R.), p. 1008
101	17	Autobiog., p. 114
102	10	*Ibid.*, p. 140
102	17	*Ibid.*, p. 141

Page	Line	
102	19	*Ibid.*, p. 142
102	19	*Ibid.*, p. 143
102	12	*Diary & Autobiography of John Adams*, ed. L. H. Butterfield (Cambridge, Mass., The Belknap Press of Harvard University Press, 1963), Vol. 2, p. 182
103	15	Autobiog., pp. 112–113
103	18	*Ibid.*, p. 113
103	6	L. I (B.R.), p. 328
103	3	Autobiog., p. 116
104	3	*Ibid.*
104	8	*Ibid.*
105	1	L. I (B.R.), pp. 327–328
105	16	L. I (B.R.), p. 96
105	13	*Ibid.*, p. 100
106	7	Quoted in *John Adams and the American Revolution*, Catherine Drinker Bowen (Boston, 1950), p. 578
106	14	O. F. L.
107	1	L. I (B.R.), pp. 101–102
107	16	L. I (B.R.), p. 107, f.n. 2, from the *Journal of the Continental Congress*, V, pp. 603–604
107	1	*Pennsylvania Constitution of 1776*, J. Paul Selsam (Philadelphia, 1963)
109	7	Autobiog., p. 119
110	7	*Ibid.*
110	19	*Ibid.*, p. 120
110	9	L. I (B.R.), p. 109

CHAPTER 6

Page	Line	
113	18	Autobiog., p. 124
115	11	*Ibid.*, p. 128
115	12	*The Battles of Trenton and Princeton*, William S. Stryker (Boston and New York, 1898)
115	3	L. I (B.R.), p. 125
116	13	Autobiog., p. 129
117	19	L. I (B.R.), p. 326
117	17	Autobiog., p. 129
117	5	L. I (B.R.), p. 358
118	9	*Ibid.*, p. 130
118	15	*Ibid.*, p. 131
118	16	*Ibid.*
119	8	*Ibid.*, p. 139
120	4	*Ibid.*, p. 163, f.n. 5

Page	Line	
120	12	*The Early History of Medicine in Philadelphia*, George W. Norris (Philadelphia, 1886)
121	8	Flex., p. 25
121	7	W. J. B., p. 190. Cf. Norris, p. 197
122	9	W. J. B., p. 195
122	17	Flex., p. 32
123	9	*Ibid.*, p. 43
123	13	W. J. B., p. 203. Cf. Flex., p. 44
123	6	Flex., p. 44. Cf. W. J. B., p. 204
124	4	L. I (B.R.), p. 140
125	14	*Ibid.*, p. 141

Page Line
125 19 *Ibid.*
126 12 *Ibid.*, pp. 143-144
126   5 *Ibid.*, p. 143
127   4 *Ibid.*
127   4 *Ibid.*, p. 153
128 19 *Ibid.*, p. 154
128 17 *Ibid.*, p. 155
129   6 *Ibid.*, p. 156

Page Line
129 10 *Ibid.*, pp. 156-157
129 13 *Ibid.*
129   3 "Historical Notes of Dr. Benjamin Rush, 1777," *Pennsylvania Magazine*, V, 27 (1903)
130   3 L. I (B.R.), pp. 156-157

CHAPTER 7

Page Line
131   5 L. I (B.R.), p. 161
132 13 *Ibid.*, pp. 173-174
132   5 *Ibid.*, p. 181
133   6 *The Writings of George Washington*, ed. John C. Fitzpatrick, Vol. X, p. 297 (Washington, D.C., 1933)
134 15 L. I (B.R.), pp. 182-183
134   6 *The Writings of George Washington*, ed. Jared Sparks (Boston, 1834), p. 513
134   3 L. II (B.R.), Appendix I; also *Washington and the Revolution: a reappraisal*, Bernard Knollenberg, New York, 1940
135 11 Sparks, *op. cit.*, p. 514
135 13 Sparks, *op. cit.*, p. 515
136   9 L. I (B.R.), p. 191
137 17 John C. Fitzpatrick, ed., *op. cit.* (1933) Vol. X, p. 265
139   4 L. I (B.R.), p. 185
139 18 *Letters of Members of the Continental Congress*, ed. Edmund C. Burnett, Vol. III, p. 66 (Washington, D.C., 1921-1936)
140   7 L. I (B.R.), p. 197
140 14 *Ibid.*, p. 200

Page Line
141   2 *Ibid.*, p. 360, f.n. 4
141 11 *Ibid.*, p. 206. See also *Annals of Medical History*, William S. Middleton, Vol. IV, New Series (New York, Harper and Row, Hoeber Medical Division, 1932)
142   7 L. I (B.R.), p. 227
142 12 *The Early History of Medicine in Philadelphia*, George W. Norris (Philadelphia, 1886), p. 83
143   3 L. I (B.R.), p. 248, f.n. 1
143 15 *Ibid.*, p. 248
143 18 Quoted in L. II (B.R.), p. 1205
144 11 L. I (B.R.), p. 259
144 19 Quoted in Flex., p. 85. See also *John Morgan, A Vindication of his Public Character in the Station of Director-General of the Military Hospitals and Physician in Chief to the American Army* (Boston, 1777)
144 16 John C. Fitzpatrick, ed., *op. cit.* (1931-1944), Vol. XXI, p. 218
145   7 Autobiog., p. 180

CHAPTER 8

Page Line
146 10 Autobiog., p. 137
147   1 *Ibid.*, p. 36
147 13 L. I (B.R.), p. 216
147   2 *Ibid.*, p. 219
148   9 *Ibid.*, p. 237
149   9 *Ibid.*, p. 240
149 14 *Ibid.*, p. 242
149 17 Autobiog., p. 85
149   2 Med. Inq. & Obs. I (B.R.), p. 123
150 11 *Ibid.*, pp. 127-128
150   5 *Ibid.*, p. 125, f.n.

Page Line
152 15 *Ibid.*, pp. 134-135
152   8 Autobiog., pp. 85-86
153 12 *Ibid.*, p. 85
153   7 Goodm., p. 72
154   7 Autobiog., p. 167
155   4 *Ibid.*
155   1 L. I (B.R.), p. 431
156   7 Autobiog., p. 311
156   8 *Ibid.*, p. 257
156   3 L. I (B.R.), p. 274
157   8 *Ibid.*, p. 267
157 18 *Ibid.*, p. 278

Page	Line		Page	Line	
157	11	*Ibid.,* p. 281	158	11	*Ibid.,* p. 282
157	9	*Ibid.,* p. 279	159	6	*Ibid.,* p. 286
158	2	*Ibid.,* p. 280	159	6	For further elaboration, cf. Autobiog., p. 130, f.n. 61
158	7	*Ibid.*			
158	9	*Ibid.,* p. 278	160	11	Autobiog., p. 158, f.n. 2
158	12	*Ibid.,* p. 281	160	10	L. I (B.R.), p. 371
158	13	*Ibid.,* p. 279	160	1	*Ibid.,* pp. 389–390
158	17	*Ibid.,* p. 281			

CHAPTER 9

Page	Line		Page	Line	
161	5	L. I (B.R.), p. 336			ed. Dagobert D. Runes (New York, Philosophical Library, 1947), p. 29
162	14	*Ibid.,* p. 337			
162	12	*Ibid.,* p. 379			
163	8	*Ibid.,* p. 337	169	5	L. I (B.R.), p. 366
163	17	*Ibid.*	170	16	Essays (B.R.), p. 8
163	13	*Ibid.,* p. 379	170	3	*Ibid.,* p. 14
163	2	*Ibid.,* pp. 338–339	171	14	*Ibid.,* p. 44
164	12	*Early Dickinsoniana,* The Boyd Lee Spahr Lectures, Dickinson College (Carlisle, Pennsylvania, 1961), p. 104	171	12	*Ibid.,* p. 92
			171	2	Med. Inq. & Obs. II (B.R.), p. 3 ff.
164	2	L. I (B.R.), p. 46	172	11	*Ibid.,* p. 28
165	6	*Ibid.,* p. 357	173	1	*Ibid.,* p. 51
165	14	*Ibid.,* p. 315	173	10	Essays (B.R.), p. 139
165	7	Autobiog., p. 314	174	6	Med. Inq. & Obs. I (B.R.), p. 320
166	16	L. I (B.R.), p. 314			
166	6	L. H. B., p. 447	174	10	Autobiog., pp. 161–162
168	10	L. I (B.R.), p. 416	176	1	L. I (B.R.), pp. 435–436
169	4	Quoted in *The Selected Writings of Benjamin Rush,*	176	4	*Ibid.,* p. 437
			176	1	*Ibid.,* p. 432

CHAPTER 10

Page	Line		Page	Line	
177	2	L. I (B.R.), p. 443			quoted in Goodm., pp. 145–146
177	4	Goodm., p. 299			
178	4	L. I (B.R.), p. 441	185	8	Goodm., p. 153
179	4	Med. Inq. & Obs. I (B.R.), p. 240	187	5	L. I (B.R.), p. 530
			187	14	*Ibid.,* p. 513
179	13	*Ibid.,* p. 202	187	16	*Ibid.,* p. 506
179	8	Med. Inq. & Obs. II (B.R.), p. 134	187	20	*The Life and Selected Writings of Thomas Jefferson,* ed. Adrienne Koch and William Peden (New York, 1944), p. 131
181	15	Med. Inq. & Obs. I (B.R.), p. 331			
181	20	*Ibid.,* p. 332			
181	5	*Ibid.,* p. 333	187	5	L. I (B.R.), p. 508
182	15	*Ibid.,* p. 335	188	7	*Ibid.,* p. 531
182	6	*Ibid.,* p. 337	189	19	*Ibid.,* p. 536
183	10	*Autobiography of Charles Caldwell, M.D.,* ed. Harriot W. Warner (Philadelphia, 1855), p. 116	189	2	Med. Inq. & Obs. II (B.R.), p. 359
			190	2	*Ibid.,* p. 365
183	3	*Ibid.,* p. 246	190	14	Autobiog., p. 174
184	9	Goodm., p. 132	190	18	*Ibid.,* p. 175
185	12	Rush Manuscript in Library Company of Philadelphia;	190	19	*Ibid.,* p. 176
			190	11	*Ibid.,* p. 177
			190	7	*Ibid.,* p. 180

Page Line
191 1   *Ibid.*, p. 181
191 8   *Ibid.*, p. 182
191 16 *Ibid.*, p. 183
191 14 *Ibid.*, p. 221
192 14 Med. Inq. & Obs. II (B.R.),
193 15 L. II (B.R.), pp. 627-628
         p. 367
193 18 *Ibid.*
193 9   L. I (B.R.), p. 455
194 18 Med. Inq. & Obs. II (B.R.),
         p. 449
195 11 *Ibid.*, p. 430
195 19 *John* V:26
195 6   L. I (B.R.), p. 454
196 4   *Ibid.*

Page Line
196 12 *Ibid.*, p. 451
196 16 *Ibid.*, pp. 468-469
196 19 *Ibid.*, p. 471
197 10 *Ibid.*, p. 457
197 6   *Ibid.*, p. 482
198 5   *Ibid.*, p. 460
200 12 Reprinted in *A New Deal in
         Liquor*, Yandell Henderson
         (New York, Doubleday,
         1934), p. 194, p. 197
200 11 L. I (B.R.), facing p. 512
201 15 *Ibid.*, p. 482
201 18 Essays (B.R.), pp. 271-272
202 7   *Ibid.*, pp. 340-341

CHAPTER 11

Page Line
203 19 Yellow Fev., p. 8
203 1   *Ibid.*, p. 10
204 5   *Ibid.*, p. 11
205 12 L. II (B.R.), p. 637
205 9   *Ibid.*
206 1   *Ibid.*, p. 639
206 4   Autobiog., p. 228
206 11 L. II (B.R.), p. 639
206 1   *Ibid.*, p. 641
208 17 Yellow Fev., p. 23
208 11 *Ibid.*, p. 29
211 14 Quoted from *American Daily
         Advertiser* of August 29, 1793,
         in "Yellow Fever Epidemic
         of 1793 in Philadelphia," Wil-
         liam S. Middleton, *Annals of
         Medical History*, Vol. 10
         (1928), p. 140
211 14 L. II (B.R.), p. 643
211 2   Yellow Fev., p. 37
213 1   *Ibid.*, p. 124
213 4   L. II (B.R.), p. 646
213 12 Yellow Fev., p. 197
213 7   *Ibid.*, p. 201
214 14 *Ibid.*, p. 202
214 8   Lectures (B.R.), p. 45
215 3   "The Black Death," William
         Langer, *Scientific American*

Page Line
         (February 1964)
215 16 Lectures (B.R.), p. 48
217 7   Yellow Fev., p. 266
218 6   L. II (B.R.), p. 655
218 9   *Ibid.*, p. 656
218 6   Yellow Fev., p. 341
219 19 Quoted in Goodm., pp. 180-
         181
219 16 Yellow Fev., p. 342
220 18 *Ibid.*, pp. 343-344
220 8   *Ibid.*, p. 346
220 1   *Ibid.*
221 14 L. II (B.R.), p. 747
221 17 Yellow Fev., p. 348
222 23 Autobiog., p. 235
223 18 *Bring Out Your Dead: The
         Great Plague of Yellow Fever
         in Philadelphia in 1793*, John
         H. Powell (Philadelphia,
         1949)
223 17 L. II (B.R.), p. 685
223 14 *Ibid.*, p. 673
223 8   *Ibid.*, p. 702, f.n. 1
224 19 *Ibid.*, p. 687
224 13 *Ibid.*
225 6   Yellow Fev., pp. 360-362
226 14 L. II (B.R.), pp. 745-746

CHAPTER 12

Page Line
227 1   Autobiog., p. 97
228 9   *Autobiography of Charles
         Caldwell, M.D.*, Harriot W.
         Warner (Philadelphia, 1855),
         p. 184
228 14 Yellow Fev., p. 337

Page Line
229 6   *Benjamin Rush's Theories on
         Bloodletting after One Hun-
         dred and Fifty Years*, O. H.
         Perry Pepper, Mütter Lec-
         ture LIX, The College of

Page Line

Physicians (Philadelphia, November 1946)

230 6 John H. Powell, *op. cit.*

232 15 Quoted in "The Influence of Benjamin Rush on the Practice of Bleeding in South Carolina," Joseph I. Waring, *Bulletin of Medical History,* No. 35 (1961) p. 235

232 19 Yellow Fev., p. 271

232 1 C. K. D., p. 126

233 4 *Ibid.*

233 18 Yellow Fev., p. 10

234 8 *Ibid.,* p. 240

234 19 *The Enigma of Yellow Fever* in *The Conquest of Epidemic Disease,* Charles-Edward A. Winslow (Princeton, 1943)

235 5 Autobiog., p. 102

236 14 Quoted in L. II (B.R.), p. 791 (from the Pickering Papers, Massachusetts Historical Society, Boston)

236 17 *Ibid.,* p. 794

237 2 *Ibid.,* p. 795

237 3 Autobiog., p. 103, f.n. 48

Page Line

238 5 *Ibid.,* p. 103

238 12 O. F. L., p. 84

239 3 L. II (B.R.), p. 803

239 14 *Ibid.,* p. 805

241 10 *An Eulogium Intended to Perpetuate the Memory of David Rittenhouse,* Benjamin Rush (Philadelphia, 1796), p. 33. See also Essays (B.R.), p. 368

241 16 Action. Quoted also in Verdict, p. 125

241 19 L. II (B.R.), p. 793

241 1 *Ibid.,* p. 818, f.n. 5

242 14 Verdict, p. 146. See also Action

242 19 *Ibid.,* p. 135. See also Action

242 12 *Ibid.,* p. 134

243 16 Action

243 2 *Ibid.*

244 12 *Ibid.*

245 6 *Ibid.*

245 19 *Ibid.*

245 5 *Ibid.*

246 14 Autobiog., pp. 248–249

246 1 Verdict, p. 208

CHAPTER 13

Page Line

248 11 L. II (B.R.), p. 1218

248 6 *Ibid.,* p. 825

249 1 *Ibid.,* p. 850

249 14 Zilb.

250 5 L. II (B.R.), p. 847

250 14 *In Search of Philippe Pinel,* John C. Nemiah, unpublished manuscript

251 8 Braintree, Mass. Town Records, 1640–1793. Quoted in *The Mentally Ill in America,* Albert Deutsch, (New York, Columbia University Press, 1949), p. 42

252 16 Quoted in Deutsch, *op. cit.,* p. 181

253 8 *Providence Journal,* April 10, 1844

253 4 Quoted in Deutsch, *op. cit.,* p. 52

254 10 *Some Account of the Pennsylvania Hospital from its First Rise to the Beginning of the Fifth Month, called May 1754,* printed by Benjamin Franklin and D. Hall,

Page Line

MDCCLIV, facsimile (Baltimore, The Johns Hopkins Press), p. 4. See also Deutsch, *op. cit.,* p. 59

255 15 *The History of the Pennsylvania Hospital, 1751–1895,* Thomas G. Morton (Philadelphia, 1897), p. 125

256 12 L. I (B.R.), p. 529

256 16 Quoted in Zilb., p. 317

257 15 *The Treatment of the Insane Without Mechanical Restraints,* John Conolly (London, 1856), pp. 4–5

257 7 *Three Hundred Years of Psychiatry, 1535–1860,* Richard Hunter and Ida Macalpine (New York and London, Oxford University Press, 1963), p. 423

258 2 *Ibid.,* pp. 561–562. See also *An Inquiry into the Nature and Origin of Mental Derangement,* Sir Alexander Crichton (London, 1798); "The Insanity of King

3I4

REVOLUTIONARY DOCTOR

Page Line
George III," Isaac Ray,
American Journal of Insanity,
XII, No. 1 (July 1855), pp.
1-29; and *America's Last
King: An Interpretation of
the Madness of George III,*
Manfred S. Guttmacher

CHAPTER 14

Page Line
264 5 Lectures (B.R.), pp. 293-294
264 10 *Ibid.,* p. 286
264 7 *The Ever-Present Past,* Edith
Hamilton (New York, 1964),
p. 189
264 1 Cf. *The Lost World of
Thomas Jefferson,* Daniel J.
Boorstin (New York, 1948)
265 18 Lectures (B.R.), p. 276
265 16 *Ibid.,* pp. 286-287
266 16 Dis. of Mind (B.R.), pp. 78-
79
266 13 *Ibid.,* p. 80
266 7 *Ibid.,* p. 82
268 12 *Ibid.,* p. 220
268 16 *Ibid.,* p. 160
268 14 *Ibid.,* p. 158
268 5 *Ibid.,* p. 136
269 4 *Ibid.,* p. 262
269 14 *Ibid.,* p. 263
269 20 *Ibid.*
269 9 *Ibid.,* p. 265
270 9 *Ibid.,* p. 239
270 16 *Ibid.,* pp. 239-240
270 12 *Ibid.,* p. 42
270 4 *Ibid.,* p. 41
271 1 *Ibid.,* p. 44
271 10 *Ibid.,* p. 341
272 12 *Ibid.,* p. 61
272 2 "The Definition of Mental
Illness, Benjamin Rush, 1745-
1813," Eric T. Carlson and
Meribeth M. Simpson, *American Journal of Psychiatry,*

CHAPTER 15

Page Line
281 13 L. II (B.R.), pp. 1164-1165
282 2 *Ibid.,* p. 1169
282 9 Autobiog., p. 261
282 19 *Ibid.,* p. 370
282 7 *Ibid.,* p. 288
283 6 L. II (B.R.), p. 1074
284 17 O. F. L., p. 196
284 16 L. II (B.R.), pp. 1143-44, f.n.
1

Page Line
(New York, 1941)
259 8 "Philippe Pinel and the Reform of Insane Asylums,"
Raymond de Saussure, *Ciba
Symposium,* II, No. 3 (1950),
pp. 1222-52

Page Line
Vol. 121 (September 1964),
pp. 209-214
273 19 Dis. of Mind (B.R.), p. 176
274 11 Quoted in "The Contribution of Benjamin Rush to
Psychiatry," Fritz Wittles,
*Bulletin of the History of
Medicine,* No. 20, 1946, p.
163. See also *Lecture on the
Mind,* by Benjamin Rush
274 9 Dis. of Mind (B.R.), p. 7
274 1 Quoted in "Benjamin Rush
and American Psychiatry,"
Clifford B. Farr, *American
Journal of Psychiatry,* Vol.
100 (January 1944)
275 15 Dis. of Mind (B.R.), pp. 9-
14
275 18 *Ibid.*
276 2 *Ibid.,* p. 103
277 8 Lectures (B.R.), p. 384 ff.
278 13 *Ibid.,* p. 380
278 17 R. H. S. 2
278 1 Quoted by Wittles, p. 160
279 4 *Ibid.,* p. 165
280 6 Quoted in "Benjamin Rush's
Medical Use of the Moral
Faculty," Eric T. Carlson
and Meribeth M. Simpson,
*Bulletin of the History of
Medicine,* XXXIX, No. 1,
(January-February 1965) Cf.
also Lectures (B.R.), p. 393

Page Line
284 1 *Ibid.,* p. 1143
285 3 *Ibid.,* p. 1142
285 17 *Ibid.,* p. 971
285 19 *Ibid.,* p. 1190
285 14 *Ibid.,* p. 1188
286 9 Lectures (B.R.), pp. 164-180
286 18 *Ibid.,* p. 253
286 20 *Ibid.,* p. 295
286 18 *Ibid.,* p. 355 ff.

Page Line

287 10 *Ibid.*, p. 400
287 19 *Ibid.*, p. 256
287 9 *Ibid.*, p. 263
287 5 *Ibid.*, p. 266
287 3 *Ibid.*, p. 267
288 2 *Ibid.*, p. 355
288 *14* L. II (B.R.), p. 893
288 *11* *Ibid.*, p. 894, f.n. 4; from Horace, *Satires*
288 8 L. II (B.R.), p. 893
289 10 L. I (B.R.), p. 530
289 12 *Ibid.*, p. 531
289 19 L. II (B.R.), p. 977
290 5 *Ibid.*, p. 978
290 20 *Ibid.*, p. 979
291 9 *Ibid.*, p. 1021
291 14 *Ibid.*, p. 1023, f.n. 4. See also O. F. L., p. 246; also "The Dream of Benjamin Rush: The Reconciliation of John Adams and Thomas Jefferson," L. H. Butterfield, *Yale Review*, XL (1950–1951), pp. 297–319
291 *16* L. II (B.R.), p. 1075. Cf. O. F. L., p. 272
291 *1* *Ibid.*, p. 1075
292 10 *Ibid.*, p. 1127
292 *19* *History of the Townships of Byberry and Moreland in Philadelphia, Pa.*, Joseph C. Martindale (Philadelphia, 1901)
292 *12* L. II (B.R.), p. 1150
292 7 *Ibid.*
293 9 *Ibid.*, p. 1152
293 18 *Ibid.*

Page Line

296 1 "Benjamin Rush" by Samuel Jackson, in *Lives of Eminent American Physicians*, ed. Samuel D. Gross (Philadelphia, 1861), p. 18
296 7 *The Writings of Thomas Jefferson*, Albert Ellery Bergh, Ed., Thomas Jefferson Memorial Association of the United States (Washington, D.C., 1907), Vol. XIV, p. 200
296 17 John Adams, letter to Elbridge Gerry, April 26, 1813, from the Adams Papers by permission of the Massachusetts Historical Society
296 2 L. II (B.R.), p. 1090
297 6 *Ibid.*, p. 1095
297 14 *Ibid.*
297 18 *Ibid.*, p. 1167
297 *1* *Ibid.*, p. 1028
298 8 *Ibid.*, p. 1116
298 4 O. F. L., pp. 61–62
299 13 L. II (B.R.), p. 1101
299 20 O. F. L., p. 73
299 *19* Autobiog., p. 148
299 17 L. II (B.R.), p. 1103
299 5 L. I (B.R.), p. lxxi
300 1 L. II (B.R.), p. 1096
300 8 *Ibid.*, p. 905
300 15 *Ibid.*, p. 966
301 11 L. I (B.R.), p. 530
301 15 *Mark Van Doren on Great Poems of Western Literature* (New York, 1946), p. 30

INDEX